Teacher
Pay
&
Teacher
Quality

We dedicate this book to those teachers whose value to students will forever exceed the bounds of any compensation system.

Teacher Pay & Teacher Quality

Attracting, Developing, & Retaining the Best Teachers

James H. Stronge | Christopher R. Gareis | Catherine A. Little

CORWIN PRESS
A SAGE Publications Company
Thousand Oaks, California

For information:

Corwin Press
A Sage Publications Company
2455 Teller Road
Thousand Oaks, California 91320
E-mail: order@corwinpress.com

Sage Publications Ltd.
1 Oliver's Yard
55 City Road
London EC1Y 1SP
United Kingdom

Sage Publications India Pvt. Ltd.
B-42, Panchsheel Enclave
Post Box 4109
New Delhi 110 017 India

Printed in the United States of America.

Library of Congress Cataloging-in-Publication Data

Stronge, James H.
Teacher pay and teacher quality: attracting, developing, and retaining the best teachers / James H. Stronge, Christopher R. Gareis, Catherine A. Little.
       p. cm.
Includes bibliographical references and index.
ISBN 1-4129-1320-9 (cloth) — ISBN 1-4129-1321-7 (pbk.)
    1. Teachers—Salaries, etc.—United States. 2. Teachers—Recruiting—United States.
3. Teacher effectiveness—United States. I. Gareis, Christopher R. II. Little, Catherine A.
III. Title.
LB2842.22.S87 2006
331.2'813711'00973—dc22

                                        2005029174

This book is printed on acid-free paper.

06   07   08   09   10   11   9   8   7   6   5   4   3   2   1

Acquisitions Editor:	Elizabeth Brenkus
Editorial Assistant:	Desirée Enayati
Project Editor:	Tracy Alpern
Copy Editor:	Amy Freitag, Four Lakes Colorgraphics
Proofreader:	Theresa Kay
Typesetter:	C&M Digitals (P) Ltd.
Indexer:	Sylvia Coates
Cover Designer:	Lisa Miller

Contents

Acknowledgments

While this book involved our collaborative efforts, we would like to acknowledge the contributions made by others from beginning to end in this project. This project was born out of our work with many school districts in examining their evaluation and compensation systems. Although the school districts on which we base our practical applications remain anonymous, we do wish to acknowledge their role. Leslie Grant, a doctoral candidate and research assistant, contributed significantly to the book by refining and editing the final version of the manuscript. To everyone who assisted us in making this book possible we express our sincere gratitude.

Corwin Press gratefully acknowledges the contributions of the following individuals:

Edward Vargas
Superintendent
Hacienda La Puente USD
City of Industry, CA

Kenneth Peterson, Professor
Dept. of Curriculum and Instruction
Portland State University

Gina Segobiano
Superintendent/Principal
Signal Hill School District
Belleville, IL

John Deasy
Superintendent of Schools
Santa Monica, CA

Randel Beaver
Superintendent
Archer City ISD
Archer City, TX

Preface

School districts across the country face challenging times. School districts must maximize resources with possibly decreasing budgets. At the same time, school districts may face high teacher turnover, an aging teaching population, and mandates from state and federal government agencies. Teacher pay and teacher quality are inextricably linked. While many in the teaching profession cite intangible rewards as reasons for staying in the profession, tangible rewards such as salary, benefits, and working conditions may affect quality teachers' decisions to transfer schools, retire earlier than expected, or leave the teaching profession altogether. The purpose of *Teacher Pay and Teacher Quality* is twofold:

1. To bring together the issue of teacher pay with the important and central issue of teacher quality

2. To provide a sequential and practical approach for developing a comprehensive teacher compensation system based on research and best practice

Teacher Pay and Teacher Quality does not promote a single model of teacher compensation, but rather advocates a component-parts approach for a school district to develop a compensation system that serves its needs and goals.

Teacher Pay and Teacher Quality is designed to serve as a practical how-to book for educators on designing and implementing a teacher compensation system. The book begins with an overview of the critical issues to consider in the development of a compensation system: attracting, developing, and retaining quality teachers. The six chapters are organized sequentially, taking the reader through the definitive steps of educational planning. Scenarios and applications of concepts add to the practical nature of the book. Concepts are introduced early and developed in more depth or examined through a different lens in subsequent chapters. An example of this spiraling effect includes the objective introduction and discussion of pay options in one chapter and the evaluation and application of these pay options in a later chapter.

• Chapter 1 focuses on the connections between teacher pay and teacher quality, including linking teacher quality and student achievement; viewing pay in terms of attracting, developing, and retaining quality teachers; and examining the history of teacher compensation and theoretical frameworks for understanding teacher motivation and rewards.

• Chapter 2 investigates the relationship between teacher pay and school purposes, including how a compensation system supports the organizational purpose and goals of a school district. This chapter also identifies key objectives, evaluation questions, data sources, and quality criteria linking the goals of attracting, developing, and retaining teachers to the compensation system.

• Chapter 3 considers the school district environment in assessing the teacher compensation system, including using environmental scanning to identify strengths and weaknesses, assessing competition in compensation, and examining the impact of peripheral issues, such as working conditions and student demographics.

• Chapter 4 introduces and discusses pay options available to and used by school districts across the country. These pay options are examined in terms of assumptions and key features, advantages and highlights, disadvantages and concerns, and the focus each brings to teacher quality.

• Chapter 5 offers a model for designing a teacher compensation system. Pay options discussed in Chapter 4 are evaluated and applied in the model, which is a component-parts approach to building a teacher compensation system.

• Chapter 6 focuses on planning for implementation, offering a five-step process for developing a restructured teacher compensation system within a district.

About the Authors

James H. Stronge, PhD, is Heritage Professor in Educational Policy, Planning, and Leadership at the College of William and Mary in Virginia. His primary research interests are teacher quality and performance evaluation systems for teachers and administrators. He has worked for numerous state, regional, and local educational organizations on issues related to qualities of effective teachers, teacher selection, and performance evaluation systems for teachers and administrators. He is the author and editor of numerous articles and books, including *Linking Teacher Evaluation and Student Achievement, Evaluating Teaching: A Guide to Current Thinking and Best Practice,* and *Qualities of Effective Teachers.* He received a doctorate in educational administration and planning from the University of Alabama. He has been a teacher, counselor, and district-level administrator.

Christopher R. Gareis, EdD, is Assistant Professor of Educational Leadership at the College of William and Mary in Virginia. He is a former high school and middle school English teacher, as well as a middle school assistant principal and principal. He also directed the teacher preparation program at William and Mary as Associate Dean, and he continues the work of developing a network of partnership schools and clinical faculty in support of preservice teacher preparation and novice teachers. He has worked with school districts, state departments of education, and schools in the areas of teacher compensation, personnel evaluation, strategic planning, facilities planning, teacher preparation, mentoring, and curriculum development. In addition to these areas, his research interests include teacher leadership and principal efficacy.

 **Catherine A. Little, PhD**, is Assistant Professor in Educational Psychology in the Neag School of Education at the University of Connecticut. She teaches courses in gifted and talented education and in the teacher preparation program, including work with undergraduate honors students in education. She holds a PhD from the College of William and Mary in Educational Policy, Planning, and Leadership with an emphasis in gifted education administration, and she worked for several years as Curriculum Coordinator at the William and Mary Center for Gifted Education. Her research interests include excellence in teaching, professional development, preservice teacher preparation, curriculum differentiation, and perfectionism in gifted students. She has worked extensively with school districts in such areas as differentiation and interdisciplinary curriculum development. In 2003, she coedited the text *Content-Based Curriculum for High-Ability Learners*, which received a Legacy Book Award from the Texas Association for the Gifted and Talented.

1

Attracting, Developing, Retaining—and Paying—Quality Teachers

Teacher quality matters. It's no doubt, individual, family, community, and other beyond-school factors dramatically affect student success. Nonetheless, of all the factors within the influence of schools, teacher quality is among the most, if not the most, powerful variable affecting student achievement.

In summarizing the findings from the Tennessee Value-Added Assessment System regarding the impact of teacher quality on student achievement, Bill Sanders and his colleagues found that teacher effects were powerful and that teacher effectiveness varied widely within schools. Given the overall influence of teacher effectiveness on student achievement drawn from their analyses, they stated, "the immediate and clear implication . . . is that seemingly more can be done to improve education by improving the effectiveness of teachers than by any other single factor."[1] In fact, the teacher had a larger effect on student achievement than any other factor, including the school system, heterogeneity of ability levels within a class, and class size.

In a more recent, large-scale, experimentally designed study involving randomized assignment of teachers and students in which both teacher effects and school effects on student achievement were calculated, the researchers found that the impact of teachers was far greater than that of overall school effects. In other words, "which teacher a student gets within a school matters more than which school the student happens to attend."[2] More specifically, "if teacher effects are normally distributed, these findings would suggest that the difference in achievement gains between having a 25th percentile teacher (a not-so-effective teacher) and a 75th percentile teacher (an effective teacher) is over one-third of a standard deviation . . . in reading and almost half a standard . . . in mathematics."[3]

While the concepts embedded in the No Child Left Behind Act[4] are laudable, they are only a starting point. Yes, we need "highly qualified teachers," but more importantly, we need *highly effective* teachers in our schools.[5] And, if we are to have effective teachers working with every student every day in every school, our best hope is to attract promising teachers, substantially support these teachers in their development as quality professionals, and then keep them in our schools.

The premise of *Teacher Pay and Teacher Quality: Attracting, Developing, and Retaining the Best* is that teacher quality matters—and that it matters a great deal. If we are committed to this premise, then we must be committed to populating our schools with the highest quality teachers possible. While pay, undoubtedly, is not the sole solution to teacher quality, we contend that it *is* a vital factor that we cannot afford to neglect. Indeed, we contend that not only *how much* we pay teachers but also *how* we pay them are fundamentally important issues.

In this opening chapter, we focus on the fundamental connections between teacher pay and teacher quality. In particular, we explore the relationship between compensation and attracting, developing, and retaining teachers. But first, we offer an overview of theoretical frameworks for teacher motivation and reward, followed by a brief history of teacher compensation.

EXAMINING MOTIVATION: DO FINANCIAL INCENTIVES WORK IN PROMOTING TEACHER QUALITY?

A central issue in the debate over teacher compensation systems, particularly when discussing any form of performance-based pay, is the degree to which motivation and compensation are related. The fundamental meaning of *incentive* is that it is something that encourages people to act in such a way that they will receive the incentive as a consequence. Thus incentive-based systems presume that desirable behavior may be achieved more effectively if the individual has an expectation of a reward. A major issue in teacher compensation is to determine what role financial incentives play in teachers' decisions to join, develop, and remain in the profession—in other words, how financial incentives compare to other rewards, such as satisfaction with student growth and a feeling of personal accomplishment, in promoting higher levels of teacher quality and performance in the classroom.

Research and theory on motivation have carefully considered whether financial incentives are beneficial to productivity in the workplace. At some level, people do work because of the compensation they receive. Compensation provides a livelihood and supports professional growth and accomplishment. Moreover, the strength of a compensation structure, relative to the strength of the structure in comparable environments, is part of the basis for employee willingness to remain with a given employer.[6] Indeed, although few teachers would report entering the profession for the money, many who leave the profession dissatisfied express that the low salary was one of their reasons for leaving.[7] Teachers who move from one school district to another often cite similar concerns with salary, although in both cases working conditions are also highly influential in teachers' decisions to leave the profession or transfer.[8] The alternative compensation models discussed in this book attempt to address some of the concerns that cause teachers to leave the profession or a given school district dissatisfied with salary and working conditions, as well as to facilitate teachers' desires to achieve intrinsic rewards while providing additional extrinsic benefits. Through providing different kinds of incentives for different aspects of performance, the compensation models strive to increase motivation for higher quality teaching and to reward quality of work.

In making decisions about alternative compensation models, it is important that public policymakers, administrators, and teachers carefully consider the fundamental assumptions of such models and what they suggest about the complex relationships among motivation, performance, working environment, and compensation. Key theories about these relationships and how they may play out in the educational context are summarized below.

Intrinsic and Extrinsic Rewards

One common belief about teachers, supported by a number of studies, is that they engage and remain in their profession not primarily for extrinsic rewards—such as salary and recognition—but for intrinsic rewards, such as the satisfaction of seeing students grow and learn or collegiality with other teachers.[9] One of the major arguments against compensation plans that incorporate performance bonus components is the concern that reward structures have a tendency to erode intrinsic motivation, as well as potentially having a negative influence on collegiality among teachers.[10] However, evaluations of existing performance-based compensation programs indicate that teachers see both student learning *and* bonuses as positive outcomes of programs and do not perceive the two as antithetical.[11] Given the conflicting perspectives on the effects of performance-based programs on motivation, it is important to explore the types of reward structures more closely because their relationships to intrinsic motivation vary.

Theories of motivation acknowledge both extrinsic and intrinsic rewards as forms of *extrinsic motivation* because both provide desired consequences. However, it may be argued that the two types of reward influence intrinsic motivation—the motivation "[to do] an activity for its inherent satisfactions rather than for some separable consequence"[12]—in different ways, depending on the context in which they are presented. Key factors in this difference include

- perceived locus of control,
- competence,
- identification with goals.

When individuals feel that they have some autonomy over their engagement with a task, that they are capable of accomplishing the task, and that the goal is valuable and relevant to them, their pursuit of the goal and its consequent reward incorporates much more self-determination, the hallmark of intrinsic motivation. On the other hand, when individuals feel their behavior is largely externally controlled, or that they do not have the competence to achieve the goal, or that the goal is not valuable or relevant, then a reward is unlikely to facilitate the development of intrinsic motivation related to the goal.[13] These factors are similar to those highlighted in expectancy theory, which suggests that financial incentives can increase motivation to expend effort toward a goal, provided that employees

- believe in their own ability to achieve goals,
- see a clear connection between their individual effort and the achievement of the reward,
- value the expected reward enough to put forth the effort required to achieve it.[14]

Thus the individual's psychological connections with the goals, as well as the issue of competence as a necessary condition, emerge within this theory as well.

In the educational context, some of the conditions that are in place might allow incentives to facilitate greater intrinsic motivation. For example, when incentives are linked to desired learning outcomes for students, then they are also linked to the intrinsic rewards teachers desire and, by extension, to their enjoyment of teaching. When teachers feel competent in their ability to achieve desired outcomes—or when an incentive program also provides capacity-building resources to support teachers in developing this competence—then the extrinsic reward may be integrated with the intrinsic rewards as well. Perhaps the most challenging key element to meet within the current educational context is to ensure that teachers feel autonomy in connection with an incentive program. Such factors as deadlines, competition, directives, and threats, because they are perceived to be externally controlling and thus to limit autonomy, may undermine intrinsic motivation, an undesirable effect.[15] Therefore, although the restructuring of a compensation system may not remove some of these controlling factors, including the rigors of a school schedule and the demands of a state accountability system, such restructuring should take into account the need for teachers to feel some autonomy, through such features as choice and opportunities for self-direction.[16]

In schools, the emphasis on setting and measuring goals and outcomes—through daily objectives at the classroom level or long-term mission statements at the school or district level—suggests the worth of the expectancy theory with regard to establishing teacher compensation plans related to performance. However, the cautions mentioned above must be carefully considered to support achievement of goals and fostering of intrinsic motivation. Teachers must feel that

- the goals are achievable and measurable,
- the potential reward is worth the effort,
- they can see a clear connection between their own actions and choices and the achievement of the goals.

In other words, teachers must believe that they can make a difference.[17]

Comparison and Collaboration: Fostering Quality and Limiting Competition

As noted previously, competition is one of the elements of an incentive that may be perceived as a controlling factor and therefore undermine intrinsic motivation to engage with a task.[18] Critics of performance-based pay systems also argue that financial incentives linked to performance can carry serious threats to collegiality and collaborative work, as well as rupturing relationships between employees and supervisors.[19] Proponents of performance-based pay argue, instead, that performance rewards can function as motivators and maintain collaborative efforts provided that the awards are based on group efforts and results, rather than results for any single individual.[20] Moreover, advocates for reforming compensation argue that the traditional single-salary schedule, while potentially inspiring less competition than some proposed restructured models, also does not foster continuing development or improvement in quality among teachers and may, in fact, dishearten more talented teachers because of its lack of recognition of quality differences.[21] Concerns about fairness exist side by side with concerns about quality in reviewing and restructuring compensation systems, particularly with regard to the comparisons teachers are able to make between themselves and their peers.

According to equity theory, people are motivated to reduce inequities they observe in their work environments and thus to ensure fairness; employees who are dissatisfied or sense unfairness may change their behavior, attempt to change the behavior or decisions of others, or perhaps leave the job.[22] In education, with the use of the single-salary schedule, teachers can clearly recognize the objective basis for differences in pay, but they also have opportunities to observe one another's effort and to evaluate that effort relative to pay. This is the foundation for objections to the single-salary scale on the basis of fairness. Teachers who extend less effort may be paid more than those who work harder merely because they have been with the school longer, potentially resulting in resentment and competitive feelings among teachers, or even attrition. Equity theory is at work when high-quality teachers are disheartened when they see poor-quality teaching rewarded or feel their own efforts are undervalued by the school system.

Some compensation models attempt to respond to concerns about equity by rewarding strong performance while at the same time responding to concerns about collaboration and competition by making performance awards contingent upon outcomes for groups of teachers, rather than individuals. Although, as noted, this is the recommended route for performance-based awards, it does raise an additional issue, grounded in social dilemma theory. This is the idea that if employees are rewarded for the performance of a group instead of at an individual level, then some individuals will sense the opportunity to be "free riders."[23] This again raises the equity issue, at a more intimate level, if teachers observe others on their own team being rewarded for less effort. Some research suggests that the free rider problem is more a theoretical problem than an actual problem; however, it is a reminder of the importance of carefully structuring and communicating the compensation system, the choices it encompasses, and the teams in which teachers are to work.[24]

One implication of social dilemma theory is that if performance-based compensation is to be used, it should be emphasized at an individual and not at a group level in order to maintain fairness and avoid the problem of some doing the work for all. However, contemporary organizational understandings, particularly in education, acknowledge the idea that achievement of goals is necessarily the result of the performance of many individuals, and that extricating the performance of one over a group is a difficult endeavor. Balancing the concerns of individual versus group performance is an important consideration in any teacher compensation system. Framed in terms of teacher quality, we must remember a central finding of seminal work in Tennessee on value-added assessment: The most significant outcomes in student achievement occurred when students had three effective teachers *in consecutive years*. The message is clear: Student achievement is correlated with the *cumulative* effect of *individual* quality teachers.[25]

Other Extrinsic Motivators

Opponents of performance-based pay systems also argue that because of the nature of the teaching profession and the assumption that teachers do not go into the field for financial reasons in the first place, their motivation to achieve would be better served through providing alternative incentives that improve working conditions and job satisfaction—such as more planning time, resources, and administrative support.[26] Indeed, given the limited funding available for school reform efforts, some recommend that funds be used to promote other types of rewards, such as smaller class sizes, instead of making changes to teacher salary systems.[27] Regardless, a critical consideration is the effect that rewards linked to performance have on teacher motivation to accomplish their jobs successfully. Again, motivation theorists emphasize autonomy and competence, suggesting that performance-based incentives that provide information and positive feedback and that promote a sense of competence more strongly than they represent control (i.e., limiting autonomy) are more likely to support intrinsic motivation and engagement with the tasks and desired goals.[28] The obvious conclusion is that careful consideration must be given to the best ways to align funding patterns with school and district goals and to ensure that teachers reap some external benefits, financial or otherwise, from changes in funding packages so that the laudable internal motivations and desire for intrinsic rewards that brought many teachers to the classroom in the first place are not eroded.

HOW WE PAY TEACHERS: A BRIEF HISTORY OF TEACHER COMPENSATION

The question of how teachers should be compensated for their practice and to what degree that compensation should be tied directly to performance measures and to individual teacher characteristics and behaviors is one that has been discussed and debated in the United States for more than a century. The advantages and disadvantages of different types of pay systems, including the implementation challenges inherent in each, have emerged as various models have been tested and maintained or tried and discarded. Yet, the same questions are revisited again and again as educators, policymakers, and taxpayers consider their goals and the most facilitative mechanisms for meeting them. At the center of the debate over teacher compensation has always been the issue of *fairness,* with the ongoing question of how to ensure objectivity in recognizing and responding to variations in teacher performance.

Merit Pay and the Single-Salary Schedule: A Swinging Pendulum

Throughout much of the twentieth century, the compensation debate focused on the relative advantages and disadvantages of the single-salary schedule and merit pay models. Key points in this debate are discussed below and summarized in Figure 1.1. Although today the single-salary schedule is the "default" compensation model in use in American schools, forms of the merit pay system actually predate it. As the nation industrialized and urbanized in the late nineteenth and early twentieth centuries, schools grew larger and more complex in administration, and teaching began to emerge as a more long-term and legitimate career. During this period, salaries for teachers began to be somewhat standardized within school districts based on academic preparation and experience—laying the groundwork for the single-salary schedule—but also with different levels of pay for elementary and secondary teachers, for women and men, and for teachers of different racial and ethnic backgrounds.[29] Some districts also paid teachers differently depending on their political party affiliation.[30] In addition, these compensation systems often included opportunities for teachers to earn merit pay, with merit based on subjective assessments by administrators, often considered to be arbitrary in nature.

Objections from emerging teacher unions, along with and including the rising voices of female educators concerned with issues of equity, eventually led to the development of the single-salary schedule.[31] This model determined pay for teachers solely based on years of experience and level of academic preparation, not on administrator judgment of merit, with the assumption that these factors bore a positive relationship with teacher effectiveness and student learning, while also being measurable and objective. In addition, the "steps" and "lanes" of the single-salary schedule, representing increasing years of experience and increasing acquisition of graduate coursework, were intended as an incentive for teachers to gain higher education and to remain longer in the profession.[32] This model of compensation was introduced in Denver and Des Moines as early as 1921 and was used by 97 percent of school districts in the United States by 1950.[33]

Even as the single-salary schedule was growing in popularity during this period, merit pay plans were still in widespread use until at least the mid-1930s. The emphasis on scientific management and efficiency during this period influenced teacher compensation structures, with the notion that the most effective and efficient teachers should be identifiable and could be compensated for their work.[34] However, throughout their history, the central problem with merit pay plans has been the issue of defining the behaviors to be used for recognizing "merit." Defining good teaching has

Figure 1.1   Key Issues in the Debate: Single-Salary Schedule Versus Merit Pay

	Single-Salary Schedule	*Merit Pay*
Fairness—Basis for Judgment	Based on objective measures of educational background and teaching experience	Based on more subjective measures, often including administrator ratings that historically have been perceived as arbitrary
Fairness-Quality Differences	No direct linkage between compensation and quality; no differential pay for stronger or weaker teachers	Direct attention paid to the quality of the work, with stronger teachers theoretically receiving higher compensation
Collaboration and Collegiality	No direct influence	May promote competition for limited rewards among teachers, potentially limiting collegiality in the school environment
Funding	Easier to allocate funding because salaries are based on input characteristics of teachers	Funding limits may lead to insufficient funds to reward all teachers deemed deserving of merit pay and/or to quota systems that create competition by limiting reward availability from the outset
Ease of Administration	Straightforward administration; primarily requires record keeping on teacher input characteristics and any acquired education	Complex administration, including close linkages to the system of teacher evaluation and/or student performance measures

traditionally proved elusive because "no single set of teacher characteristics, teacher behaviors, curricular approaches, or organizational devices guarantees a high probability of success in the classroom."[35] Moreover, the traditional reliance of merit pay plans on administrator ratings, often gathered through a limited number of classroom observations and informal interactions, has consistently raised questions about their fairness. These concerns, along with a chronic problem of insufficient funds to support merit pay programs, have led to a history of limited effectiveness; indeed, the failure of many merit pay plans in the past is the basis for much of the opposition to recent compensation reform efforts.[36]

The single-salary schedule, easier to implement and more concrete in its definitions of fairness, was thus the dominant compensation model for teachers at the midpoint of the century. Nevertheless, although the single-salary system was developed partially in reaction to concerns about the fairness of previous systems, concerns about its own fairness emerged as well, for a related reason. Acknowledging the different levels of skill and competency that teachers demonstrate, some began to raise concerns that a system paying teachers based solely on experience and academic preparation with no performance measure was unfair to those teachers who demonstrated exceptional performance. Moreover, such a system offered little incentive for exemplary performance and little recourse to require change in minimally competent performance.[37]

These concerns about the single-salary schedule have been most prominent during periods considered to be educational crises in the country, when society called out for better results from schools and teachers. In the late 1950s, after the launch of Sputnik, merit pay plans again emerged for discussion, with an emphasis on how to ensure that high-quality teachers were providing the kind of high-quality education needed to prepare the next generation of cold war scientists and innovators.[38] These plans, however, like their predecessors, also disappeared from use, until the school reform initiatives of the 1980s and 1990s brought the issue of compensation linked to results back into discussion. The 1983 report *A Nation at Risk* recommended that teacher pay be "professionally competitive, market-sensitive, and performance-based."[39] This aspect of the report, coupled with the larger quality concerns it raised, contributed to another movement toward establishing alternative compensation structures for teachers.

Compensation Reform Efforts: Changing the System

Compensation reform efforts following *A Nation at Risk* generally eschewed the term *merit pay* and advocated that models including performance components for teachers use multiple data sources for evaluation and attempt to limit subjectivity. Career ladders, which began to grow in popularity during the 1980s, incorporate the basic structure of the single-salary schedule but make it more flexible, attempting to accomplish three primary goals:

- To add greater relevance and accountability to the steps and lanes of the salary scale
- To identify and support those teachers developing and performing at a high level
- To reward these high-performing teachers with opportunities for leadership roles as well as financial incentives

Career ladder models establish a series of career steps for teachers to achieve, usually designated by titles such as teacher leader, expert teacher, and master teacher. Teachers move up a career ladder by demonstrating professional growth and differentiated roles based on a set of specific criteria. In most career ladder models, movement up the steps results in increased salary and also opportunities for involvement in curriculum development, professional development, or other leadership responsibilities.[40]

However, many career ladder models established in the mid- to late 1980s were abandoned after only a few years, primarily due to lack of funding. Moreover, many teachers opposed career ladder systems for the same reasons that merit pay systems were opposed: the subjective nature of some of the measures, particularly the notion of involving supervisor ratings of teaching performance and the issue of competition.[41] Because of their structure and emphasis on moving teachers into leadership positions, most career ladder systems have quotas, which may exacerbate the competition issue and engender resentment among some teachers for those who are so visibly recognized.

Over the last century, the pendulum swing between the single-salary schedule and merit pay programs has allowed exploration of the issues of fairness and feasibility in implementating compensation options. Over the last 25 years, additional compensation options have emerged in efforts to respond to the concerns that limit the two traditional models; career ladder models represent one of these options. Other recent efforts to identify and collect data on specific behaviors fundamental to good teaching are beginning to earn respect among teachers, administrators, and teacher unions. The framework set forth by the National Board for Professional Teaching Standards and results of teacher effectiveness studies are legitimizing and standardizing the idea of objective assessment of teacher performance.[42] Moreover, within the accountability context begun with the standards movement and sustained by the No Child Left Behind Act, we have reached another era of high concern for teacher development, quality, and accountability, necessitating further close examination of compensation structures and their relationship to supporting the goals of attracting, developing, and retaining quality teachers.

CURRENT ISSUES AND TRENDS IN TEACHER COMPENSATION

In the mid- to late 1990s and extending through this present time, another wave of alternative compensation systems has continued to emerge in America in conjunction with movements for standards and accountability across the educational system. School districts currently, in an effort to respond both to predicted teacher shortages and to teachers' concerns about the history of unsuccessful teacher pay programs, appear to be relying more on theories of motivation and organizational management, recent research on teacher effectiveness, and lessons learned from the past as the basis for new frameworks for alternative compensation models.

The educational climate of the last decade or so has been characterized by an emphasis on establishing challenging content standards for students and accountability systems to measure performance against those standards. Likewise, contemporary models for changing teacher compensation reflect attention to identifying performance standards and measures, as well as a focus on linking teacher performance to student achievement. In addition, many emerging models place a strong emphasis on teacher growth and development, focusing attention on the professionalism of teaching.

The various emerging systems for alternative compensation may be classified into two major categories of emphasis, although many systems incorporate aspects of both in practice:

- School-based performance awards
- Knowledge- and skills-based pay

The first category primarily reflects the emphasis on student achievement, the second on professional development.

School-Based Performance Awards

Programs emphasizing school-based performance awards (SBPA) are grounded in the notion that the mission, goals, and major emphases across school programs should be focused on improving student achievement. Such compensation systems delineate specific goals for growth and then reward the schools achieving the goals. Most SBPA programs emphasize measurement of the achievement of a *group*, encouraging grade-level, departmental, or schoolwide teams in achieving goals, based on a philosophy that teaching should be a collaborative effort and that a climate of competition should be avoided.

Financial rewards from SBPA programs may go directly to the staff individually or to the school budget, as individual bonuses or to support improvements for the school as a whole. The incentive of individual bonuses seems to be a strong motivator, however, and many programs are designed to provide bonuses not only to teachers but to support staff as well.[43] For example, in the early 1990s, a school district in North Carolina awarded bonuses to every employee in the school district if the employee met individual and school performance goals. Employees could earn a bonus of up to six percent of their annual salary.[44] Conversely, a SBPA program came under fire in Houston when 81 percent of the employees in the school district were eligible for bonuses based on student achievement goals set by the individual schools. The program did not serve as an incentive, but as a joke to the community.[45] Most SBPA programs use a format in which rewards are bonuses to be added to base pay and must be re-earned each period in the program. Ideally, this encourages ongoing efforts to strive toward the goals of improvement and achievement.

One key aspect of school-based performance award programs is the need to establish clear, attainable goals and specific means for measuring the goals. Because most programs recognize the performance of groups at a grade, team, or schoolwide level, they provide the opportunity to streamline multiple initiatives and to leverage various resources, including professional development funds, to support these goals.[46] SBPA systems also align various goals that teachers view as positive, including student achievement, professional development opportunities, and financial rewards. According to case study research collected by the Consortium for Policy Research in Education (CPRE), aligned goal emphasis and leveraged resources in SBPA programs are contributing to improved school performance in some districts implementing the plans.[47]

The CPRE postulated several conditions that must be present to support the success of SBPA programs, based on their case study research and its relationship to motivation theory:

- Teachers must believe in their ability to achieve the program goals, and those goals must be in line with the goals of other programs in place at the school.
- Teachers must also perceive the program as fair, well implemented, and consistent with other goals they maintain, such as student achievement.
- The possible positive outcomes of the program must be greater than its potential negative outcomes, such as stress and increased workload.[48]

Although some districts are cautious about implementing SBPA programs because of a perception that teachers may feel threatened by them or may demonstrate an inappropriately competitive response, several existing programs have found extensive support from teachers in their implementation. In the North Carolina school district discussed previously in this section, teachers voted to continue a differentiated pay plan for all employees rather than change to awarding equal bonuses to only certified employees during a statewide financial crisis. One teacher explained, "We don't want people to say we just got a handout. We can show we are accountable for the dollars we get."[49] In addition, teachers who supported new plans in Denver and Minneapolis stated that they feel a lack of public respect and increasing pressure from accountability efforts. Performance-based programs allow teachers to exert more control over their own destiny and strengthen their sense of professionalism.[50]

Knowledge- and Skills-Based Pay

A second category of contemporary performance award programs being explored in teacher compensation systems is knowledge- and skills-based pay (KSBP). This type of program, sometimes known as competency pay, reflects an emphasis on demonstrated professional growth and development as a basis for compensation. Thus it rewards teachers for acquiring and using professional expertise. In this way, it resembles the traditional single-salary schedule that pays teachers higher salaries based on acquisition of graduate credits and degrees. Therefore, while KSBP incorporates various new elements into teacher pay, its underlying concepts are relatively familiar to most teachers.

In KSBP systems, teachers receive compensation for professional development that is linked to their teaching assignment and for demonstration of good teaching as determined by specific standards. In some cases, those standards are locally determined. However, many KSBP systems also use externally determined standards, such as those of the National Board for Professional Teaching Standards (NBPTS), singly or in combination with local standards. Such incorporation of externally determined standards, with external evaluators assessing teacher work, is generally supported by teachers as a way to promote fairness within the system.

Most KSBP systems identify knowledge or skill blocks—for example, in content area reading or in instructional technology applications—and define valid and reliable ways for teachers to demonstrate achievement of those blocks. The types of blocks may be categorized as *depth skills, breadth skills,* and *vertical skills.* Within this categorization,

- depth skills are intended to strengthen expertise in a given functional or discipline area, such as increasing content knowledge in a subject;
- breadth skills refer to lateral knowledge, such as increasing a teacher's expertise in subject areas other than their primary emphasis or in working more effectively with special needs students;
- vertical skills refer to the development of leadership and management competencies.

These three categories may also overlap to some degree, with the development of skills in such areas as peer mentoring, curriculum development, or staff development reflecting aspects of multiple categories.

Knowledge and skills blocks can then be assigned relative value in terms of how much bonus or advancement pay they merit, based on the difficulty of achieving each block and its value to the school. For example, in KSBP systems that acknowledge National Board Certification, teachers who achieve certification would be likely to receive a higher bonus for that than for a more condensed, specific block because of the extensive NBPTS requirements. Or, in a different KSBP system that has identified a significant need for differentiated instruction, teachers who complete a district-selected training regimen and demonstrate appropriate use of new knowledge and skills in this area would receive additional pay.

In KSBP, teacher evaluation methods may incorporate classroom observation by an administrator or peer but usually also involve a portfolio approach in which teachers must use multiple means to demonstrate their achievement. As with the use of externally determined standards, the review of teacher portfolios by a more external group, rather than a teacher's immediate supervisor alone, promotes a sense of fairness and objectivity in the system.

Because of the nature of teaching as a practice, KSBP programs require careful attention to the standards against which knowledge and skill will be assessed. In addition, teacher unions have emphasized that for such programs to be fair, administrators must ensure that teachers will have appropriate opportunities to demonstrate their competency and that the supervision will be held to an appropriately high quality.[51]

Compensation in Public Education and in Private Industry

Pay-for-performance programs, productivity bonuses, and similar compensation strategies designed to improve performance and motivate employees are common practice in the business sector and represent one source from which educators may draw guidelines and frameworks for alternative compensation programs.[52] However, concerns about the validity of comparing public education and private industry on these issues are often voiced, based on several key issues:

- The variability among the resources (students) that teachers have to work with in order to generate results (achievement)
- Fear of industrializing or mechanizing the process of education
- The determination of what product is desired and how productivity should be measured[53]

Thus, again, concerns center around fairness and the different contexts in which teachers work, given the different experiences students bring to the classroom.[54]

Another concern is the public nature of pay information for public employees. Corporate pay plans may be kept confidential, but teacher pay and that of other government employees is a matter of public record.[55] A further, less tangible area of concern about performance-related pay in the private versus the public sector is the fundamental assumption and purpose behind such a pay system: whether the purpose is to *reward* some employees for outstanding performance or to *weed out or punish* other employees for poor performance.[56] Within the crisis-oriented context of today's public education system, performance-based pay systems are frequently interpreted by teachers as representing the stick rather than the carrot.

Proponents of connecting pay to performance argue that other nonprofit organizations and government agencies also use pay-for-performance systems.[57] Indeed, they also point to the success in improving achievement of for-profit educational firms, such as Sylvan Learning Systems, suggesting that the link between public and private sector productivity is not as distant as opponents suggest.[58] Looking at other methods for linking teacher pay to performance measures, supporters have argued that few professional jobs may be directly linked to specific measures of productivity, and that the establishment of *competency-based pay* makes performance pay a reasonable system for professional positions, including teaching.[59]

A final area of concern around the difference between performance-based compensation in public education and in private industry is basic finance. Private industry is able to provide bonuses for productivity largely because productivity results in higher revenue. In private industry, the alignment between compensation and performance is clear. The "bottom line" is, quite literally, money; therefore, performance that contributes to the company's "bottom line" is rewarded with an increased share of the "bottom line"—that is, money. In education, the alignment is less evident. The "bottom line" in education is student achievement. Thus the age-old assumption that student learning is "its own reward" for quality teachers and the criticism that linking pay to teacher effectiveness is somehow an affront to teachers' inherent altruism.

Public education systems hoping to establish performance-based pay programs must find other ways of funding the initiatives, because loss of funding has been the downfall of many innovative compensation programs in the past. Nevertheless, dedicated funding to the program over time, whether through profit projections or through reallocation of funds, is central to the successful establishment of alternative compensation systems.

TEACHER PAY AND TEACHER QUALITY

In a societal context emphasizing educational reform, within which key goals are improving student achievement and ensuring qualified teachers in every classroom, teacher compensation systems are being examined as an avenue for change with the potential to support both of those goals. Moreover, policymakers and policy researchers predict that offering alternative compensation systems may facilitate the related goals of recruiting and retaining quality teachers despite the attractions of other professions.

Given these goals, the rationale for restructuring the teacher compensation system in a school district may be addressed in light of three teacher quality factors:

- Attracting quality teacher candidates to the profession
- Developing professionals across the career span
- Retaining quality teachers in the classroom

Each of these fundamentally important factors is addressed in the following pages.

Attracting Quality Teachers

Teacher salaries, both at the beginning teacher pay level as well as cumulative pay across the teaching career, put the education profession at a disadvantage in attracting candidates of high potential. Teacher salaries remain somewhat low compared to those of professionals with similar educational preparation. Studies comparing salary rates have consistently demonstrated that teacher salaries are more comparable to salaries in technical fields than to the professions, and few occupations requiring college degrees have salaries lower than those found in teaching.[60] In 2002, beginning teachers earned much less than their classmates who entered other occupations. Consider the following occupations and salaries for those beginning a career in the given field:

Teaching	$30,719
Liberal arts	$34,568
Sales/marketing	$37,946
Business administration	$40,242
Accounting	$41,162
Computer science	$46,495
Math/statistics	$46,744
Engineering	$49,702[61]

A beginning engineer earns more than 50 percent more than a beginning teacher, although both individuals may have spent the same amount of time and money on their postsecondary education.

In addition, the broadening of career opportunities for women and minorities over the last several decades has influenced young people's professional decision making, requiring school systems to focus additional attention on recruitment practices to entice candidates to the profession.[62] Yet, the dire predictions of teacher shortages are also connected to the issue of aging and retiring teachers, not solely to data regarding teacher preparation programs. Many college students still enter and graduate from these programs, and there is also a trend of professionals from other fields entering education as a second career. Consequently, candidates are available; school districts must then find ways to attract the most talented candidates to their schools. Although conventional wisdom suggests that teachers enter the field for the intrinsic rewards and the service orientation, not for the financial incentives, salary is, nevertheless, an important consideration, and noncompetitive salaries have been found to be one of several significant factors that contribute to novice teachers' departures from the profession during the first five years in the classroom.[63]

Salaries vary considerably from one school district or state to another, both in terms of starting salaries and rate of increase. School districts must carefully examine the degree to which their initial offerings are competitive and sufficiently attractive to new teachers, as well as how quickly and through what means teachers will be able to earn higher pay. Many school districts and states are seeking innovative ways to make entrance into the teaching profession a more attractive proposition. Some current innovations include the following:

- Signing bonuses, such as those used by Massachusetts
- Bonuses for those teaching in hard-to-staff schools in Denver
- Scholarships or loan forgiveness, by which college students in education pledge to teach for a certain period in a state's high need areas in exchange for tuition support and/or loan forgiveness, as used in North Carolina
- Increases to the overall salary system, such as those implemented in Connecticut, whereby teacher salaries are given a higher fiscal priority statewide
- Alternative salary scales, such as the system piloted in Cincinnati, which offers a reasonable starting salary but also offers novice teachers the opportunity to move more quickly up the steps of the scale[64]

Each of these options, by offering teachers immediate financial incentives and/or pledging financial flexibility over the career span, makes the profession more attractive to entering teachers than a traditional salary schedule and thus has the potential to increase the applicant pool.

Developing Teachers

A second key area of focus is the need to ensure quality among practicing teachers and to encourage continuous improvement over the career span. A growing body of research continues to amass evidence that teachers influence student achievement more than any other factor, emphasizing both the positive effect of stronger teachers and the negative effect of weaker teachers.[65] We know through empirical evidence that effective teachers use classroom time carefully, effectively manage student behavior, ask questions that support student learning, and provide timely and useful feedback to students.[66] This research strengthens the argument for supporting teacher growth and acknowledging exemplary practice. Moreover, some motivation theories suggest that even in occupations with high potential for intrinsic rewards—such as the emotional benefits teachers gain while supporting student learning—there is still a relationship between compensation and job satisfaction.[67]

The traditional salary schedule provides incentives for teachers to remain over time by compensating them based on longevity, and it encourages teachers to gain more education through graduate coursework, but it does not necessarily promote teacher development tied directly to job assignment. Moreover, the traditional salary schedule rewards *putting in time* far more than exerting exceptional effort, and it rewards exemplary and mediocre performance at approximately the same level. Compensation that is linked directly to demonstration of professional growth and/or professional performance, on the other hand, has the potential to respond to public demands for improvement in teaching in return for tax dollars spent. Linking compensation to professional development has the capacity to stimulate the acquisition of the knowledge and skills necessary to teach to the rigorous standards in today's schools.

Not only might a compensation system encourage professional growth and development in teachers, but it can also potentially influence the role and development of administrators. If administrators must play a crucial role in assessing teachers fairly and accurately for a system that incorporates performance evaluation, then they must give primary focus to their own role as instructional leaders.[68] Indeed, proponents of alternative compensation systems suggest that linking compensation more directly to professional development and improvement efforts can promote increased discussion of quality instruction throughout a school and a school system.[69]

Retaining Quality Teachers

Just as it is in a school district's best interest to invest in developing teacher talent through professional development and incentives for growth, it is also in the district's best interest to encourage teachers to remain with the district over time. Moreover, it is in the best interest of the education profession to encourage teachers to remain in practice over the long term due to the effects of teacher experience (or lack thereof) on student achievement. In a review of the extant literature on teacher experience, Stronge reported that experienced teachers are more effective in the classroom than novice teachers.[70] Experienced teachers have better planning skills, use a variety of teaching strategies, are better organized, and deal with discipline issues more effectively. Consequently, a third area of focus in restructuring compensation systems is the need to retain quality teachers by avoiding reaching the maximum income range on the salary scale too quickly.

Studies investigating teacher attrition have documented that among those teachers who leave the profession, newer teachers—who receive lower pay—leave most quickly,[71] and frequently they cite low pay as a major reason for their attrition.[72] The traditional single-salary schedule is perhaps most disadvantageous to novice teachers in their early years; most salary schedules are *back-loaded,* meaning that salaries rise more steeply at the higher levels, representing more experienced teachers, than at the lower levels where novice teachers are placed. Given this structure, it may take newer teachers many years to achieve a competitive salary. Yet some teachers, even in their earliest years in the profession, demonstrate high effectiveness along with high motivation. Alternative salary systems have the potential to reward these effective teachers and to encourage them to remain in the profession over time.

At the other end of the career span, more experienced teachers also are influenced by the salary schedule and may be disadvantaged by it. Most single-salary schedules allow a teacher to continue to move up a scale over a number of years; but after 15 or 20 years in the system, teachers generally reach the highest salary possible within their lane and can receive additional raises only through cost-of-living increases or gaining higher education. Other options for these career teachers to increase their salary are to leave the classroom for administrative positions or to leave education altogether and pursue a new career. Thus the system promotes the removal of high-quality, motivated, experienced teachers from the setting in which they may have the greatest influence over individual student learning. Alternative compensation systems, by employing levels of teacher performance in a ladder-type system or by providing bonuses for specific performance demonstrations, can help to maintain teacher motivation over time and can help to eliminate the topping-out problem by linking extra compensation to yearly performance.

CONCLUDING THOUGHTS: WHERE DO WE GO FROM HERE?

Although some theories would suggest that there is a danger in emphasizing extrinsic over intrinsic motivation by implementing a system that uses performance-based awards, the theories that illustrate a clear emphasis on goal setting and the achievability of goals at individual and group levels are important to acknowledge and consider in terms of planning an alternative compensation system.

Teachers may not enter the profession of teaching for monetary gain. However, opportunities in the marketplace are too open and varied in today's world to necessitate that individuals feel that teaching is their only option. In fact, many teachers who leave the profession cite low salary as part of their reason for leaving, especially if they feel ineffective in their role.[73] With this in mind, a teacher compensation system that places emphasis on professional development and related performance goals as primary motivators, with financial rewards as an added incentive, has the potential to promote good will in teaching as well as enhancing performance throughout the system.

Compensation as Part of a Total Educational System

One important aspect of the rationale for changing teacher compensation systems is recognition that teacher compensation should be linked to *other organizational changes* within school districts and within the field of education as a whole.[74] Recent reform emphases in education include

- a results orientation linked to clear performance standards and regular measurement,
- teaching to high standards for all students,
- greater participation by teachers in school management, with corresponding greater emphasis on teamwork.[75]

Within a standards-based reform environment, standards for teacher performance are a natural outgrowth, and professional development to help teachers support student achievement of standards is also a necessity. Similarly, organizational and management frameworks that promote more decision making and empowerment at the school level also support compensation systems that encourage teachers to take charge of their own placement on a salary scale or their own receipt of bonuses for performance.

Next Steps

In *Teacher Pay and Teacher Quality: Attracting, Developing, and Retaining the Best*, we focus on the practical aspects of connecting issues of quality with issues of compensation. In the book, we don't attempt to carve out new theoretical territory; rather, our interest is in providing our readers with practical applications of how to proceed in a step-by-step fashion in the important work of focusing financial resources on attracting, supporting, and retaining a quality teacher workforce. In this introductory chapter, we offer a brief overview of teacher pay in terms of where we've come from, where we are, where we might want to go, and why we might want to go there. Indeed, throughout the book, our focus is on the all-important nexus of teacher pay and teacher quality.

2

Teacher Pay and School Purposes

How Do They Relate?

Chapter 1 explored the history of teacher compensation structures and some key issues in attracting, developing, and retaining quality teachers in today's school systems. Based on this broad survey, it is clear that schools have a wide range of options related to teacher compensation, as well as a considerable number of challenges to face in achieving the goals of attracting, developing, and retaining quality teachers. As noted in the first chapter, the purpose of this book is to provide practical guidelines and step-by-step suggestions for reviewing and strengthening teacher compensation systems to respond to these challenges.

At the beginning of any set of steps, as at the beginning of any purposeful journey, we must first examine where we are going and how we will assess our progress along the way. Consequently, this chapter begins with an exploration of how goals for compensation systems linking teacher pay and teacher quality fit within the big picture of a school district's overall goals and direction. We will then address initial steps critical to launching a review and potential restructuring of a compensation system, specifically focusing on an examination of the assumptions and shared beliefs that characterize the work of the school district and, by extension, the teacher compensation system. Finally, we will identify key principles to consider in examining teacher compensation systems, as well as considerations for quality criteria that form the basis for evaluation.

ALIGNING TEACHER COMPENSATION WITH ORGANIZATIONAL PURPOSE AND DIRECTION

Of course, the central purpose of schools is not to compensate teachers; nor, as noted in Chapter 1, do most teachers pursue careers in education primarily because of the compensation they will receive. Nevertheless, the teacher compensation system is an important part of the set of structures and policies school districts put in place to work toward their central purposes. Attracting, developing, and retaining quality teachers are considerations much closer to the central purposes of schools than compensation per se because of the influence these quality teachers have on students and learning. An organization gains strength when its many components and elements are directed toward a common, central mission and when each component can be acknowledged as part of that effort. Therefore, a first critical consideration in exploring a school district's teacher compensation system is how it is or may be directed toward supporting the mission and goals of the school district at large.

Mission, Vision, and Teacher Compensation

In the language of organizations, *mission* and *vision* are critical, interrelated elements that should infuse the work of a given organization at every level and within every unit. A *mission* is a sense of purpose, infused with the shared beliefs of the organization's members, and guided by a *vision* of an ideal future for the organization and those it serves. Vision and mission are influenced by past events and traditions; relevant external factors, priorities, and values of the members of the organization; and the intuition of leaders and members about what the future will bring and the role the organization may play in that future.[1] When vision and mission are articulated and shared by the members of an organization, they support motivation and energy, a proactive orientation, and direction for action.[2]

An organization's mission statement may be read as the collective response to the question, "Why do we exist?"[3] The development of a mission statement requires careful reflection by members of an organization on what they most value, what they hope to achieve, what they believe it is possible to achieve, and what will be involved in working toward those values and possibilities. Mission statements of schools and school districts generally focus attention on varied purposes and philosophies of education, with emphasis on students, their learning and capabilities in the present and future, and the future of society. Some of the elements that frequently appear in school mission statements include *helping each child achieve his or her full potential, striving for high academic standards, promoting lifelong learning, encouraging responsible citizenship, respecting and celebrating diversity, maintaining safe and nurturing environments, working in partnership with families and community,* and *preparing for the challenges of the future.*[4]

Although a mission statement may not make specific reference to personnel roles or responsibilities, building a mission as a shared sense of purpose requires careful consideration of what the members of the organization can and must do to realize that mission.[5] This, then, is a critical linkage to beliefs about the characteristics and quality of those who work within the organization. In the case of schools, mission statements often do not specifically state anything about teacher quality; yet they say much about intended outcomes and imply that the quality of the school and its teachers influences the achievement of those outcomes.

Once articulated, a mission statement provides the basis for developing strategic goals and measures of evaluation to assess progress and achievement. For example, a school district that includes striving for high academic standards in its mission statement might have strategic goals specifically identifying desired performance levels on standardized tests and desired rates of participation in advanced courses. A mission statement incorporating emphasis on partnership with families and community might have strategic goals focused on increasing parental involvement in school activities and on developing school-business partnerships and local internship opportunities for students.

To support alignment with and progress toward strategic goals, the mission statement should be shared and used as a fundamental consideration for all initiatives of the school district, with attention to how each unit within the organization is striving toward the mission with its goals, plans, and activities. Thus all human resource functions, including the policies and procedures for teacher compensation, should be linked directly to the mission and to the strategic goals it informs. Key human resource goals and functions include the recruitment, selection, and induction of new teachers for the district and the retention of quality teachers, as well as monitoring and acknowledging the progress teachers make in their professional development while employed by the district. As a result, exploring the role of compensation systems in attracting, developing, and retaining quality teachers ties to these human resource imperatives. At a more global level, the teacher compensation system—and the human resource imperatives—should all be aligned with the larger school district goals and mission of increased student learning, which are presumed to be in large part related to enhanced teacher quality.[6]

An Example

Throughout the chapters of this book, we will be providing examples from a hypothetical school district to illustrate key ideas. This hypothetical district, which we call *Lincoln Public Schools* (LPS), is based on our

Figure 2.1   Mission Statement for Lincoln Public Schools

The mission of the Lincoln Public Schools is to provide an excellent education, in partnership with families and community in order to prepare all students to meet high academic standards, to strive toward their individual potential; and to function effectively as responsible citizens in the changing society of the twenty-first century.

experiences with a variety of real school districts and reflects no single district, but rather a conglomeration of elements from many districts across multiple states and regions. Figure 2.1 offers a mission statement for the hypothetical LPS.

This mission statement focuses on three key elements of student development—meeting high academic standards, reaching potential, and developing responsible citizenship. It highlights the involvement of families and community as partners with the school system in the educational endeavor. The statement also addresses awareness of changing societal needs in the future that students will face. Given this mission statement, Figure 2.2 illustrates how the elements of the mission and one or two selected goals for each element influence some key considerations in attracting, developing, and retaining quality teachers, and may in turn influence the compensation system.

Thus, for any school district's mission and related goals, linkages should be made to attract, develop, and retain quality teachers. These implications then form a key set of considerations for how a teacher compensation system must be structured to promote the intended outcomes.

Vision, Mission, and Change

A vision represents an ideal future toward which an organization strives; a mission statement articulates purpose and direction toward that vision. Purpose and direction imply movement and growth; therefore vision and mission by their nature emphasize a desire for change. In examining a compensation system with an eye to pursuing the organizational mission, the emphasis should likewise be on assessing need for change and how to link any changes in a compensation system to other organizational changes within school districts and within the field of education as a whole.[7] Recent reform emphases in education include (a) a results orientation linked to clear performance standards and regular measurement; (b) teaching to high standards for all students; and (c) greater participation by teachers in school management, with corresponding greater emphasis on teamwork.[8] Within a standards-based reform environment, standards for teacher performance are a natural outgrowth, including definitions of key elements and measures of teacher quality. Moreover, professional development to help teachers support student achievement of standards is also a necessity in increasing teacher quality; by extension, compensation

Figure 2.2   Linking Mission and Goals With Attracting, Developing, and Retaining Quality Teachers

Mission Statement Elements	Selected Goals	Considerations for Teacher Quality and Human Resource Imperatives
Meeting high academic standards	• To increase student achievement rates on standardized tests • To increase student participation in advanced courses at high school level	• How to *attract* and *retain* teachers whose students show high achievement rates • How to *attract* and *retain* sufficient teachers qualified to teach advanced courses • How to *develop* teacher capacity to teach to high academic standards and in advanced courses
Striving for individual potential	• To demonstrate evidence of student growth gains across varied groups within the population, including students with special needs, students with advanced abilities, and students from economically disadvantaged backgrounds	• How to *attract* and *retain* teachers with qualifications to work with special populations of students • How to *develop* in teachers the skills needed to respond to the individual needs of special populations of learners • How to *attract* and *retain* quality teachers in critical shortage and specialty areas
Developing responsible citizens	• To demonstrate increasing evidence of student awareness of and involvement in the roles and responsibilities of citizenship, including improved school behavior and increased involvement of students in school and community initiatives	• How to *develop* teacher skills in maintaining discipline and promoting student involvement • How to *attract* and *retain* teachers who contribute to and involve students in school initiatives beyond the classroom
Partnerships with families and community	• To increase parental involvement in school initiatives • To develop community partnerships focused on student learning with local businesses and organizations	• How to *attract* and *retain* teachers who promote quality relationships with parents and the community • How to *develop* teacher skills in promoting community partnerships
Preparation for changing needs of twenty-first-century society	• To demonstrate evidence of learning goals among staff to maintain updated knowledge and to model lifelong learning for students • To increase technological competency among students and school staff	• How to *attract* and *retain* teachers who proactively seek opportunities for learning and professional growth • How to *develop* specific skills and competencies among staff and promote ongoing skill development

systems should reflect recognition and support of such professional development and increasing quality. Similarly, organizational and management frameworks that promote more decision making and empowerment at the school level also support compensation systems that encourage teachers to take charge of their own placement on a salary scale or their own pursuit of bonuses for exceptional performance.

Schools and school districts are complex environments, and any process of purposeful change within them is likewise complex. For successful change to occur, critical elements that must be in place or developed include *vision, skills, incentives, resources,* and *an action plan;* without a clear sense of vision, confusion results, and without incentive to change, resistance results.[9] Compensation systems represent, in part, incentives for growth and change; and the more directly the teacher compensation system relates to the school district's ideal vision, the stronger and more influential an incentive it is likely to be.

Launching the Process: Examining What We Believe About Teacher Quality and Compensation

Beyond a basic understanding of compensation as payment for services rendered, the form and elements of a teacher compensation system are grounded in assumptions and beliefs about teacher practice, the profession of teaching, and what influences teacher quality. In a quite literal sense, a compensation system demonstrates what a school district *values* in terms of teacher characteristics, behaviors, and professional choices. Moreover, the way a compensation system is structured illuminates beliefs about how teacher quality *develops* and how it is *demonstrated,* as illustrated in the following examples:

- A compensation system that is based strictly or primarily on longevity demonstrates value placed on long-term commitment to the profession and assumes that quality develops with experience.
- A compensation system that provides different salary scales based on degrees earned demonstrates an assumption that a teacher's quality improves as he or she gains more formal education.
- A compensation system that provides extra pay for engaging in extra tasks, such as coaching a team or taking on a leadership role on a committee or a task force, fundamentally assumes that compensation should be tied to quantity of tasks undertaken and that quality relates to total sum contributions to the work of the school district.

These examples reflect elements of traditional teacher compensation systems, which pay teachers based on their experience and their education while providing additional compensation for additional work.

Alternative compensation systems, briefly addressed in Chapter 1 and in further detail in Chapters 4 and 5, reflect additional assumptions about compensation and teacher quality, as illustrated in these examples:

- A compensation system that provides rewards for student outcomes reveals an emphasis on teachers' influence on student learning, with the assumption that teacher quality is demonstrated primarily in the achievements of students.
- A compensation system that provides differential pay for different teaching roles (e.g., providing differential pay for teachers in math, science, or other shortage areas) reflects an assumption that level of demand is an element of defining quality, even if indirectly.
- A compensation system that incorporates specific funds to support pursuit of new knowledge and skills, as well as rewarding such growth with salary increases, incorporates attention both to *incentives* and to *capacity building*,[10] while assuming that teacher learning and teacher quality are interrelated.

Fundamentally, characteristics of a compensation system communicate assumptions about and value placed upon each of the key goals discussed in this text—attracting, developing, and retaining teachers. For example, a school system demonstrates strong emphasis on *attracting* teachers with such compensation elements as signing bonuses, highly competitive salaries at the initial steps, and special incentives for teachers in critical shortage areas. Emphasis on *developing* teachers is reflected in the options available for increasing pay through professional development or specific performance evidence linked to individual or group growth efforts. A compensation system's emphasis on *retaining* teachers is revealed in such details as the rate of progression across steps on a salary scale and in methods that prevent experienced and highly educated teachers from "topping out" in salary. As we will see throughout this book, an effective compensation system should reflect attention to all three key goals in its structure, demonstrating comprehensiveness and flexibility and serving as an incentive for teachers entering and progressing through the school district.

Because compensation systems reflect and communicate assumptions about teacher quality, it is critical that school leaders carefully consider what those communicated assumptions are, and whether the assumptions embedded within the compensation system are the same beliefs communicated by the mission statement and shared among the members of the organization as a whole. Consequently, any review and restructuring of a compensation system should *begin* with reflection upon questions such as those given in Figure 2.3.

Although individual educators and school leaders may differ in their beliefs and their responses to these questions, and although different

Figure 2.3   Examining Assumptions and the Messages of the
Compensation System

Examining Overarching Beliefs	Examining Assumptions Communicated About Teacher Quality
What do we believe about teacher quality? What are the elements that define teacher quality?	• What role does experience play in defining teacher quality? What type(s) of experience is/are relevant? • What role does teacher education play in defining teacher quality? • What role does pursuit of further professional development play in defining teacher quality? • What role does demonstration of developed knowledge and skills play in defining teacher quality? • What role does student achievement play in defining teacher quality? • What role does involvement in school district initiatives beyond specific job expectations play in defining teacher quality? • What evidence demonstrates levels of and increases in teacher quality, relative to each of the elements noted above?
What do we believe about the relationship between teacher compensation and teacher quality?	• Should teachers be compensated for demonstrated increases in quality, given definitions of teacher quality determined above? • What types of connections between quality and compensation exist in our current compensation system? • What incentives does the current compensation system provide for teachers of high quality to apply to and enter the school district? • What incentives does the current compensation system provide for teachers to increase in quality, given definitions of quality determined above? • Do incentives exist for teachers to do more than meet minimum job expectations? • What incentives does the current compensation system provide for quality teachers to remain with the school district over time?

school districts may vary in their decisions about compensation systems, the guidelines for considering compensation systems in this book rely on the core assumptions that compensation and teacher quality are linked, that strengthening compensation systems provides incentive for strengthening teacher quality, and that teacher quality is critical in promoting student learning, which is fundamental to the mission of schools. Therefore, a school district's responses to the above questions are critical in determining how the district will define teacher quality and how the compensation system must be structured to reflect and communicate that definition, thus providing support for the goals of attracting, developing, and retaining quality teachers.

MOVING FORWARD: KEY CONSIDERATIONS FOR DEVELOPING A COMPENSATION SYSTEM

The previous discussion focused on exploration of core beliefs and assumptions about teacher quality and teacher compensation. Such consideration of beliefs and assumptions should occur both at the beginning of a review and restructuring of a compensation system and also as an ongoing reflection throughout the process. This will help to ensure that the compensation system, in the end, communicates the desired message to the teachers whom the school district wishes to attract, develop, and retain. To support communication of the desired message and, ultimately, to support the central goals of attracting, developing, and retaining quality teachers, the process of reviewing and restructuring should be guided by shared assumptions about how an effective compensation system should be developed and what it should look like. Although some aspects of these shared assumptions may vary across different school districts, embedded within them are several essential principles that should be considered. The following statements represent some assumptions and key considerations about the process of restructuring compensation systems and about the outcomes of that process; a summary of essential principles for developing a comprehensive compensation system appears at the end of the section.

Assumptions and Key Considerations About the Process

• The process of designing a teacher compensation system should be collaborative, involving and soliciting input from multiple stakeholders.

• The process of designing a teacher compensation system should include assessment of current and projected needs through data collection from multiple sources.

• The process of designing a teacher compensation system should include attention to feasibility and resource allocation.

• The process of designing a teacher compensation system should include consideration of allocating resources for *capacity building* (investing in teacher development) as well as for *inducements* (rewards for actions or performance).[11]

• The process of designing a teacher compensation system should explore and address stakeholder assumptions about potentially divisive issues in compensation. These issues include (a) definitions of teacher quality as demonstrated through varied performance indicators; (b) acknowledgement of *group* versus *individual* performance; and (c) differential pay for teaching positions in critical shortage areas, including specific content areas or with special populations of students.

• The process of designing a teacher compensation system should explore the alignment of design elements to teacher responsibilities and school district goals in order to ensure that the compensation system supports and does not conflict with these responsibilities and goals. For example, a compensation system that fosters competition among individual teachers for performance rewards may conflict with goals emphasizing the collaborative efforts of school teams toward supporting learning for all students.

Assumptions and Key Considerations for the Compensation System

• A teacher compensation system should align with the school district's mission and goals.

• A teacher compensation system should provide opportunities for teachers to receive greater compensation relative to greater demonstrations of teaching quality, rather than allowing equal compensation for all, regardless of quality.

• A teacher compensation system should incorporate attention to each of the goals of attracting, developing, and retaining quality teachers.

• A teacher compensation system should be *competitive* at all stages of teacher career development.

• A teacher compensation system should reflect attention not only to salary but also to other elements of compensation, including benefits and working conditions.

• A teacher compensation system designed to promote teacher quality should incorporate specific, reliable, valid measures of teacher quality linked to compensation.

• A teacher compensation system should provide recognition for multiple ways that quality may be demonstrated, which is linked to the specific roles and responsibilities defined for teachers.

• A teacher compensation system should be *flexible* at an organizational and individual level, allowing the organization to respond to changing needs and allowing some individual choice with regard to compensation options to be pursued.

• A teacher compensation system should be *clear* and easily *communicated.*

• A teacher compensation system should be supported in implementation by facilitative administrative structures, organized data-gathering and evaluation systems, and effective communication procedures.

Across all of these assumptions and considerations, a few essential design principles emerge for consideration in teacher compensation systems:

- *Competitiveness*, with attention to providing incentives for teachers at all stages of their careers to maintain employment and ongoing growth within the school district
- *Strategic flexibility*, with assessment of current and future organizational needs and multiple options for teacher pursuit of increased quality and compensation
- *Comprehensiveness*, with emphasis on all three goals of the system (attracting, developing, and retaining quality teachers); on the complex nature of teaching and multiple ways of demonstrating quality; and on a concept of compensation that encompasses more than just salary
- *Clarity*, with emphasis on involvement of stakeholders throughout the process, planning for implementation, and facilitative channels of communication
- *Appropriateness*, specifically linking teacher compensation to the varied roles and responsibilities of the teaching position, to the teacher evaluation system, and to the mission and goals of the school system

These design principles, essential to the development of a strong compensation system linked to teacher quality, should guide the assessment of current systems, plans for restructuring, and development of evaluation structures. The principles will be revisited in the next section and throughout the remaining chapters of the book as we continue exploring practical considerations and steps in strengthening compensation systems.

ESTABLISHING CRITERIA: DEFINING AND MEASURING QUALITY

So far in this chapter, we have explored the issues of aligning compensation with overall organizational purpose and goals, and we have examined some design principles fundamental to developing quality compensation systems. At this point, we must also address the issue of planning for assessment and evaluation, considering how to know the degree to which the compensation system holds to the design principles, and how to know if the system is achieving its purpose and goals. Thus we must consider *measures of quality* and *performance criteria*—elements of how to evaluate a compensation system, with consideration of the part played by teacher evaluation.

Planning for evaluation must occur along with the other big picture considerations at the outset of developing a compensation system. As with all other aspects of the compensation system, the quality criteria developed to assess it must focus on the nexus of teacher pay and teacher quality— does the system, in fact, represent and respond to a positive relationship between the quality of work that teachers do and the compensation they receive for that work? Furthermore, to ensure appropriate responses to that question, quality criteria must be in place to assess teacher performance. Therefore, the design of a compensation system must include consideration of individual and program evaluation—the evaluation of teachers and the evaluation of the compensation system itself as a program within the school district.

The purpose of program evaluation is twofold. First, evaluation provides data and a standard of judgment by which to assess the effectiveness of a program and to identify areas of strength and weakness. This is typically referred to as *formative* or *enabling evaluation*. Second, program evaluation provides data and a standard of judgment by which to assess the worth, value, or merit of a program. This is typically referred to as *summative evaluation*. Evaluation of a teacher compensation system should include both types, and quality criteria must be established as part of the planning process. Whether formative or summative in nature, evaluation methods should be tied to the goals of the intended program. The goals of the compensation program are to attract, develop, and retain quality teachers. Therefore, the quality criteria established should assess whether the program is working to achieve those goals, and the measures of quality identified must be able to provide specific evidence to support that assessment process.

For each of the major goals of the compensation program—to attract, develop, and retain quality teachers—a set of guiding questions, possible data sources, and performance criteria may be established. A school district striving to develop or change its compensation system should consider these questions and criteria at the beginning of the process and then throughout, both to establish baseline data and to determine the effectiveness of the system in action.

Attracting Teachers

The goal of attracting quality teachers to a school district encompasses several practical, strategic objectives that form a foundation for the development of quality criteria and evaluation parameters. Key objectives within the goal of attracting quality teachers include the following:

- A large applicant pool, including many high-quality candidates
- Sufficient quality applicants to meet the school district's current and projected needs
- Efficient recruitment structures resulting in a high yield of quality applications

- High rate of acceptances of initial offers (to top-choice candidates)
- Sufficient acceptances by quality candidates

In addition to these key objectives, with specific consideration of the compensation system, an additional objective would be to find limited evidence that compensation is influential in *decline* of offers and perhaps some evidence that compensation is highlighted as a key factor in *acceptance* of offers.

Given the goal of attracting quality teachers and the objectives noted, evaluation related to this goal must focus on several fundamental questions: Does the school district attract an adequate applicant pool of quality teachers to respond to existing and projected needs? What recruitment sources are most effective in providing a quality applicant pool? Why do quality teachers accept or decline positions in the school district? To find answers to all of these questions, a school district must have structures in place that document application and hiring numbers and provide evidence on recruitment sources and reasoning behind the employment decisions made.

Connected with each of the fundamental questions listed above, more specific data-gathering questions, data sources, and performance criteria may be identified. Figure 2.4 provides sample questions and data sources, with key considerations for establishing quality criteria.

Developing Teachers

Within the context of linking teacher compensation to teacher quality, the goal of developing quality teachers is perhaps the most complex of the three emphases. Pursuit of this goal requires collaboration with the professional development function of the school district, including attention to the professional development options and resources available to teachers, the multiple methods of evaluating teacher development, and balancing funds in such a way as to not only acknowledge teacher development but also to support the process in practical, tangible ways. As with the aforementioned goal of attracting teachers, we must identify key objectives, evaluation questions, data sources, and quality criteria linking the goal of developing teachers to the compensation system. Key objectives within the goal of developing quality teachers include the following:

- Availability of professional development resources linked to student and teacher learning needs
- Access to professional development resources, including consideration of release time
- Variety in professional development resources, addressing teacher needs across a developmental and quality range, and ensuring options for pursuit of individual growth as well as collaborative development

Figure 2.4   Questions and Considerations for Quality Criteria—Attracting Quality Teachers

Questions	Data Sources	Establishing Criteria
Does the school district attract an adequate applicant pool of quality teachers to respond to existing and projected needs?		
• How many teachers apply to the school district annually? What is the ratio of applications to open positions? • What percentage of applications is considered viable for possible employment (i.e., what percentage of applications represent "quality teachers" based on entry qualifications)? What is the ratio of these applications to open positions?	• Application data (including records over several years) • Records of position openings over several years and projected needs	• What changes would the school district like to see in the size of the applicant pool overall, relative to open and projected positions? • What degree of increase in the number of viable applications or the ratio of viable applications to open positions does the school district desire?
What recruitment sources are most effective in providing a quality applicant pool?		
• What recruitment sources are in place, and how does the school district determine the relationship between recruitment sources and teacher applicants? • What do teachers say attracts them to apply to the school district? • What relationships exist between applicant quality and recruitment sources?	• Recruitment records • Application data (including records over several years) • Survey/interview data	• What relationships between recruitment sources and applications does the school district desire? • What application yield would be considered successful for each recruitment source? What employment yield would be considered successful for each source?
Why do quality teachers accept or decline positions in the school district?		
• What percentage of quality applicants accepts the school district's offer of employment? • How frequently does the school district need to make offers to second- or third-choice applicants? • What reasons do teachers give for accepting or not accepting positions with the school district? • How often do teachers include compensation when sharing reasons for accepting or not accepting positions within the school district?	• Application data (including records over several years) • Hiring data • Survey/interview data	• What degree of increase in the percentage of employment offers accepted does the school district desire? • What percentage of decline, based on compensation issues, does the school district consider acceptable?

- Participation of increasing numbers of teachers in professional development options, with specific linkage to needs and goals at individual and team or school levels

- Evidence of change in classroom practice linked to professional development
- Evidence of increasing teacher involvement in professional development beyond minimum expectations
- Evidence of increasing student achievement

Evaluation related to the goal of developing quality teachers should focus on key questions such as the following: Are current teachers able to achieve professional development goals related to teacher and student needs? Is there evidence that teacher effectiveness is improving or being sustained? Is student achievement improving? Responses to these questions link to the compensation system in several ways, including evidence of how the system supports and rewards pursuit of professional development beyond minimum expectations, what measures are in place to assess and acknowledge increasing teacher quality, and the flexibility of the system in rewarding development of teacher quality at multiple career stages and across varied roles and responsibilities in teaching.

Figure 2.5 provides sample questions and data sources related to developing quality teachers, with key considerations for establishing quality criteria.

Figure 2.5   Questions and Considerations for Quality Criteria—Developing Quality Teachers

Questions	Data Sources	Establishing Criteria
Are current teachers able to achieve professional development goals related to teacher and student needs?		
• What professional development opportunities are available to teachers within and beyond the school district? • How do available professional development options relate to data-based evidence of professional development needs? • Do teachers take advantage of opportunities to pursue professional development, individually and collectively? • What evidence are teachers asked to provide to demonstrate achievement of professional development goals?	• Professional development records of opportunities and participation • Needs assessment of school personnel regarding professional development needs • Student achievement and teacher evaluation data sources	• What level of participation in professional development does the school district require for teachers? • What increase in participation in professional development does the school district desire? • What levels and forms of participation in professional development will the school district designate as meeting and exceeding expectations? • What evidence of increasing goal achievement and developing quality does the school district desire among teachers? • What relationships exist between forms of quality compensation awarded and ongoing evidence of teacher professional development?

Figure 2.5 (Continued)

Questions	Data Sources	Establishing Criteria
Is there evidence that teacher effectiveness is improving or being sustained?		
• How does the system define teacher effectiveness, and how do teachers demonstrate evidence? • Do teachers demonstrate growth gains relative to results in the evaluation system? • Do teachers demonstrate growth gains against individually determined goals? • Do teachers at all levels of quality and all stages of development demonstrate evidence of sustained or improved effectiveness?	• Structure and components of evaluation system • Student achievement and teacher evaluation data sources • Goal-setting results • Survey data (teachers, administrators, clients)	• What levels of performance within the teacher evaluation system does the school district consider to meet and to exceed expectations for effectiveness? • What relationship exists between demonstrated teacher effectiveness and teacher use of resources for professional development? • What degree of improvement in effectiveness does the school district desire for teachers at varied stages of career development and at varied levels of initial demonstrated quality? • What relationships exist between forms of quality compensation awarded and other evidence of teacher effectiveness?
Is student achievement improving?		
• Are student achievement results meeting expectations against standards? • Are student achievement results demonstrating continuous progress, both for groups of students and for the school district as a whole? • What relationships exist between evaluations of teacher quality across multiple indicators and achievement of the specific groups of students with whom teachers work?	• Student achievement data • Teacher evaluation data sources	• What levels of student achievement does the school district consider to meet and exceed expectations for performance and growth? • What degree of gain in student achievement does the school district desire? • What relationships exist between demonstrated student achievement gains and other forms of quality compensation that are awarded?

Retaining Teachers

The third key goal to consider in linking teacher compensation and teacher quality is the issue of retaining quality teachers with the school district and in the profession. Attention to this goal requires structures and data-gathering efforts to explore teachers satisfaction with their jobs and to understand reasons why teachers choose to leave or stay with the school district. Moreover, progress toward this goal requires reflection back on the previous two, with careful consideration of the varied indicators of teacher quality, for the emphasis is not just on teacher retention generally but on retention of *quality teachers.*

Once again, we must identify key objectives, evaluation questions, data sources, and quality criteria linking the goal of retaining teachers to the compensation system. Key objectives within the goal of retaining quality teachers include the following:

- Limited attrition of quality teachers
- Increasing rate of retention for quality teachers
- High levels of teacher job satisfaction
- Strong positive relationship between teacher quality indicators and teacher job satisfaction
- Strong positive relationship between increasing teacher pursuit of professional development and teacher job satisfaction

Evaluation related to this goal should focus on key questions such as the following: Does the school district retain quality teachers? Why do teachers choose to leave or stay with the school district? What would make the school district a more attractive working environment? Figure 2.6 provides sample questions and data sources related to retaining quality teachers, with key considerations for establishing quality criteria.

Teacher Quality and Teacher Evaluation

The goals of attracting, developing, and retaining quality teachers and efforts to link compensation to quality must be clearly connected with the school district's policies and procedures for teacher evaluation. Although it is not the purpose of this text to provide detailed guidelines around teacher evaluation systems, a brief overview is in order to address some key considerations related to teacher evaluation within a context linking teacher compensation to teacher quality.

A primary goal of a teacher evaluation system should be to encourage continuous growth and improvement at an individualized level by collecting and analyzing pertinent data and utilizing those data as the foundation for meaningful feedback and, by extension, as a foundation for flexible compensation. Such a system conceptualizes evaluation as an ongoing process of measuring performance against goals and developing and implementing plans for continuous improvement.[12] The evaluation system, like the compensation system, should be clear, fair, and consistent to guide effective practice for multiple individuals over time, yet should also be sufficiently flexible to encourage individual initiative and creativity. To achieve its goals, an effective system of teacher evaluation should incorporate several key features:

Figure 2.6   Questions and Considerations for Quality Criteria—Retaining Quality Teachers

Questions	Data Sources	Establishing Criteria
Does the school district retain quality teachers?		
• How many teachers leave the school district annually? • What percentage of teachers leaving the district (a) retire, (b) transfer to other districts, or (c) leave the profession? • What are the relative attrition and retention rates for teachers? • What relationships exist between attrition and retention rates and indicators of teacher quality?	• Teacher retention and attrition data • Exit interview data • Teacher evaluation data and other quality indicators	• What changes does the school district wish to see in attrition/retention rates? • What relative percentages of teacher attrition for each major reason does the school district consider to be acceptable? • Are retention rates higher for teachers who have demonstrated stronger evidence of teacher quality? What improvement does the school district desire in retention rates for these teachers specifically? • Are retention rates higher for teachers who have received compensation linked to specific evidence of teacher quality?
Why do teachers choose to leave or stay with the school district?		
• What reasons do teachers give for leaving the school district? • What reasons do teachers give for staying with the district? • What relationships exist between the quality of the teacher and reasons for leaving?	• Exit interview data • Teacher satisfaction survey/interview data	• What percentage of attrition based on compensation issues does the school district consider acceptable? • What evidence of satisfaction relative to the compensation system does the school district consider to be acceptable? What improvement in satisfaction relative to the compensation system does the school district desire?
What would make the school district a more attractive working environment?		
• What do teachers like about their working environment? • What do teachers dislike about their working environment? • What relationships exist between teacher satisfaction data and key elements of teacher quality, including level of experience, student performance, and others?	• Exit interview data • Teacher satisfaction survey/interview data	• What degree of increase in teacher satisfaction does the school district desire? For what specific components of teacher satisfaction? • In what areas are quality teachers most and least satisfied?

- Carefully defined benchmark behaviors tied to each domain of performance (e.g., instruction, assessment, communication, community relations, professionalism, and learning environment) to demonstrate professional responsibilities
- Use of multiple data sources for information on teacher performance, including such sources as *goal setting and performance against individual goals, student achievement results, formal observations, informal observations,* and *portfolios*
- An emphasis on the relationship of teacher performance to improved academic achievement for students
- A procedure for performance review that increases teacher involvement, stresses accountability, and promotes professional improvement as the primary goal
- Flexibility to ensure opportunities for growth for different teachers depending on their stage of professional development and particular areas of need and interest

As noted in the figures in this chapter, some of these key features are also integral to evaluation of the compensation system relative to the goals of attracting, developing, and retaining quality teachers. These two evaluation systems—the system for evaluating teachers and that for evaluating the compensation system—should include some overlap in *goals, relevant key features, relevant data sources,* and *use of formative and summative emphases.* Such a linkage not only contributes to efficiency, it also promotes the key design principle of appropriateness.

SUMMARY: TEACHER COMPENSATION IN THE BIG PICTURE OF SCHOOL PURPOSE

This chapter has approached critical first steps in reviewing and restructuring a compensation system by looking at the big picture and at the endgame: What is the school district trying to accomplish? How does teacher compensation fit within the school district's overall mission and goals? What do the goals of the school district and the goals of the compensation system reveal regarding our assumptions about teaching and learning? What should we look for in establishing a baseline and evaluating progress?

By addressing teacher compensation within a clear sense of the school district's mission and goals, and by examining key assumptions and questions throughout the process, we maintain a careful awareness of what we most value and how we communicate those values. Moreover, with ongoing reflection on shared assumptions and essential design principles, the process of developing or restructuring a compensation system becomes more integrally and seamlessly connected with overall efforts toward the vision and mission. Thus a compensation system should work to attract, develop, and retain quality teachers by linking teacher pay and teacher quality in a *clearly communicated* structure that is *comprehensive, appropriate, flexible,* and *competitive.* With all of these design principles as a starting place, and having examined core assumptions and beliefs, the next chapter will turn specific attention to the principle of *competitiveness* in teacher compensation.

3

Competitive Salaries and Benefits

How Do We Stack Up?

T eacher pay, ultimately, is all about fairly and adequately supporting and maintaining a quality teaching force. Unfortunately, typical problems that often exist with traditional teacher compensation systems are numerous. In particular, contemporary teacher pay systems are inflexible and fail to adequately promote individual development, teamwork, and collegiality. In addition, traditional teacher compensation programs fail to differentiate pay based on a number of factors (see Figure 3.1).

Although these are typical of most compensation packages, each school district faces unique challenges. Therefore, it is imperative that a school district assess its own competitiveness in relation to neighboring school districts.

In this chapter, we explore key elements of competitiveness for teacher compensation. In particular, we address the following questions:

1. How do principles of environmental scanning apply to teacher compensation systems?

2. How can the competitiveness of teacher salaries be assessed?

3. How can nonsalary benefits contribute to a competitive salary package?

4. What role can working conditions play in a competing job market?

Figure 3.1   Factors Neglected or Minimized in Traditional Teacher
Compensation Systems

- Complexity of jobs
- Differentiated responsibilities
- Market forces, such as critical shortage areas
- Evaluation results or promotion/demotion
- Individual effort
- Student performance
- Areas of specialization
- Overall ability of teachers

HOW DO PRINCIPLES OF ENVIRONMENTAL SCANNING APPLY TO TEACHER COMPENSATION SYSTEMS?

Environmental scanning offers a well-established strategic planning tool for school districts to use in determining how they stack up in relation to other school districts as well as in relation to trends within the teaching profession. Essentially, a school district asks: Where are we now with our compensation system?[1] How is the current compensation system meeting the mission and goals of the school district and its future needs?

One key approach for conducting an environmental scan is through a *SWOT* analysis: <u>S</u>trengths, <u>W</u>eaknesses, <u>O</u>pportunities, and <u>T</u>hreats.[2] The first phase of a SWOT analysis is for the school district to conduct a thorough internal analysis by examining the strengths and weaknesses of its own compensation system. Then, the school district must examine the external environment for opportunities and threats, particularly in relation to competing school districts.

During the first phase of a SWOT analysis, school districts look inward. In other words, what is the current compensation system in the school district? Strengths and weaknesses of each school district's compensation system are unique. Some factors to consider include

- the current salary structure,
- the competitiveness of the salary structure,
- the strengths and weaknesses of nonsalary benefits,
- the current working conditions that either positively or negatively affect teacher morale.

By looking inward, school districts have a better understanding of those factors that contribute to teachers continuing to teach in the school district and those factors that contribute to teachers leaving the school district.

During the second phase of the SWOT analysis, school districts look outward. Competition from area school districts, as well as trends affecting education, in general, and teaching as a career, in particular, shed light on both opportunities and threats. In other words, what trends are likely to affect the school district's ability to attract and retain quality teachers and what is the impact of the existing compensation structure on these trends? Examining salary rates of competing school districts and anticipating teacher shortage areas are examples of factors to consider as part of this thorough review process. Other factors may include the following:

- Enrollment predictions
- Budget shortfall/surplus
- Economic growth or decline
- Changes in student demographics
- Changes in teacher demographics

Considering opportunities and threats involves forward thinking, and forward thinking involves anticipating the future effects of currently made decisions. For example, a school district could decide to increase its starting salary and compress the salary step increases in a purposeful effort to make the pay schedule more attractive to new teachers. However, what began as an incentive in recruitment for new teachers could have an unintended consequence resulting in teacher retention problems down the road. By compressing the salary schedule, the school district, indeed, is able to promise faster and more substantial pay raises to new teachers. However, what happens when those same teachers reach the top of the salary schedule in a few years while neighboring districts continue to provide salary step increases for more experienced teachers? One likely result is that the new teachers hired a few years ago will begin leaving the district in favor of the greener pastures for experienced teachers in the neighboring school districts where the scale is not as compressed. Engaging in environmental scanning can be a vital part of maintaining the organizational health of the school district. Ultimately, a compensation system that evolves based on strengths, weaknesses, opportunities, and threats is more likely to support the recruitment and retention of high quality teachers because the process engages a school district in these key activities:

- Identifying potential barriers
- Exploring promising alternatives
- Questioning conventional assumptions about compensation
- Aligning compensation processes with organizational goals
- Viewing compensation as an internal system that is, in fact, acted upon by the external context

For each school district, a SWOT analysis is unique; however, there are at least three issues central to the processes related to compensation: salary, benefits, and working conditions.

HOW CAN THE COMPETITIVENESS OF TEACHER SALARIES BE ASSESSED?

The competition for quality teachers is becoming fierce. Teachers are in demand as enrollment increases, reductions in class size are mandated, and the teacher workforce nears retirement. By 2005, K–12 enrollment in public and private schools was expected to increase to 53.5 million students, up an estimated 1 million students from 1998.[3] In many school districts, even as enrollment increases, teachers are retiring and leaving the profession faster than certified new hires can be secured. Contributing to the problem is the fact that the average age of a teacher is 44, compared to other workers nationwide at 39, which means, comparatively, more teachers will be eligible to retire in the next decade than other professions.[4] In addition, 39 percent of newly prepared teachers elect not to teach.[5] Of additional concern is the fact that many new teachers do not remain in the profession past their third year. These factors contribute to the growing need to attract new teachers and to retain the teachers who are already with the school district.

For a school district to ensure its competitiveness in an increasingly constricted labor market, several factors must be considered. Obviously, teacher pay is an essential factor in attracting and retaining a quality teaching force. In this section of the chapter, we address the competitiveness of teacher compensation from various perspectives. In particular, we use a case study to highlight competitive teacher pay in terms of

- salary benchmarking,
- per diem salary rates,
- salary at face value,
- salary adjusted for cost of living.

In the case study, we provide a comparative analysis of our hypothetical school district, *Lincoln Public Schools* (LPS), in relation to its neighboring— that is, competing—school districts. This district is located adjacent to a state boundary, and thus some competing school districts are located within the same state (State 1), while others are located in a neighboring state (State 2). The overall purpose of the case analysis is to assess the existing salary schedules for teachers in neighboring school districts as compared with teachers in LPS.

Salary Benchmarking: Breaking Down the Salary Schedules

Direct salary, of course, is the central consideration of any compensation system. A review of current salary schedules among comparison school districts indicates that LPS is comparable in initial and early to midcareer salary, but differences become more evident when considering other factors, such as length of service, continuing education, and cost of living.

The beginning teacher salary available to LPS teachers is comparable to surrounding areas. Figures 3.2 and 3.3 present the salary data for the minimum starting salary, 15 years of experience, and maximum salary available for teachers with bachelor's or master's degrees, respectively. In Figure 3.3, the master's + 30 lane and doctoral degree salary add-ons are presented as elements added to the appropriate step on the bachelor's scale. The averages for each category are listed.

The most telling indications of teacher salaries over time are visually apparent in Figures 3.4 and 3.5. In Figure 3.4, a beginning teacher with a bachelor's degree will earn comparable salaries at LPS as compared with two of the adjacent school districts. However, a teacher with ten years' experience will earn progressively less with LPS than with the adjacent school districts. Figure 3.5 demonstrates a similar but less stark picture for a teacher with a master's degree. LPS offers a comparable salary in the first 13 years, but then the salary seems frozen after that time, whereas the two adjacent school district salaries surpass the salary offered by LPS.

Figure 3.2   Teacher Salary Schedule for LPS

Initial Placement for New Hires With the Following Years of Experience	Step	BA*	BA + 15	MA	MA + 30	PhD
1	1	33,000	34,648	38,277	42,237	44,218
2	2	34,648	36,298	40,260	44,218	46,197
3	3	36,298	37,946	42,237	46,197	48,178
4	4	37,946	39,596	44,218	48,178	50,157
5, 6, 7	5	39,596	41,247	46,197	50,157	52,138
8, 9	6	41,247	42,897	48,178	52,138	54,117
10	7	42,897	44,547	50,157	54,117	56,098
	8	44,547	46,797	52,138	56,098	58,076
	9	46,197	47,847	54,117	58,076	60,057
	10	47,847	49,497	56,098	60,057	62,034
	11		51,147	58,077	62,034	64,015
	12		52,797	60,057	64,015	65,994
	13		54,447	62,034	65,994	67,977
	14			64,015	67,977	69,954

Figure 3.3   Actual 2001–2002 Salary Offerings for Selected School Districts

	School District	Bachelor's Degree			Master's Degree			Added to Bachelor's Degree Starting Salary	
		Minimum	15 Years	Maximum	Minimum	15 Years	Maximum	MA +30	Doctorate
State 1	LPS	33,000	47,847[a]	47,847	38,277	64,015	65,015	9,237	11,218
	District 1	34,297	49,752	50,994	37,920	66,671	68,337	5,572	7,620
	District 2	34,069	52,449	65,387	38,416	56,796	73,737	5,843	7,525
	District 3	33,660	45,240	45,240	38,610	57,282	69,730	6,435	None listed
	District 4	32,945	51,539	68,431	37,249	55,843	72,735	5,786	7,453
	District 5	32,516	46,026	69,743	36,016	49,526	73,243	4,500	5,500
	District 6	33,115	47,132	59,288	37,365	51,382	63,538	5,750	6,750
State 2	District 7	33,308	40,287[b]	40,287	35,388	52,322	58,923	4,098	6,123
	District 8	35,087	47,025[c]	47,025	38,655	63,699	73,306	4,696	None listed
	District 9	33,548	46,190[d]	46,190	36,775	55,250	63,895	6,765	7,168
	Area Average	**$33,555**	**$47,349**	**$54,916**	**$37,467**	**$57,279**	**$68,246**	**$5,284**	**$7,423**

Notes: Salary maximum reached at year: [a]13, [b]9, [c]10, [d]12
Figures are rounded to the dollar.

Figure 3.4   Comparison of Earnings by Bachelor's Degree

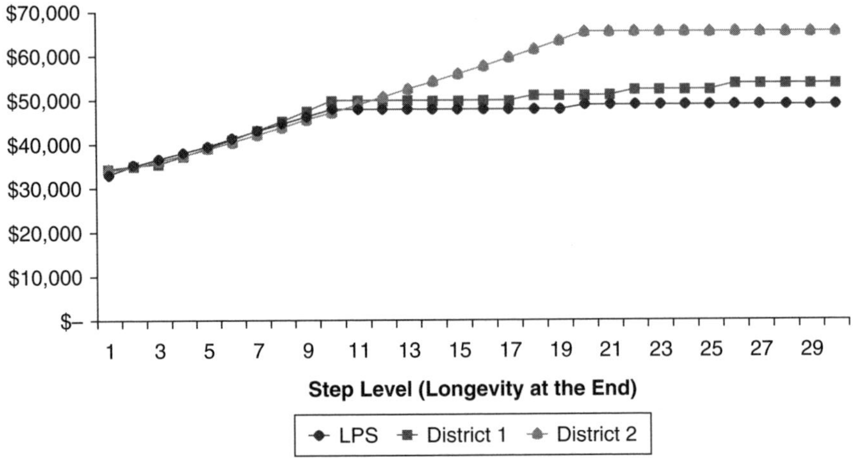

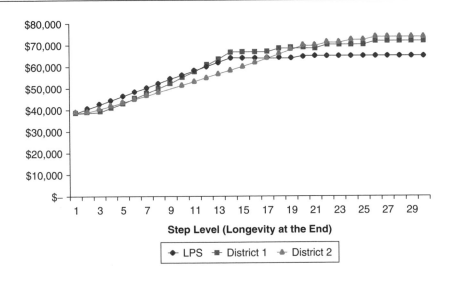

Figure 3.5   Comparison of Earnings by Master's Degree

Per Diem Salary Rates: Does More Pay Mean More Workdays?

Teacher salaries typically are based upon a yearly contract, in most cases a ten-month contract. Thus the salary paid to the teacher is based upon services rendered during those ten months. Focusing merely on a yearly salary or even a ten-month salary and making comparisons based

Figure 3.6 Per Diem Rates for State 1 School Districts*

School Districts	Number of Contract Days	Bachelor's Degree			Master's Degree		
		Minimum	15 Years	Maximum	Minimum	15 Years	Maximum
LPS	190	$174	$252	$252	$201	$337	$342
District 1	200	$171	$249	$255	$190	$333	$342
District 2	193	$177	$272	$339	$199	$294	$382
District 3	200	$168	$226	$226	$193	$286	$349
District 4	198	$166	$260	$346	$188	$282	$367
District 5	200	$163	$230	$349	$180	$248	$366
District 6	195	$170	$242	$304	$192	$263	$326
Average	**196**	**$171**	**$249**	**$298**	**$193**	**$294**	**$356**

* The same data as Figure 3.3 are used for salaries; school district figures are rounded to the nearest dollar.

upon those amounts can be misleading. While yearly salaries are useful in comparing work over the contract period, the fact is that school districts vary considerably in their contracted number of days, typically ranging from 185 to 200 or more. Per diem salary rates provide valuable information in comparing how much teachers make each day during that contract period.

School districts differ in the number of contract days. Therefore, a teacher in one district may be working more days than a teacher in another district. For example, Figure 3.6 shows that teachers in Districts 1 , 3, and 5 work ten more days than do teachers in our hypothetical district, LPS. Per diem salary rates can shed light on whether teachers in LPS are working more or less than teachers in other school districts and whether the differences in the number of contract days are reflected in yearly salary rates.

Examining salary on a per diem basis shows that some school districts that pay more are actually adjusting for requiring teachers to work longer contracts. Figure 3.6 illustrates the differences in per diem offerings when the applicable salary is divided by the number of contract days. In addition, Figure 3.6 summarizes the per diem rate offered at each of the same levels for teachers who have a bachelor's or master's degree.

Figure 3.7 depicts selected State 1's school districts' per diem offerings relative to LPS. Note that the per diem offering at District 6 Public Schools for teachers with bachelor's degrees and 15 years of experience raised that school district's offerings above LPS's offerings; however, District 6's maximum salary then falls beneath LPS. Also, note that there is greater variation

Figure 3.7   LPS Per Diem Salary Offerings Compared With Selected School
Districts

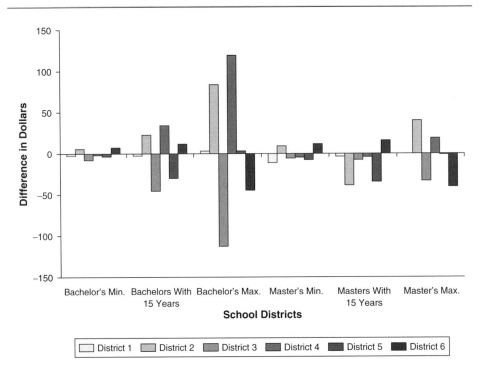

in per diem amounts among school districts' master's level salaries than
their bachelor's level offerings. For example, District 6 rises above LPS for
both the minimum and the 15 years' experience marks, while District 3 falls
below LPS for the maximum salary offering on a per diem basis. Another
notable finding is that the starting salary for teachers with bachelor's
degrees is virtually the same across the selected school districts when per
diem basis is considered.

Salary as Face Value: What Is the Pay?

Experienced teachers are more likely than first-year teachers to consider
issues such as planning time, contract time, cost of living, and per diem
rates. For the experienced teacher, benefits and cost of living may have a
significant bearing on retention. The beginning teacher may be more likely
to consider the face value salary offer and make a decision on that basis.

Prospective teacher applicants often request school district salary
information or seek it out on the Internet. Figures 3.2, 3.3, and 3.6 present
the same LPS salary data analyzed in different ways. How individuals use
the information in their job search differs. For example, using Figure 3.2,
teachers with more than ten years of experience may be concerned about

Figure 3.8   LPS Bachelor's Degree Salary Offerings Compared With
Competing School Districts

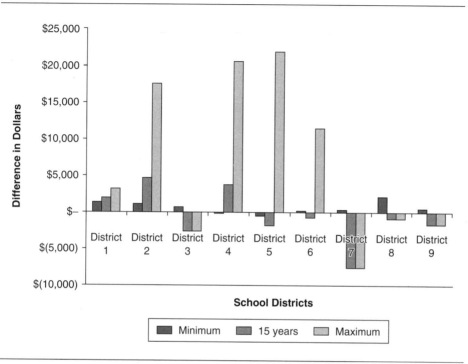

Note: Midcareer teachers have 15 years of experience.

the lack of parity in being located at a comparable step in the LPS salary
scale. As another example, consider novice versus experienced teachers:
Teachers who apply to LPS for their first teaching job may be more concerned with the total salary (Figure 3.3), whereas someone with more
experience in seeking a teaching position may be more interested in the
per diem rate (Figure 3.6).

For teachers who have earned a bachelor's degree, the LPS starting
salary is comparable to surrounding districts, but as teachers gain experience the salary scale becomes increasingly less competitive based on dollar values. Figures 3.3 and 3.6 illustrate the differences in earning potential
on an annual salary and a per diem basis. While many of its competitor
school districts continue to increase salaries throughout the teacher's
career, LPS caps the bachelor's degree teacher salary at Step 10 (as noted
in Figure 3.2). Consequently, the differences evident at Step 11 and beyond
result in various school districts (notably District 2, District 4, District 5,
District 6, and District 8) being more attractive for teachers with more
years of experience.

The following three scenarios illustrate some of the unintended consequences of the current LPS salary schedule upon teachers and some of the
options available to LPS in response.

Scenario 1: Teacher with a bachelor's degree

Maureen started teaching in LPS after graduating with a bachelor's degree in mathematics. She has been loyal to the district for 19 years, loves her school, and meets or exceeds expectations on the performance evaluation. Lately, she has been looking at other school districts, as she is falling behind in salary. She knows a master's degree would boost her salary; but she just doesn't have the time right now with three kids, the oldest of whom is starting college in two years.

What does Maureen see?

Other teachers in neighboring school districts get paid for their experience. She will be eligible for full retirement in 11 years. The last three years' salary will be used to calculate the teacher's retirement benefits. Given these issues, Maureen is attracted to higher paying districts.

What can LPS do?

Without restructuring the salary schedule to value experienced teachers, LPS is likely to lose Maureen.

Scenario 2: New teacher with a master's degree

Sasha will be graduating with a K–6 elementary certificate. She went through a five-year bachelor's/master's program. Her bachelor's degree is in chemistry and her master's degree is in education. This will be her first full-time teaching position.

What does Sasha see?

She is especially impressed with salary offerings she found online for LPS and District 3. Both school districts are offering approximately $5,000 more for having a master's degree. Her first choice is District 3 because they pay more initially.

What does Sasha not see?

Sasha did not think to calculate the per diem rate. If she had, she would have found that LPS pays $8.00 more a day or $1,520.00 over the course of the year on a per diem basis. This is her first job and everything is new.

What can LPS do?

Share per diem information along with the salary schedule. Alternatively, add days to the teacher contract—days that may be used either for instruction or as days designated for activities related to development of professional knowledge and skills—and increase the salary on a commensurate basis.

Scenario 3: Veteran teacher with a master's degree

Andrew had already taught for 17 years in other states when he moved to Lincoln County to be closer to his parents. His undergraduate work was in English and his master's degree was in special education, a critical shortage area both nationally and at LPS.

What does Andrew see?

As a traditional practice for attempting to discourage district jumping, LPS does not match teacher experience with the salary step for new hires with more than 14 years' experience. Neighboring school districts (e.g., District 2) tend to follow this same practice, but often give teachers more credit for years of experience than does LPS.

What does Andrew not see?

In an effort to ensure against charges of inequity in pay, LPS does not provide flexibility in its compensation system for hard-to-fill areas.

What can LPS do?

Make one-to-one correspondence for years of experience and step placement. Use flexible placement on the salary schedule to attract teachers in critical shortage areas, such as special education.

For teachers who have earned advanced degrees, LPS provides quality compensation relative to competitor school districts. The entry-level salary for an LPS teacher is higher than what is offered in most of the other districts, as seen in Figure 3.9. On a per diem basis, the first-year teacher with a master's degree makes more in LPS than in any of the comparative school districts. Teachers with 15 years of experience are generally still earning more than their counterparts in other districts. However, nine school districts offer higher compensation at the end of a teacher's career than LPS. Teachers who transfer into LPS with more than six years of experience are also at a disadvantage, as the steps are compressed for new hires. Thus the early salary advantages do not last throughout a LPS teacher's career, and experienced teachers are not attracted to LPS. Hence, the LPS salary schedule is essentially designed to attract novice teachers, entice them to stay during the first years of their careers, and hope that they develop enough of sense of loyalty to the school system to stay for the remaining 24 years of their careers. This is a shaky—but all too common—basis for attracting, promoting, and retaining quality teachers.

Figure 3.9   LPS Master's Degree Salary Offerings Compared With Selected
Area School Districts

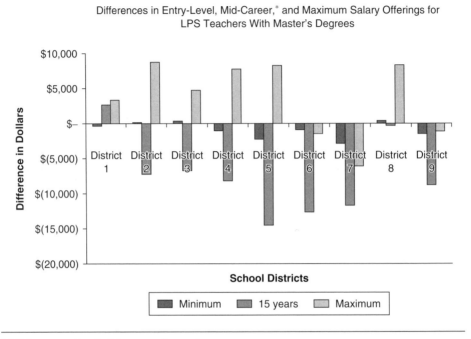

Differences in Entry-Level, Mid-Career,* and Maximum Salary Offerings for
LPS Teachers With Master's Degrees

* Midcareer refers to 15 years of experience.

Salary Adjusted for Cost of Living: How Far Will the Salary Go?

Another consideration associated with salary is the impact cost of living has on the actual buying power of the employee. The national average cost of living index figure is pegged at 100, using the Consumer Price Index published by the Bureau of Labor Statistics (BLS). The BLS collects data regarding how much consumers spend for food, housing, apparel, transportation, medical care, entertainment, and goods.[6]

The cost of living adjustment (COLA) figures for each of the ten school districts in this analysis appear in Figure 3.10. Salaries were adjusted by dividing the published salary figures by the COLA. For example, LPS has a published COLA of 141 (or 1.41 when converted), meaning it is a high-cost area in which to live. For a teacher with 15 years of experience and a master's degree, the cost of living adjustment is the following:

$$\$64{,}015 \div 1.41 = \$45{,}401$$

Consequently, the purchasing power of this teacher, relative to the national average, is approximately $19,000 less than the actual face-value salary.

Note: Because COLA is reported by cities, for county school districts, one would be required to select a city within the given county for estimating the applicable COLA.

Figure 3.10   Cost of Living Index for Selected School Districts

| | School District | COLA | Sample Impact for a Teacher With 15 Years of Experience and a Master's Degree | |
			Published Salary	Adjusted*
State 1	LPS	141	$64,015	$45,401
	District 1	151	$66,671	$44,153
	District 2	157	$56,796	$36,176
	District 3	159	$57,282	$36,026
	District 4	110	$55,843	$50,766
	District 5	139	$49,526	$35,630
	District 6	139	$51,382	$36,965
State 2	District 7	103	$52,322	$50,798
	District 8	149	$63,699	$42,751
	District 9	173	$55,250	$31,936
	Average	**142**	**$57,279**	**$41,060**

* Adjusted to the national average of 100 by dividing the published salary by the COLA.

The following scenario illustrates a potential effect of the LPS salary schedule related to the issue of cost of living.

Scenario 4: Impact of cost of living adjustments on teacher's spending power

Terrell teaches kindergarten in a metropolitan area in another part of the state. He has a master's degree in Early Childhood Development. Terrell has five years of teaching experience and is moving to the Lincoln County area after he gets married. He likes what he sees in Lincoln County and District 1 in terms of compensation.

What does Terrell see?

On a per diem basis, both school districts start pretty close; it is only after the middle of one's career that the divide widens substantially.

What does Terrell not see?

The cost of living in District 1 is generally higher than Lincoln County.

What can LPS do?

Share cost of living examples with prospective teachers.

For LPS teachers with a bachelor's degree, the COLA is competitive at the start of their careers, but due to LPS's capped salary structure, the teachers have less spending power in later years than colleagues teaching in neighboring districts (Figure 3.11). For teachers with master's degrees and above, LPS, District 1, District 2, District 3, and District 6 tend to be comparable in light of cost of living (Figure 3.12).

It is important to note that cost of living is heavily influenced by the cost of housing in an area. Consequently, teachers, especially new hires, may find it difficult to live within the LPS attendance zone, resulting in longer than desired commutes. A thorough analysis would be needed to determine where teachers live, why they choose to live there, and implications for quality of work (e.g., commute distance and time, teacher retention, and absenteeism rates disaggregated by travel distance).

The discussion and scenarios in this section amplify the importance of school districts providing more than a copy of the salary schedule to prospective employees. Benchmarking, per diem rates, and cost of living adjustments illuminate the differences among school districts and can either encourage or discourage a prospective employee's decision, depending on that person's circumstances. Using this type of data can help a school district determine its competitiveness in recruiting and retaining quality teachers.

Figure 3.11   Bachelor's Degree Salary Cost of Living Adjustments*

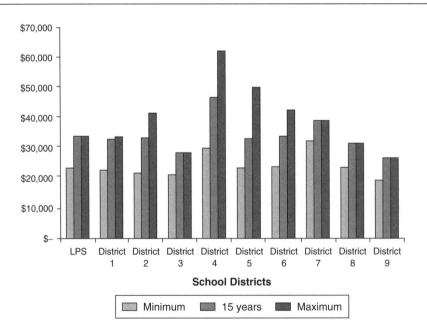

* All cost of living adjustments were retrieved March 5, 2002, from http://list.realestate.yahoo.com.

Figure 3.12   Master's Degree Salary Cost of Living Adjustments*

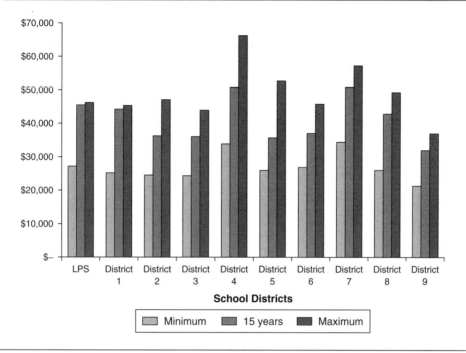

* All cost of living adjustments were retrieved March 5, 2002, from http://list.realestate.yahoo.com

HOW CAN NONSALARY BENEFITS CONTRIBUTE TO A COMPETITIVE SALARY PACKAGE?

While direct salary is the obvious starting point in a teacher compensation package, indirect (i.e., fringe) benefits also contribute to salary competitiveness. Benefits can affect the overall value of the salary package, even though they are not compensation paid directly to the employee. Typical types of benefits include

- protection programs,
- paid time-off benefits,
- accommodation and enhancement benefits.[7]

Protection programs protect the employee's income. Paid time off provides compensation even when the employee is not working, and accommodation and enhancement benefits offer programs to enhance quality of life for the employee. Examples of these types of benefits offered by school districts are listed in Figure 3.13. Benefits offered by school districts typically

Figure 3.13   Types and Examples of Typical Nonsalary Benefits

Protection	Paid Time Off	Accommodation and Enhancement

Insurance
   Health
   Dental
   Group life
 	
Long-term disability
 	
Professional liability protection
 	
Retirement contribution
 	
Tax-deferred annuities
 	
Workers' compensation
	Academic and professional leave
	
	Personal leave
	
	Sick leave
		Credit union
		
		Flexible spending account
		
		Direct deposit
		
		Sick leave bank
		
		Employee Assistance Program
		
		Staff development offerings, including a mentor program
		
		Tuition reimbursement program

are funded through three methods: total amount paid by the school district, shared cost with the employee, and an employee-paid option.

For our hypothetical case study, a summary of the benefits offered by LPS and each competitor school district is provided in Figure 3.14. At the bottom of Figure 3.14 is a category for the portion of a teacher's salary that each respective school district pays for benefits, including social security, retirement, and insurance (life and health). The average for the large metropolitan area near LPS is 30.02 percent of a teacher's salary, which is slightly higher than LPS (28.54 percent). However, the median is 29.01 percent; therefore, LPS may best be described as in the low-average range.

In the case study, LPS offers a range of benefit options that are comparable to other area school districts. All school districts in our case analysis offer the following benefits: credit union, group life insurance policies, health insurance, sick leave, personal leave, sick leave bank, and retirement contributions. In all cases, the employer and employee share the cost of health insurance. In most cases, the school system pays the employee's contribution to the retirement system and premiums for group life insurance. Most school districts offer flexible spending accounts, a separate dental plan, tax-deferred annuities, and tuition reimbursement. Each school district also has unique benefits listed that are not typically addressed by the other districts, such as free parking, no city residency requirement, or financial support for home buying within the district.

The following scenario illustrates a potential effect of the LPS benefits offerings.

Figure 3.14 Summary of Benefits of Selected Area School Districts

Benefits	LPS	State 1							State 2	
		District 1	District 2	District 3	District 4	District 5	District 6	District 7	District 8	District 9
Credit Union	O	O	O	O	O	O	O	O	O	O
Flexible Spending Account	O	O	O	✓	O	O	O	O		O
Insurance: Dental	$	$	$	$	$		O	✓	O	$
Insurance: Long Term Disability	$	✓	✓	✓						
Insurance: Group Life	$	✓		$	✓	✓	✓	✓	$	✓
Insurance: Health	$	$	$	$	$	$	$	$	$	$
Insurance: Prescription (separate)								$	O	$
Insurance: Vision (separate)		O (no premiums)					O	✓	O	$
Leave: Academic and Professional	✓		✓	✓				$	✓	✓
Leave: Personal	✓	✓	✓	✓	✓	✓	✓	✓	✓	✓
Leave: Sick	✓	✓	✓	✓	✓	✓	✓	✓	✓	✓
Leave: Sick Leave Bank	O	✓	✓	✓	✓	O	O	O	✓	O
Orientation Workshop (paid)*			✓					✓	✓	$
Professional Liability Protection	$	✓	$	✓	✓	✓	✓		✓	$
Retirement	✓	$	$	✓	✓	✓	✓	✓	✓	$
Staff Development Offerings	O		✓					✓	O	
Tax Deferred Annuity	O	✓	O	O	O	O	O	O	O	O

* For teachers new to the school district: ✓ = provided to all; $ = shared cost between employer and employee; O = employee funded/choice option.

Figure 3.14 (Continued)

Benefits		State 1						State 2		
	LPS	District 1	District 2	District 3	District 4	District 5	District 6	District 7	District 8	District 9
Tuition Reimbursement	✓	✓	✓	✓	$	✓		$	$	✓
Other: year-round salary option, U.S. Savings bonds, tenure, city homeownership program, no city residency requirement, signing bonuses, direct deposit, day care facility, employee assistance, workers' compensation, cancer insurance, free parking, out-of-state withholding, sick leave conversion (cash-out)	O	O	O	O	O	O	O	O	O	O
Total Benefits as a Function of Salary (social security, retirement, life insurance, and health insurance)	28.54	27.75	27.61	29.01	30.41	30.95	34.75	31.24	32.65	28.56

Scenario 5: Impact of protection benefits offered

Nathan successfully taught elementary school for eleven years before moving to the metropolitan area adjacent to LPS. His wife carries the health insurance for the family through her employer. However, one of Nathan's children requires extensive medication for a medical condition and his wife's health insurance does not cover all of the costs. Nathan would like insurance coverage options that fit his family's needs.

What does Nathan see?

Nathan sees that every district in the metropolitan area shares the cost of health insurance with the employee. Districts 7 and 8 offer separate prescription insurance plans at a shared cost with the employee, whereas LPS does not offer prescription insurance to its employees. None of the districts offer a "cafeteria style" benefits plan in which employees may choose benefit options.

What can LPS do?

Unless LPS offers options in insurance selections, LPS may lose Nathan to a school district that offers a prescription plan.

Scenario 6: Impact of enhancement and paid time-off benefits offered

Katrina is moving to the LPS area from overseas. She spent seven years teaching French in a Department of Defense School in Germany. Katrina would like to further her education by pursuing a master's degree and she values attending professional conferences. In particular, she wants to seek out professional development opportunities for improving foreign language instruction.

What does Katrina see?

Katrina sees that LPS, District 2, and District 9 offer tuition reimbursement and academic and professional leave to all employees. However, only District 7 provides staff development offerings to all employees. LPS provides choices for staff development.

What can LPS do?

Share with Katrina the staff development opportunities offered as choices through the school district. LPS can highlight the amount of tuition reimbursed and the amount of professional and academic leave time provided to employees.

WHAT ROLE CAN WORKING
CONDITIONS PLAY IN A COMPETING MARKET?

Organizational health refers to the atmosphere—or environment—of a workplace, in this case a school district. Components affecting an organization's health include the accessibility of resources, goals, and the possibility of attaining them; preserving the values of a group; and fitting individuals into the organization as a whole.[8] Strategies to improve organizational health often focus on morale, consideration for others, leadership influence, and academic emphasis. In a healthy school system, for example, if teachers genuinely like their coworkers and feel valued, then the organizational health would be considered more robust. While working conditions are not the same as salary, they, nonetheless, are important issues to consider in attracting, developing, and retaining a high-quality teacher workforce. For another example, teachers may choose to accept a position in one district over another due to a variety of factors other than salary. These factors include quality of the school buildings, resources available, and academic levels of students.[9]

School systems with a healthy climate tend to foster a high level of trust. In a healthy work environment, teachers and others benefit by being able to feel more readily that they are making a worthwhile contribution. The organization benefits in that the employees understand the overall goals, are motivated to achieve them, and assume ownership of the goals. This mutually beneficial relationship is built on a solid vision conveyed and supported by clear, credible communication that, in turn, builds trust.

Among the key factors related to organizational health and working conditions are student demographics, class size, and contract time. Within the context of our case study, each of these factors will be reviewed briefly, in turn.

Student Demographics

The school districts used for comparison with LPS in the case study were selected based on their geographic proximity because teachers in the same metropolitan area would be likely to compare neighboring school districts. Issues such as school size, class size, and socioeconomic characteristics become important distinguishing features among school districts for current and prospective employees. Teachers, especially those in high-demand subject and specialization areas, do consider the socioeconomic levels and the academic levels of students in making employment decisions.[10]

Among the comparison school districts, LPS has the highest percentage of students receiving free and reduced lunch and the second highest percentage of English as a Second Language (ESL) students (Figure 3.15). Teachers working with challenging demographics, such as those in LPS,

Figure 3.15   Demographic Comparison Data for Selected School Districts

	School District	Student			
		Enrollment	Cost per Pupil Spending	Free and Reduced Lunch (%)	English as a Second Language (%)
State 1	LPS	11,712	$12,467	50	14.7
	District 1	19,299	$11,756	40	26.2
	District 2	165,016	$10,862	19.6	10.9
	District 3	1,773	$9,645	8.6	10.3
	District 4	35,349	$8,938	8.4	3.1
	District 5	6,791	$8,515	18.7	10.4
	District 6	57,190	$6,072	22	7.2
State 2	District 7	102,334	$7,492	46.7	13.8
	District 8	136,653	$7,894	23.7	6.9
	District 9	137,597	$7,107	44.1	6.0

Note: Percentages are based on total student enrollments.

are more likely to face stress in the classroom. This matter must be considered in any analysis of attracting and retaining quality teachers.

The best teachers should be teaching the most challenging students. However, one traditional reward system in schools is to reward longevity and excellence with the more preferred (i.e., upper level) teaching assignments. Poor and minority students are more likely to have teachers who are uncertified, teaching out of their field, inexperienced, or perform poorly on tests for college admissions and teacher licensure.[11] If LPS wants high-quality teachers in place to meet the needs of LPS students, a new reward system must replace the old one. LPS needs to consider paying its best teachers to teach its most challenging students.

Class Size

Figure 3.16 shows average class sizes in the various districts. It is important to note that average class size may be misleading, as some classes, such as special education, are capped at much lower numbers than others, resulting in higher numbers in general education classrooms. At any rate, larger class sizes mean more demands are placed on teachers, with more time spent on activities such as grading and less on one-on-one contact with students. And, obviously, in larger classes, there are more students and families to get to know in order to meet students' educational

Figure 3.16   Class Size for Selected School Districts

	School District	Average Class Size per Classroom Teacher		
		Elementary Schools	Middle Schools	High Schools
State 1	LPS	20.30	19.10	21.10
	District 1	17.56	19.69	17.57
	District 2	21.70	24.70	24.60
	District 3	20.60	15.90	20.80
	District 4	22.00	21.60	26.60
	District 5	20.50	23.60	23.30
	District 6	22.10	19.60	17.60
State 2	District 7	21.49	23.32	18.60
	District 8	22.61	24.60	25.50
	District 9	25.20	24.30	25.30

needs. Consequently, not only do smaller classes impact the quality of working conditions for teachers, but also they allow teachers to offer more direct support for the students under their charge. Teachers are able to focus more on engaging students in learning instead of managing classroom behavior. And, ultimately, decreased class size can lead to improved student achievement.[12]

Teacher Contract Time

Figure 3.17 displays how selected school districts in the case analysis use teachers' contract days and time. For example, District 3 emphasizes early release time in lieu of full staff development days. LPS staff development days, workdays, and conference days, in general, are comparable to those in other school districts. However, District 4 has the most student days and the second longest teacher calendar, but offers the highest number of full days without students. Overall, LPS has the shortest faculty calendar and is below the median for days without students.

Planning time among school districts varies greatly. The LPS workday is slightly shorter than those of most competing school districts (Figure 3.18). Finally, for new teachers, LPS offers one of the longest new teacher orientation programs. However, the extra five workdays for new teachers are not accompanied by additional compensation. As with the other factors related to working conditions, the amount of work time required, along with how that time is allocated and compensated, will have direct implications for attracting and retaining a quality teacher workforce. One

Figure 3.17   Allocation of Teacher Contract Days

	School District	Student Days	Contract Days	Conference/Workdays/ Inservice		New Teacher Orientation	Inclement Weather
				Full Days	Early Release		
State 1	LPS	180	190	7	4	5	6
	District 1	182	196	9	10	3	9
	District 2	180	193	10	0	3	3
	District 3	180	200	0	54	5	24
	District 4	185	198	15	1	3	5
	District 5	184	200	11	1	1	9
	District 6	184	195	10	0	1	4
State 2	District 7	180	196	9	2	5	3
	District 8	182	198	8	5	1	6
	District 9	185	194	10	0	3	6
	Average (rounded)	**182**	**196**	**9**	**8***	**3**	**7.5****

* District 3's emphasis on early release days skews the average.

** Numbers will not add up, as some days incorporate dual roles of being both inclement weather and teacher workdays.

survey of teacher working conditions noted that when teachers felt they had enough time to accomplish their work, achievement in the school increased.[13] As teacher quality is related to student achievement, time can also be a factor in teacher satisfaction.

SUMMARY: TEACHER QUALITY AND COMPETITIVE PAY

The primary purpose for a competitive total teacher compensation package is to guarantee that the best teaching cadre possible is employed. Through examination of salary benchmarking, per diem pay, cost of living adjustments, and the role of benefits and working conditions, school districts are better equipped to attract, entice, and negotiate with both new recruits and current employees. By arraying its financial and nonfinancial

Figure 3.18   Teacher Contract Time During the School Day

	School District	Elementary		Middle/Jr. High/High School	
		Workday Length (Hours)	Planning Time/Week (Minutes)	Workday Length (Hours)	Planning Time/Week (Minutes)
	LPS	6.8	150	7.3	225–275 (250 midpoint)
State 1	District 1	7.2	175	7.4	275
	District 2	7.5	150*	7.5	235*
	District 3	7.5	675	7.5	680
	District 4	7	200	7.25	230
	District 5	7.5	225	7.5	250–460 (355 midpoint)
	District 6	7.5	110	7	250
State 2	District 7	7.5	160	7.5	260
	District 8	7	200	7.3	285
	District 9	7	175	7.4	250
	Average (rounded)	**7.2**	**222**	**7.4**	**307**

* Did not indicate if planning time was duty-free.

resources adeptly, a school district, clearly, can enhance the likelihood of attracting and retaining high quality teachers. By doing so, the district can

- improve the quality of instruction by emphasizing effective class-room performance;
- contribute to the successful achievement of the organization's goals and objectives;
- promote self-growth, instructional effectiveness, and overall performance improvement of its teachers.

Ultimately, the compensation system of a school district is a means to an end, not an end in itself. Its purpose should be to develop and maintain a high quality workforce in order to serve the needs of students. With this overriding goal in mind, a school district would be well served to consider the competitiveness of its total compensation package in light of attracting, supporting, and retaining its most valuable asset—its teachers.

4

Considering Options for Teacher Pay

What Are the Promising Possibilities?

Teacher compensation models may be classified several different ways, based on such features as whether additional compensation appears as a bonus or a lasting salary increase; whether compensation increases as a result of longevity, additional responsibilities, continuing education, and/or performance; and whether additional compensation is available on an individual or group basis. All of these elements are considerations in reviewing and restructuring compensation programs to support the goals of attracting, developing, and retaining quality teachers more effectively. The purpose of this chapter is to provide background information, analysis, and examples of the major current models of teacher compensation, addressing key underlying assumptions and the advantages and disadvantages of each. Chapter 5 will then continue the discussion of compensation options, with a focus on judging and applying the various models within a specific school district context.

Seven types of compensation models will be explored in the pages that follow, clustered by the type of teacher behaviors and outcome measures to which they correspond. First we will explore two traditional models of teacher compensation, focusing on paying teachers for fulfilling the teaching role and additional duties associated with the work of schools: the *single-salary schedule* and *additional responsibility* or *extra duty pay.* Then we turn to two models that differentiate compensation more directly based on the professional learning and growth that teachers pursue and demonstrate: *career ladders* and *knowledge- and skills-based pay*. Third, we address compensation models that provide compensation directly linked to outcomes, including teacher and student outcomes: *individual responsibility pay* and *performance-based pay*.[1] Finally, we will explore a different direction in compensation options, addressing possibilities for "creative compensation" that may provide bonuses and benefits that do not necessarily fall within the previous six categories.

These seven types or models of teacher compensation are addressed separately for purposes of clarity; however, it should be noted that many school districts use a combination of compensation options, incorporating relevant features of several different models to meet their specific local needs and interests. Following each model overview, some examples of the model in action will be shared,[2] along with a discussion of how the model relates to the key emphases of this book on attracting, developing, and retaining quality teachers.

SINGLE-SALARY SCHEDULE[3]

Key Features and Assumptions

The single-salary schedule is considered to be the traditional model of teacher compensation. It first emerged early in the twentieth century and was used by 97 percent of American school systems by 1950.[4] Under a single-salary schedule, teachers across a school district are paid according to a scale that acknowledges years of experience and educational units (i.e., degrees and additional graduate coursework obtained). Teachers are placed into lanes on the scale based on their acquired education, and they move up steps on the scale each year that they remain in the district, shifting lanes as they obtain further coursework and degrees. The salary schedule for our hypothetical Lincoln Public Schools (LPS) is an example of this model (see Figure 3.2 in Chapter 3).

The single-salary schedule was developed to respond to concerns about the fairness of earlier methods of paying teachers, which relied heavily on administrator judgment of teacher merit and varied by specific teaching role in a school district.[5] The single-salary schedule relies on the assumptions that two primary influences are important in developing teacher quality: *experience* and *continuing education*. Through acquiring greater experience or further education, teachers increase their salary; provided that teachers accomplish the minimum expectations of their job, their salary increases over time, and they may enhance that increase through furthering their education. With its reliance on graduate education as the primary method of moving across lanes, the single-salary schedule uses an *indirect* measure of professional development rather than a direct assessment of teacher knowledge and skills by the district. Research supports the assumption that experience and continuing education are positively correlated to teacher effectiveness.[6] However, research is less clear about *how much* experience, *how much* continuing education, or *what kind* of continuing education is characteristic of highly effective teachers.

The single-salary schedule is uncomplicated to administer and requires minimal data management. Record keeping is required only around teachers' years in the district and acquired graduate hours; hence, the experiential data may easily be maintained centrally, and the responsibility for reporting graduate hours is on the teacher.

Several important issues must be addressed in the decision-making process around this compensation model. First, the scale must be established such that it is *competitive at the entry level* in order to compete with other school districts and organizations around the goal of *attracting* quality teachers. Second, school divisions must consider where on the scale to place *experienced teachers new to a school district*—in other words, how much credit to give for teaching experience outside of the district. Note that in the LPS salary schedule depicted in Figure 3.2, new hires are placed on the step directly commensurate with their experience through the first five years of teaching. Beyond the fifth year, however, experienced teachers moving into LPS essentially "lose" one or more of their years of experience upon entering the school district. Similarly, with an influx of *second-career teachers* entering the profession after years of experience in another field, school districts must consider whether and how to acknowledge the previous experience these individuals bring in placing them on the salary schedule.

Another consideration in the use of a single-salary schedule is whether to employ a *front-loaded* or *back-loaded* model. The front-loaded model uses a steeper scale in the early years of teaching, allowing less experienced teachers to increase their salaries more quickly, while the back-loaded model is steeper at later stages, providing higher salary percentage gains for more experienced teachers. The single-salary schedule can also be designed as a *midloaded* model in which greater salary increases occur after some number of years of experience (e.g., 8–14 years' experience) but prior to approaching retirement.

Deciding what "loading" to place on the model and where to place experienced teachers new to the district depends to some extent on whether the district is choosing to emphasize attracting teachers with more experience or with less experience, and on the emphasis the district places on retaining its more experienced teachers. Finally, this last point about retaining experienced teachers is particularly influential: school districts must consider how to avoid a topping-out problem—how to continue to offer reasonable and growing compensation to teachers who have been working for the district for many years and have already completed

Figure 4.1   Advantages of the Single-Salary Schedule

- ***Ease of administration and record keeping:*** The model is straightforward and simple to administer. Movement through the steps primarily occurs through automatic advancement based on years of experience in the school district, and the teacher can achieve additional movement based on education credits with documentation from the university attended. In addition, the single-salary schedule's long history and familiarity to educators makes it more convenient to maintain than a new model is to implement.

- ***Clarity:*** The model may be clearly outlined and understood with minimal explanation. Because of this, it is communicated to prospective employees without difficulty.

- ***Ease of alignment with other models:*** The single-salary schedule may be easily combined with alternative compensation models, using the traditional schedule as a baseline or as a default or safety system. Such security can facilitate support from teachers for testing alternative compensation programs because it maintains stability while new options are piloted.

- ***Promotes pursuit of higher education:*** By rewarding teachers for achieving graduate credits and degrees, the model encourages teachers to take initiative toward their own professional growth and development. In this way, the single-salary schedule may be seen as including a form of knowledge- and skills-based pay, albeit an indirect one.

- ***Promotes loyalty and longevity within the school district:*** Depending to some degree on its rate of salary growth, the model acknowledges long-term commitment to the school district by rewarding teachers who achieve more advanced steps within each lane.

- ***Fairness:*** The model was originally designed based on a principle of fairness, attempting to avoid the problems created by previous compensation models that contained performance components often administered somewhat arbitrarily. Consequently, a strength of this model is its appearance of fairness and the fact that it does not create the competitive environment that is a potential of other models. However, the assumption that this model is actually fair to teachers is challenged by concerns about teacher effectiveness—thus the focus on alternative compensation options.

advanced degrees. Most salary schedules in the United States limit the total number of steps possible, with an average of 16 years for maximum longevity increases.[7] Therefore, a district must consider how to determine compensation for teachers whose years of service extend beyond the salary schedule.

Advantages and Highlights

The simplicity and clarity of the single-salary schedule have contributed to its long history and widespread use. Some specific advantages of the system are noted in Figure 4.1.

Disadvantages and Concerns

Concerns about the fairness of the single-salary schedule and its capacity for promoting improvement have given rise to consideration of alternative models in many districts across the country and in the educational literature. Some specific disadvantages of the single-salary schedule appear in Figure 4.2.

Figure 4.2   Disadvantages of the Single-Salary Schedule

- *Fairness:* Although the model was designed based on a fairness principle, as noted above, questions have arisen as to whether it is actually fair. This is primarily because the model does not specifically and directly address teacher quality. Thus some teachers who have been teaching for many years but are ineffective receive greater compensation than those who have less experience but greater results in terms of student performance and related measures.

- *Response to market demands:* Again, based on its original design, the single-salary schedule pays for the job of teaching, without differentiating based on particular specialty or critical shortage areas, except perhaps indirectly through payment for specialized degrees. Therefore the model has a limited capacity to attract teachers for positions in critical shortage areas.

- *Applicability of additional education:* Most single-salary schedules reward teachers for achieving advanced degrees or graduate credits, but there is rarely attention given to how well the graduate education relates to the specific teaching assignment. Consequently teachers are rewarded for advanced education that may or may not specifically influence their practice.*

- *Getting started and topping out:* Many single-salary schedules present special challenges to teachers at one or both ends of their career spectrum. One issue is rate of percentage gain on salary scales. Many districts use a *back-loaded* model, which allows greater gains for more experienced teachers, thus elongating the time it takes newer teachers to achieve higher salaries. On the other hand, *front-loaded* models are less attractive to experienced teachers, whose salary gains may flatten out as they progress in the school district. Moreover, often the single-salary schedule leads to a topping-out problem, by which individuals who have been teaching for many years and have amassed several graduate degrees are no longer able to increase their salary unless they choose to move out of the classroom and into administrative positions.

- *Relationship to school reform:* The single-salary schedule, with its nearly automatic advancement, does not specifically encourage or reward the kinds of improvements demanded of the educational system by the administration and the public. In an era of accountability, in which student achievement is under close scrutiny and teachers are under intense pressure to promote this achievement, a salary model that does not align with this central goal of the school and the educational system in general may be problematic.

- *Taxpayer resistance:* Some proponents of performance-based pay argue that the single-salary schedule requires taxpayers to reward ineffective teachers, while an alternative model could link more closely with accountability initiatives.** As public demand for performance improvement continues, this issue of taxpayer resistance to the single-salary schedule may increase in the coming years.

* Ramirez, 2001.

** Firestone, 1994; Hoerr, 1998.

Focus on Teacher Quality

In most of the emerging alternative models for teacher compensation, a form of the single-salary schedule remains as a default scale, with teachers advancing up the steps from year to year as they have traditionally done, but with opportunities to accelerate their progress or add bonuses to their salaries through other compensation options. Such a use of the single-salary schedule provides both stability and flexibility to the compensation system, relieving teachers of some of their fears of unfairness yet building in opportunities for individuals who demonstrate above average or exceptional teaching to earn additional compensation for their efforts.

EXTRA DUTY/ADDITIONAL RESPONSIBILITY PAY[8]

Key Features and Assumptions

Extra duty pay is an option for teacher compensation that has been in place for many years as a *supplement* to the traditional salary schedule. This model provides supplementary pay for teachers who take on responsibilities or duties in addition to what is expected of their job or position. Traditionally, extra duty pay has compensated teachers for such responsibilities as coaching athletic teams, serving as department chair, sponsoring clubs, and similar activities.

Extra duty pay generally takes the form of bonuses added to a teacher's salary on a year-to-year basis, depending on the responsibilities fulfilled. It may be used in conjunction with any of the other compensation models; by its nature as *extra* pay, this model is *supplementary* and does not denote an entire compensation system on its own.

The concept of extra duty pay can be broadened from a focus primarily on extracurricular activities to incorporate more responsibilities linked directly to school and division goals, such as professional development leader, curriculum leader, or new teacher mentor. Such an approach is often referred to as job enlargement[9] and primarily uses pay as a *facilitator* rather than an incentive, providing teachers the support they need to engage in extra tasks they find interesting and intrinsically rewarding.

One of the key considerations of implementing extra duty pay, particularly as the concept broadens to encompass responsibilities beyond extracurricular student activities, is determining when teachers will perform their additional responsibilities. Extra duty scheduling might include some of the following options:

- Commitments before or after school
- Responsibilities within the context of the school day, with consideration of how to balance the extra duties with regular duties
- Activities during the summer or on work days

Given the range of responsibilities and time commitments, districts might consider a wider range of options for compensating teachers for additional responsibilities—for example, extra planning time or course buy-out might be compensation options considered in lieu of salary increases or bonuses.

Of the compensation models, extra duty pay most closely reflects traditional *job-based compensation* rather than *person-based compensation*—it pays for specific tasks to be performed in an add-on model rather than acknowledging and rewarding the competencies a person demonstrates related to his or her primary position. This basic assumption raises some concerns about the model, because of a fear it might lead to reluctance among teachers to engage in any extra tasks unless they are paid specifically for those tasks. However, extra duty pay—in the form of actual payment or in the form of extra planning time or similar benefits granted—can help to alleviate the overload teachers feel if they must be involved in multiple activities beyond the classroom. Moreover, this form of compensation can be linked with other alternative models to use additional responsibility pay as a way of promoting teacher quality. For example, it might be linked to a career ladder model through a structure that only entitles teachers to take on certain responsibilities when they have reached designated levels on the ladder. Likewise, school districts may use an application and evaluation process to determine who is eligible for extra opportunities, thus adding further accountability to the option.

Advantages and Highlights

Major advantages of a model incorporating extra duty pay include that it rewards effort and initiative and that it promotes leadership and involvement of teachers in school district activities beyond their expected work in the classroom. Some specific advantages are addressed in Figure 4.3.

Figure 4.3   Advantages of Extra Duty Pay

- *Ease of administration:* Although record keeping around extra duty pay is more cumbersome than with a single-salary schedule alone, the option is relatively easy to administer. Specific duties or responsibilities are matched to specific compensation, and teacher participation in their roles is documented. Unless the model is defined in such a way that it includes an evaluative component, participation in a given role of extra responsibility is the determination of compensation.

- *Clarity and flexibility:* Local applications of this model may be clearly outlined as a menu of additional compensation options and easily understood by current and prospective employees. Moreover, as a supplementary feature, this model may be easily added onto any existing or restructured compensation model.

- *Promotes involvement and leadership:* By providing compensation for participation in additional responsibilities, school districts directly encourage and reward teachers for involvement in more aspects of the school culture than only their specific job assignment. Therefore teachers may have opportunities to work with different staff and students than they would otherwise and to diversify their career experience. Moreover, because many of the roles incorporated into extra duty pay options are leadership roles, the model encourages teachers in the development of leadership skills.

- *Rewards effort:* An extra duty pay model directly links specific activities to specific compensation. In this way, it compensates teachers commensurate to the effort they expend. School districts can also reward effort by making extra duty options available only for teachers who perform their expected responsibilities at and above a designated level.

- *Alignment with school goals:* As noted above, extra duty pay models can incorporate options for teachers to take on responsibilities related to overall school goals and to be compensated for their efforts. The idea of the incentive can also be expanded to align with other goals through providing such benefits as extra planning time instead of financial compensation.

Disadvantages and Concerns

The disadvantages of extra duty pay models echo those of other models in terms of issues of fairness. In addition, the emphasis on payment for fulfilling a role often implies limited accountability, thus limiting the model's effectiveness in promoting professional development and teacher quality. Some specific disadvantages are noted in Figure 4.4.

Figure 4.4   Disadvantages of Extra Duty Pay Models

- ***Fairness:*** The fairness issue emerges in two main ways regarding extra duty pay. First, there is the issue of determining how much pay is linked to different duties and ensuring that this determination is equitable and fair according to the demands of the roles. Second, and similar to concerns with the single-salary schedule, the model does not generally acknowledge differences in performance around the additional responsibilities; rather, it rewards teachers for taking on the roles but not for meeting or exceeding the expectations of the roles or demonstrating particular efforts to increase quality.

- ***Expectations for pay:*** The more extra duty pay is expanded to incorporate many different types of responsibilities for teachers, the greater the possibility that teachers will begin to expect extra duty pay for any additional responsibilities asked of them. This can discourage an atmosphere of volunteerism around school initiatives and place the emphasis on working for rewards instead of for school improvement or other related goals.

- ***Overload:*** Extra duty pay systems encourage teachers to take on assignments above and beyond their regular job responsibilities and compensate them for doing so. In some cases, this may lead to situations in which teachers take on too much and their classroom practice—the central goal of their employment—suffers as a consequence.

Examples of Extra Duty/Additional Responsibility Pay

As previously noted, school districts have traditionally provided teachers with additional compensation for extra duties, such as coaching sports, sponsoring academic clubs, providing after-school tutoring, and serving as department chair. The stipends or bonuses provided for these responsibilities generally vary as widely as the duties themselves. Continuing with our LPS example, Figure 4.5 illustrates stipends for selected extra duties provided by LPS and several nearby school districts.

Another example of additional responsibility pay may be found in the compensation system utilized in Douglas County, Colorado, a leading school district in the implementation of alternative compensation models.[10] Douglas County's compensation model has received much attention and positive press in the general media and educational literature since its establishment in the mid-1990s because of the comprehensiveness of the model. We will return to it several times to illustrate examples of different compensation options. In this section, we specifically address Douglas County's responsibility pay component.

Beyond contract responsibilities, which may include coaching or extracurricular options as previously explored, the responsibility pay

Figure 4.5   Stipends for Selected Extra Duties in LPS and Nearby School
Districts

School Division	Baseball Head Coach	Softball Head Coach	Band Director	Newspaper	Teacher Specialists/ Dept. Chair
LPS	$2,936	$2,936	$1,098	—	$200–$2,375
District 1	$4,169	$4,169	$2,405	—	$320–$1,123
District 2	$3,498	$3,498	$3,498	$3,498	—
District 3	$3,927	$3,927	$1,088–$3,813	$2,616	$1,500–$3,000
District 4	$2,462–$2,975	$2,462–$2,975	$1,949–$3,885	$744–$1,366	—
Average*	$3,449.70	$3,449.70	$2,473.70	$2,389.67	$1,419.67

* For cases in which there is a range given in the table, the midpoint of each cell was figured
in order to calculate the average for a given duty.

component recognizes teachers for engaging in a variety of activities, including committee work, curriculum work, and mentorship of colleagues. The
district encourages teachers to be involved in site-based and district-based
responsibilities, with emphasis on utilizing professional knowledge and
skills to support school and district goals. The district has a segment of the
budget specifically earmarked for responsibility pay. This funding is provided to schools based on number of students, with schools informed each
fall of the sum available to them. Individual schools develop a site plan each
fall with collaborative involvement from administrators and teachers,
and then they file the plan with the district. As individuals complete their
assigned responsibilities, they submit forms detailing their efforts for school
and district records. At the district level, the district office and the local
teacher union negotiate an amount of responsibility pay for each year to
compensate teachers for involvement in committees that serve the larger
interests of the district.[11] Responsibility-based bonuses for specific extra
assignments in Douglas County are not large, but they may add from $35 to
over $200 to teacher salaries, depending on the responsibility performed.

Focus on Teacher Quality

Compensation models that incorporate options for additional responsibility pay have the capacity to promote attracting, developing, and
retaining quality teachers through implementation of these options. These
models generally allow for a great deal of individual decision making
regarding extra responsibilities assumed; such autonomy and flexibility
may be an attractive feature to teachers considering employment with the

school district among several competitive options. Furthermore, the model allows pay to increase more quickly than with a single-salary schedule alone, another feature that may both attract and retain teachers with the district over time. These advantages acknowledge such elements of quality as contributions to the school district and involvement with students beyond the minimal expectations of the classroom role. However, additional responsibility models traditionally do not address teacher quality directly, especially in regard to classroom practice.

Models for additional responsibility pay have the capacity to promote goals for teacher quality more directly if they (a) acknowledge and compensate for responsibilities tied to specific district goals and (b) require demonstration of readiness levels to take on additional responsibilities. Highly motivated teachers may be attracted to a district in which teachers are encouraged, tangibly, to expand their professional involvement in the practice of teaching beyond the scope of their regular responsibilities. By requiring threshold performance levels in order to engage in particular responsibilities, districts encourage teachers to develop quality by providing an incentive that not only pays for that professional development but also results in additional efforts toward school district goals. Moreover, as teachers increase in their experience and professional expertise, they are likely to be able to take on more responsibilities than might be feasible for beginning teachers; as a result, the model promotes both development and retention of quality teachers. Finally, additional responsibility pay may alleviate some of the concerns related to flattening rates of salary increase and topping out for more experienced teachers; by providing options for ongoing increases in compensation or at least for bonuses, the additional responsibility pay model contributes to the goal of retaining teachers.

To a large extent, however, the model for additional responsibility or extra duty pay is likely to reward teachers of greater and lesser quality at similar levels, depending more on which teachers are most motivated to take on extra responsibilities than on their quality of classroom practice or performance. Nevertheless, particularly when used in combination with other alternative compensation models that address quality more directly, additional responsibility pay provides a straightforward option for quality teachers to increase the compensation they receive.

CAREER LADDER[12]

Key Features and Assumptions

The traditional salary schedule generally allows teachers to advance across lanes only through achievement of educational milestones and "up the steps" only by years of employment. Some alternative compensation models, attempting to increase flexibility and to respond to individual professional development and performance, expand on the idea of lanes and steps through designation of different levels of teacher status and expertise. This concept of a *career ladder* model designates levels of teacher status, in terms of title and compensation, by acknowledging teachers for achievement in specified areas of performance. In career ladder systems, or *master teacher pay* systems, the steps on the ladder are usually designated by titles such as novice, apprentice, teacher leader, expert teacher, distinguished teacher, or master teacher. Teachers can move up the steps by demonstrating professional growth based on a set of specific criteria. These might include exemplary classroom practice, as evaluated by superiors; high-level performance relative to external standards, such as the National Board for Professional Teaching Standards (NBPTS); or pursuit of graduate coursework, advanced degrees, and/or other evidence of exceptional professional development efforts.

School districts may choose a wide range of sources of evidence for teachers to use in attempting to attain status levels; those sources of evidence will depend on how the district chooses to define the most important indicators of teacher quality. With the flexibility it incorporates for teachers to progress, however, the career ladder model reflects an understanding that professional growth and development occur at different rates and to different degrees across individuals. It attempts to support newer teachers who are exceptionally talented by allowing them to advance more quickly, while also providing opportunities for more seasoned teachers to use their knowledge and experience.

The career ladder model emerged in the 1980s, representing an attempt to identify and support teachers performing at a high level and to reward them with leadership positions and opportunities, as well as financial bonuses. Teachers who achieve higher levels on a career ladder might become involved with curriculum development, professional development, or other administrative responsibilities. In this way, they reflect some of the expanded notion of additional responsibility pay described in the previous section; however, in a career ladder model, usually additional responsibility requires achievement of specific steps on the career ladder, and with the added responsibility also comes added status.

Although some career ladder plans prioritize the presence of the teacher leader in the classroom, many remove these teachers from the classroom, for at least some time, to engage in other tasks. However, most recent career ladder programs have focused on classroom practice and on mentoring in achieving higher steps on the career ladder, rather than tasks that are less instructionally related.

The career ladder model assumes that the elements that would be used to define levels of quality teaching are identifiable and measurable in teacher practice. It also requires careful communication and management to ensure that a climate of collegiality results, in which teachers may take advantage of one another's expertise and support, rather than a climate of competition and resentment. Other factors that may lead to positive results for career ladder models include teacher cooperation in the planning process and the incorporation of both extrinsic and intrinsic incentives to improve skills.[13]

Many career ladder plans incorporate the traditional salary schedule, linking placement in a lane and minimum movement up steps to education and years of service. However, they also allow teachers to accelerate their movement up the steps of the scale by demonstrating exemplary performance against the criteria, thereby achieving higher levels of pay before they have put in the designated number of years. Alternatively, some master teacher pay models use a bonus pay approach to teacher compensation, adding one-time bonuses for achievement against specified criteria.

Advantages and Highlights

The career ladder model's major advantages center on its capacity to promote professional growth in teaching practice and to acknowledge and encourage achievement among quality teachers. Some specific advantages are discussed in Figure 4.6.

Figure 4.6   Advantages of the Career Ladder Model

- *Emphasis on professional development:* Most career ladder models require that teachers clearly demonstrate increasingly high levels of professional growth and performance as determined by specific internal or external standards. The requirements for such recognitions as NBPTS certification, the Milken Award, or Teacher of the Year are extensive and incorporate professional development, classroom performance, and teacher reflection. Thus, by incorporating such measures into the career ladder systems, school districts promote high levels of professional development and individualized growth.

- *Leadership opportunities:* Career ladder models generally incorporate not only increased compensation for higher steps on the ladder but also various leadership opportunities for teachers. These may include serving as mentor teachers to less experienced colleagues, engaging in school- or districtwide curriculum development initiatives, providing professional development opportunities, or moving part-time or for a short term into a district-level position.

- *Removes lockstep of the single-salary schedule:* By allowing teachers to move more quickly up a salary scale and by designating levels around performance instead of merely years of experience, a career ladder model acknowledges talent and initiative in younger teachers. This has the potential not only to promote professional growth and performance but also to retain quality teachers in the field and in a given district by providing a more accelerated salary scale. In addition, the structure of the ladder still acknowledges different developmental levels in teaching across the career span, such that even though newer teachers can move quickly up a ladder, experienced teachers may be able to advance to the higher levels of the ladder shortly after implementation of a new career ladder program.[*]

- *Rewards initiative and competence:* With all teachers, not only the ones newer to the field, the career ladder model acknowledges teachers who show initiative and strong performance and rewards them for their efforts.

- *Promotes mentorship and collaboration:* Although critics suggest that career ladder systems can create competition because of limited numbers of positions available at higher levels, by emphasizing the mentorship role of more proficient teachers these systems can also support collaboration and promote sharing of professional ideas and practices.

* Conley & Odden, 1995.

Disadvantages and Concerns

The disadvantages of the career ladder model include its potential to create competition, its demands for funding and administrative record keeping, and a limited track record of success. The model also raises questions about how teachers of the highest quality spend their time, considering whether master teachers should spend more of their time teaching students or mentoring other teachers. Some specific disadvantages are discussed in Figure 4.7.

Figure 4.7   Disadvantages of Career Ladder Models

- **Competition:** As with any model that evaluates individual teacher performance for compensation purposes, the career ladder model has the capacity to foster competition among teachers. Indeed, this model may carry that danger more than others because the designations of teacher levels are more visible in this system than in other kinds of systems recognizing performance differences, especially when teachers are given specific leadership opportunities based on their level or when designations are otherwise publicized.

- **Quotas:** One of the key issues in a career ladder system is determining how many teachers the school district can maintain at the different levels, especially if leadership opportunities are a component of the system. Ideally, a district would wish to be able to support as many quality teachers as possible at higher status levels on the ladder and to avoid quotas either for minimum or maximum numbers of teachers at each designated level.* However, problems with funding and a district's capacity to provide the advanced opportunities for leadership have been key reasons why many career ladder models have been discontinued in the past.**

- **Leaving the classroom:** One central argument against career ladder models in the past has been the issue that by rewarding high levels of teaching achievement with leadership opportunities outside the classroom, a district removes its best teachers from day-to-day contact with students. Although it is desirable for master teachers to share their expertise through mentoring others and providing curricular and staff development leadership, these other responsibilities do detract from the time spent in the classroom after the advanced steps have been achieved. From another perspective, the alternative responsibilities assigned on the basis of career ladder programs sometimes ask teachers to take on new responsibilities that rely on a different set of skills and knowledge, rather than more fully utilizing the skills for which teachers were recognized in the first place.

- **Fairness of assessment:** As with each of the other models involved with evaluating individual teachers for compensation purposes, the issue of fairness arises in the career ladder. Whether judgment is based on classroom observations, review of portfolios, or other measures of performance, models that utilize judgment of internal evaluators as a basis for compensation raise concerns about fair and reliable implementation of standards.

- **Overload:** The requirements of a career ladder model can be daunting for the teacher, depending on how the plan is structured. Teachers who achieve higher steps on a career ladder and have responsibilities for outside work in addition to their regular teaching assignment may become overwhelmed. In planning such a model, time allocation is an important consideration. A career ladder model can be combined with an extra duty pay plan that incorporates extra pay as compensation for extra time spent rather than as a performance bonus of some kind.

---

* Odden, 2000a.

** Keller, 2002.

Examples of Career Ladder Models

Perhaps the most highly publicized example of a career ladder model was the plan proposed for the Cincinnati Public Schools, parts of which were introduced in 1997 and explored over the subsequent five years.[14] From the outset, it is important to note that the alternative compensation proposal of the Cincinnati plan was rejected by a vote from teachers in the district, for a variety of reasons encompassing several of the disadvantages previously noted. However, the designations of levels of teacher status within the evaluation system were approved and remain in place.[15] Despite the rejection of the compensation proposal, the components of the Cincinnati model reflect many of the key features and advantages of the career ladder, and thus it will be explored here, with recognition of its inherent disadvantages as well.

Cincinnati's proposed Teacher Evaluation and Compensation System was a comprehensive, career-ladder-type program that identified five categories for teachers and linked pay to those categories. Teachers were to be paid according to their designation with the categories of *apprentice, novice, career, advanced,* or *accomplished.* Movement for teachers from one category to another was based on classroom performance, defined within a set of standards in four domains: Planning and Preparing for Student Learning, Creating an Environment for Learning, Teaching for Learning, and Professionalism. On the specific standards within the domains, teachers were to be rated according to a rubric at the levels of unsatisfactory, basic, proficient, and distinguished.

The frequency of evaluation was determined based on a teacher's status. Beginning or *apprentice* teachers would receive a comprehensive evaluation two years after hiring, at which time they had to achieve *novice* status for their contracts to be renewed. Similarly, teachers would receive a comprehensive evaluation after three years at the novice level, and again, at that time they had to qualify for the *career* level in order to be renewed. Once a teacher achieved at least the career level, he or she would receive a comprehensive evaluation every five years, although more frequent evaluations could be requested if a teacher wished to attempt to advance more quickly. A key accountability feature of the program was that teachers could move backward on the steps as well as forward. As a protection, however, teachers who moved backward would be given two years to improve before their pay would be cut to reflect the lower designation.

The evaluation component of Cincinnati's program was first proposed in 1997 and piloted in ten schools in 1999–2000. In September 2000, the school board and teacher union ratified the plan, with the agreement that although the evaluation system would move forward, the compensation changes would be delayed until the 2002–2003 school year. This agreement was intended to encourage teacher support for the plan, allowing time for the teachers to prepare for the evaluation system before they could potentially take pay cuts because of it.

Nevertheless, teachers did eventually reject the compensation plan, concerned over implementation issues and the stakes of the evaluation system. Based on teacher and administrator concerns about the system, a vote was held under which modifications to the system were proposed, including a more limited number of teachers *required* to take part, an abbreviated expectation for teachers to provide work demonstrating alignment with the teaching standards, and greater recourse for teachers who question the evaluations they receive.[16] However, teacher concerns about the career ladder model in Cincinnati persisted. In May 2002, teachers resoundingly voted against full implementation of the career ladder.

Some other examples that use comprehensive or partial career ladder emphases have been more lasting. The state of Iowa developed a set of four teacher designations, with linkage to teacher evaluation and to salary increases. Teachers start at a Beginning teacher designation and have a certain amount of time within which they must progress to Career level. They may then, over time, apply for Career II and Advanced levels based on specific performance measures, and there is a range of time within which these applications may occur.[17] Hence the program provides accelerative opportunities for quality teachers in the earlier stages of their career. However, some critics of the program argue that it has less response to the needs of more experienced teachers,[18] and the program has consistently run into funding difficulties, limiting full development and implementation.[19]

The Douglas County Public Schools in Colorado, again an exemplar of a comprehensive compensation plan, also include an aspect reflecting key features of a career ladder model. Douglas County teachers who have received positive evaluations over a given period of time are eligible to apply for the designation of Master Teacher, based on evidence of student growth and on additional evidence of quality in two or more of the areas of leadership, recognition, creativity, and innovation. The Master Teacher designation, which lasts for a period of five years, includes a salary bonus and placement in a pool of teachers available to participate in various additional responsibilities, some of which bear additional compensation.[20]

The Teacher Advancement Program (TAP) developed by the Milken Family Foundation also supports the key features of the career ladder model. TAP schools allow teachers to choose to pursue designations as career, mentor, or master teachers, and it builds in opportunities for teachers with more advanced designations to take on responsibilities for leadership and systematic, ongoing professional development.[21]

Focus on Teacher Quality

A career ladder model's flexibility and acknowledgment of individual differences in professional growth rates can make it highly attractive to teachers considering employment with a system. Although some teachers might be daunted by such accountability features as Cincinnati's backward-moving possibility, these features underscore a school district's priority on quality teaching. The model clearly promotes an emphasis on developing quality teachers because it allows for a variety of ways of demonstrating quality and using developed knowledge and skills to further the goals of the individual and the school district. Moreover, the model respects and rewards not only longevity but longevity and quality together in a school district by giving added status and compensation to those experienced teachers who have demonstrated evidence of quality at multiple levels.

Career ladder models incorporate each of the key principles for compensation models that promote attracting, developing, and retaining quality teachers. However, comprehensive versions of the model are still relatively untried, with limited evidence to suggest that they influence student learning any differently, the key outcome and pursuit of quality teaching.[22] Moreover, the experience of the Cincinnati Public Schools stands as a cautionary tale to school districts exploring this model, highlighting the necessity to ensure funding for the model, fairness and clear communication in its implementation, and efforts to ensure teachers see the model as an opportunity to grow and to demonstrate quality teaching rather than as a negative and threatening influence on their practice. (See Chapter 6 for further discussion of implementation considerations for alternative compensation models.)

KNOWLEDGE- AND SKILLS-BASED PAY[23]

Key Features and Assumptions

Knowledge- and skills-based pay (KSBP) models are among the most popular of the emerging compensation models, and many or most of the alternative compensation plans in practice today incorporate some aspect of this option. This type of compensation, also known as *competency pay*, reflects an emphasis on demonstrated professional growth and development as a basis for compensation by providing salary bonuses or increases for specific learning activities in which teachers engage. Thus it rewards teachers for acquiring and using professional expertise. It is similar to the career ladder model in its emphasis on teacher professional growth, but differs in that it generally compensates teachers for smaller "packages" of performance rather than assigning status levels based on a more cohesive assessment of overall quality and growth. The KSBP model represents an attempt to accomplish three primary goals:

1. To honor a traditional assumption that the amount of teacher education contributes favorably to teacher practice and as such should be compensated[24]

2. To promote professional development linked directly to teaching assignment by requiring that achievement of knowledge and skills be measured by practice as well as by attendance at a course or professional development session

3. To identify areas of need for professional growth in a school or division and to support teachers in their pursuit of those areas

KSBP models identify knowledge or skill blocks—for example, in content-area reading or in computer applications—and define valid and reliable ways for teachers to demonstrate achievement of those blocks, including such options as graduate courses, professional development opportunities within the district, and other learning opportunities beyond the district. Once identified, knowledge and skill blocks are then assigned relative value in terms of how much bonus or advancement pay they merit, based on the relative difficulty of achieving each block and its value to the school or district. Defining standards for performance around each block is critical. In some cases, these standards are locally determined. However, many KSBP models also use externally determined standards, such as the NBPTS, singly or in combination with local standards. Such external standards, either as they stand or adapted for local concerns, may help to streamline initial implementation of a KSBP system.[25]

Notably, achievement of knowledge and skill blocks requires more than just attendance or participation in professional development workshops or courses for recognition. Evidence of use of the knowledge and skills in practice is also essential to the structure of a KSBP model. Evaluation methods may incorporate classroom observation by an administrator or peer but usually also involve a portfolio approach, through which teachers must use multiple means beyond classroom observations to demonstrate their achievement. An external group, rather than a teacher's immediate supervisor alone, should review teacher portfolios in order to promote a sense of fairness and objectivity in the system.

Although KSBP models do provide higher salaries based on higher education levels, like a traditional salary scale, they generally add a layer of accountability around performance and course relevance. KSBP models require the development and implementation of specific standards for evaluation, with emphasis on streamlining professional development and classroom performance as linked components of practice.

Most KSBP models provide bonuses or accelerated movement up a salary scale, with annual movement based on longevity—the traditional salary schedule—as the default model. The additional pay achieved through demonstration of mastery of the knowledge or skills identified may take the form of a one-time bonus or movement to another step on the scale.

Advantages and Highlights

Among the advantages of a KSBP model are its flexibility in tailoring to individual teachers and school districts and its capacity for alignment with school division goals. Moreover, it demonstrates a clear emphasis on *developing* quality teachers by linking compensation to teacher pursuit of professional growth based on assessed school and classroom needs. Some specific advantages of KSBP models are discussed in Figure 4.8.

Disadvantages and Concerns

The KSBP model is relatively new, and so its track record is not well established. In addition, it can be a cumbersome system to design and implement, requiring detailed identification, communication, and evaluation of knowledge and skill blocks and standards. School districts employing this

Figure 4.8   Advantages of Knowledge- and Skills-Based Pay Models

- *Emphasis on professional development:* The central emphasis of the KSBP model is professional development for teachers. Teachers under such a system are encouraged to pursue education through formal graduate courses or other professional development mechanisms, and that education should be specifically linked to teachers' own job assignments and the specific needs of the school and classroom. Moreover, the focus is not only on attending professional development opportunities or courses but also on the follow-through of demonstrating the learning in action in the classroom. Ideally, then, a KSBP plan that encourages professional growth in this way not only provides financial incentives and rewards but may also result in the other kinds of intrinsic rewards that teachers value, such as improved classroom performance from students.

- *Flexibility:* KSBP models are flexible in that they can encompass a wide range of knowledge or skill blocks for teachers to pursue, thus responding to individual and group needs and interests across a wide range of teachers. Moreover, KSBP plans encourage teachers to learn a more diverse body of skills and content, preparing them to take on other responsibilities or to serve as specialists within the organizational structure.

- *Alignment to district goals:* Because KSBP models are based on the achievement of specified knowledge or skill blocks, school districts can easily define those blocks based on specific district goals and needs. Consequently, teachers will be compensated for their own growth and development around the skills and competencies the school district most wishes them to demonstrate. Moreover, the model can support collaboration goals and group professional development efforts around other district goals through designation of knowledge and skill blocks for teachers to pursue as study groups or teams.

- *Rewards initiative and competence:* KSBP systems encourage teachers to show what they know and can do and to focus on continuous improvement of practice. These systems can also help teachers work toward NBPTS certification and other external recognition by aligning local standards with the National Board and other external standards.

- *Support from experts in the field of teacher compensation:* The Consortium for Policy Research in Education (CPRE), a leading organization in the study of compensation systems around the country, advocates KSBP systems for all of the reasons given here and has laid out some specific guidelines for the development and implementation of such systems, based on expert opinion and emerging findings from KSBP case studies.*

* Odden, 200a; also see Odden et al., 2001.

Figure 4.9   Disadvantages of Knowledge- and Skills-Based Pay Models

- **_Fairness of evaluation:_** KSBP models rely on implementation of valid and reliable standards and methods for measuring them, like other models that base compensation on aspects of teacher evaluation. Teachers generally have some control over their demonstration of behaviors linked to the standards in KSBP models, but fairness remains an issue both in terms of _the standards themselves_ and _who evaluates mastery._

- **_Cumbersome:_** The very features that make KSBP models flexible also make them cumbersome. For each knowledge or skill block identified, standards for mastery and methods of demonstrating competency must also be identified, and evaluators must be trained. Moreover, record keeping can be quite extensive, and the task of keeping track of teacher mastery of given blocks grows as more teachers become involved and as they choose more blocks to pursue.

- **_Track record:_** Although many teachers are cautiously expressing support for KSBP models and the use of specific standards for teaching practice, most existing programs are still in the early stages of implementation and do not have a long track record against which schools can evaluate their flexibility.

- **_Competition:_** The KSBP model, as with any system that evaluates and compensates for teacher development and/or performance on an individual level, has the potential to lead to competition that may undermine collegial feelings in the school. Attention should be given to options for groups of teachers as well as individuals to pursue selected knowledge and skill blocks to respond to this concern.

model must take care to ensure fairness in evaluation and in opportunity for engagement. Some specific disadvantages of the model are explored in Figure 4.9.

Examples of Knowledge- and Skills-Based Pay Models

Knowledge- and skills-based pay elements form a component of many existing alternative compensation systems. Some school districts and states (e.g., California, Florida, Maryland, Ohio) incorporate KSBP by awarding teachers bonuses or salary increases for NBPTS certification. In a 1999 survey of school districts around the country, bonuses for NBPTS certification were the most frequently used form of KSBP.[26] Other districts utilize locally determined skill blocks as the basis for recognition. Indeed, such recognitions overlap with several of the previous examples given for career ladder models, and the two types of models share many similar features. The distinctions between career ladder and KSBP models are primarily that the career ladder usually includes a specific role designation and often additional responsibilities for teachers, and that a KSBP model may provide bonus options for a greater number of teachers by allocating smaller bonuses for a wider range of activities than a step or lane change might suggest. The two models may be complementary, utilized within the same school districts at the same time, as in several of the following examples.

Returning to the Douglas County model once again, the comprehensive program includes one-time bonus payouts for teacher demonstration of completion of skills blocks related to the goals of the school district, with the district designating the need areas, providing professional development opportunities, and assessing acquisition of skills.[27]

The school district of Coventry, Rhode Island, uses a traditional salary schedule but also provides bonuses for demonstration of teaching competencies according to two sets of standards: the NBPTS and a local program called RHODE. Both programs are optional for teachers, and, in fact, the portfolio preparation for RHODE is intended to help teachers prepare for National Board certification as well. Teachers prepare a portfolio encompassing nine elements of their practice, including written analyses and reflections on lesson plans and assessments, evidence of differentiated instruction, and evidence of community contact and professional development. Expectations for teachers within the district are based on National Board standards and a modified version of Danielson's Framework for Teaching.[28] The program in Coventry streamlines teachers' performance standards and the portfolio preparation process by linking the local standards directly with the national standards. In addition, by providing funding and professional leave days, the district signals to teachers the value it places on development of high-level professional competencies.

The Milken TAP program also places a strong emphasis on professional growth and provides bonuses to teachers based on demonstration of increasing knowledge and skills. In an effort to avoid some of the challenges and pitfalls of performance-based pay programs that rely on student achievement gains in determining teacher bonuses (discussed later), the TAP evaluation system designates 50 percent of available bonus funds for demonstrated knowledge and skills and 50 percent for demonstrated student achievement.[29]

Focus on Teacher Quality

Knowledge- and skills-based pay models are flexible in their implementation because of the wide range of knowledge and skills that may be designated for recognition, and they provide choice and individual determination for teachers. In addition, they are attractive for quality teachers because they focus on the acquisition and demonstration of professional competencies, addressing the specific types of behaviors and characteristics that distinguish quality teachers.

A school district that includes KSBP options within a compensation package has the capacity to attract quality teachers because it broadens the scope of what a salary schedule can provide. KSBP options also support the goal of retaining teachers, provided that the options available correspond to the particular needs of more advanced teachers and not just the learning needs of teachers earlier in their careers. Above all, KSBP models support the goal of developing quality teachers; they place emphasis on ongoing professional development for teachers, and they require a conception of professional development that includes application of skills in the classroom, not merely such activities as attending workshops. Indeed, although some early thoughts on KSBP models included the expectation that they would primarily be attractive to school districts with low performance levels and extensive teacher learning needs, in fact many early findings from studies of these models demonstrate their popularity among districts with adequate performance—districts seeking better ways to support quality teachers.[30]

INDIVIDUAL EVALUATION PAY[31]

Key Features and Assumptions

Compensation based on the evaluation of individual teacher performance has traditionally been known as *merit pay*. Merit pay systems date back to the early twentieth century and have been sporadically pursued ever since. Generally, these systems have been based on recognizing the quality of teacher characteristics and practices through observation and assessment against a set of performance standards. The individual evaluation pay system often follows the single-salary schedule in that there is standard movement along a series of steps from year to year, but *such movement usually requires demonstration of satisfactory performance*. Moreover, this model can pay bonuses to teachers for performance that exceeds the standards.

At one level, the individual evaluation or merit pay system directly responds to the central focus of this text: linking teacher pay to teacher quality. In addition, aspects of the career ladder and KSBP models just discussed incorporate elements of individual evaluation pay because of their linkage to teacher evaluation systems and assessment of skill acquisition. However, the complexity of teaching, of teacher evaluation, and of the overall mission and practices of schools has limited the extent to which individual merit pay systems—especially if called merit pay, and especially if they carry accountability for even basic salary increases—may be effectively implemented.

The individual evaluation or merit pay model is based on a fundamental assumption that good teaching and its effects can be defined, observed, and measured objectively. This basic assumption has led to the downfall of many merit pay plans because teachers and scholars debate its validity. Recent research and development efforts are moving toward defining at least some of the elements that characterize good teaching, which may in time strengthen possibilities for implementing individual evaluation pay models; however, these models can be in conflict with other emphases in the school culture, including many collaborative efforts.

The central requirement of the merit pay model is the development and implementation of a method of evaluation and a set of standards that are *valid* and *reliable*—in other words, an evaluation system that measures what it is supposed to measure (validity) and that measures it accurately and consistently (reliability). Thus a compensation system intended to reward teachers for good teaching needs to define *what good teaching is* and *how it may be fairly measured*; moreover, it is critical that teachers perceive the system to be fair and appropriate in its structure, procedures, and outcomes. Other essential features of a fair and effective evaluation system include the following:

- The use of *multiple data sources* to acknowledge the complexity of the professional role teachers fulfill and to ensure thorough documentation
- Clarity of *communication* regarding the evaluation system and its connection to other human resource and district functions, including professional development and compensation
- Structures for systematic, timely *feedback* for teachers, with careful attention to the utility of the feedback
- Attention to the *conditions of the context* within which the evaluation system is to be implemented, including time and resource constraints
- Appropriate *training* on the evaluation system for evaluators and for teachers to be evaluated[32]

Throughout their history, merit pay models have generally relied primarily or wholly on the judgment of supervising administrators in determining teacher quality, often with limited and vague standards for evaluation.[33] The contemporary individual evaluation model often increases the teacher's involvement in the compensation process, having teachers work with administrators or mentors to identify specific goals and to assess performance against those individually determined goals. Rather than basing performance on an externally imposed standard, many such models incorporate a teacher's self-evaluation as well as evaluations from administrators and/or peers.

Despite such efforts to strengthen merit pay models through teacher involvement, the model is nevertheless hampered by its tendency to foster general competition among staff members and to be tied to measures still considered somewhat subjective. Moreover, in a distinction from the career ladder and KSBP models, the individual evaluation model often gives the impression of higher stakes and less control for teachers because it focuses less on pursuit of opportunities beyond the job responsibilities and carries the risk of demotion more openly.

A key consideration around implementing this compensation model is how much of the information on teacher performance should be confidential and how much communicated. A perception exists that if individual evaluation model results are communicated—even to celebrate the accomplishments of those teachers who receive high ratings—then those teachers who did not receive bonuses will suffer negatively, including a concern that perhaps parents will request that their children not be in those teachers' classes.

Advantages and Highlights

The advantages of the individual evaluation pay model center on its inherent growth orientation and on its capacity to recognize differences in performance and therefore reward excellent teaching. Some specific advantages distinguishing this model are addressed in Figure 4.10.

Disadvantages and Concerns

The merit pay model has been controversial over its history primarily because of the difficulty of establishing fair and measurable evaluation standards tied to compensation, as well as the cumbersome administration of the model and the requisite evaluation details. Additional areas of concern include funding difficulties, the competition often fostered by individual evaluation models, and perceptions of unfairness, often based on use of limited data sources. Some specific disadvantages of the system are outlined in Figure 4.11.

Figure 4.10   Advantages of Individual Evaluation Pay Models

- *Greater teacher control than salary schedule alone:* The individual evaluation pay model allows teachers a measure of control over their compensation in that it is based on their own performance. Provided that the evaluation system fairly assesses performance, teachers are rewarded for how well they do their jobs.

- *Emphasis on teacher accountability:* Even as the model allows greater teacher control over their compensation, it also encourages teacher accountability. An individual evaluation model requires that teachers demonstrate at least satisfactory performance in order to move up on a pay scale, not merely to put in time. Moreover, the model encourages teachers in a concrete way to strive above and beyond expected levels in their classroom practice.

- *Capacity for individualization:* The individual evaluation pay model may be structured so that teachers determine their own performance goals to focus on over a given year or evaluation period. Thus the system may be tailored toward teacher growth at an individual level and support specific teacher growth and improvement needs more directly.

- *Goal alignment:* The individual evaluation pay model may be designed so that the standards for performance for teachers are specifically aligned with other goals of the school district. This alignment provides a streamlined motivational system in which teachers are directly rewarded for striving toward goals they are expected to achieve.

- *Alignment with other models:* Technically, the key structural features of the individual evaluation pay model align directly with aspects of other models that focus on development of professional skill and knowledge. Indeed, the necessity for evaluation within the career ladder and KSBP models suggests that they also are forms of the individual evaluation pay model; however, the communication of any individual evaluation plan's intent and form to teachers must be carefully considered.

Figure 4.11   Disadvantages of Individual Evaluation Pay Models

---

- ***Fairness of evaluation:*** Fairness is the central concern and the most challenging aspect of the individual evaluation pay model. Standards for evaluation must be *clear* and *valid for the teaching assignment,* and evaluators must be trained in how to use the standards for evaluation purposes. Moreover, the standards and the evaluation methods must be fairly and consistently applied to all teachers working in the district. These issues create challenges because of the need to identify and train objective evaluators who not only apply the standards fairly but are *perceived by teachers* to be applying the standards fairly.

- ***Performance problem:*** Any evaluation system that relies upon observation of teaching practice is subject to the "performance problem." This refers to the fact that classroom observations for evaluation purposes capture only a brief snapshot of a teacher's overall practice and that the snapshot is affected by the teacher's awareness of being observed. Consequently, teachers will often demonstrate behaviors to meet expectations for the observation that they do not necessarily demonstrate regularly when not being observed. Moreover, teachers who will be evaluated based on a set of specified criteria may standardize their teaching around those criteria rather than taking a broader view of pedagogical strategies and responses to student needs.

- ***Cumbersome administration:*** Teacher evaluation is always a somewhat cumbersome process, with the need for observation and other forms of data collection, review of materials, and communication with the teacher before and after review. However, when the evaluation process is linked to compensation, it may become even more cumbersome because of the higher stakes involved.

- ***Competition:*** One of the major arguments against merit pay models in the past has been that such models foster competition and friction among teachers instead of promoting collaboration and collegiality. Competition can be an even greater problem if an individual evaluation pay model has quotas for how many teachers may be rated at a level deserving additional pay. Indeed, many existing merit pay models have ended up rewarding nearly all teachers for performance, a practice that may reduce the threatening nature of an individual evaluation model but that fails to acknowledge truly outstanding work from quality teachers.[*]

- ***Funding:*** Related to the issue of quotas and competition, many individual evaluation pay models have failed because funding has not been provided to support the additional pay for the number of teachers assessed at a level exceeding expectations.

---

* Nelson, 2001.

Examples of Individual Evaluation Pay Models

Because of the historically negative connotations of the term "merit pay" in education, many school districts establishing alternative compensation programs today avoid the term, as well as the slightly more palatable "individual evaluation pay," to structure and describe their programs. Many alternative compensation models do incorporate pay decisions based on individual classroom performance. These models, however, as previously noted, generally link compensation decisions to another model such as a career ladder and/or a knowledge- and skills-based pay model. All of the districts that award bonuses for National Board certification are essentially providing compensation based on individual evaluation, although the evaluation is occurring through an external source rather than directly from the school district. Each of the KSBP examples given previously, by including application of new knowledge and skills as a condition of compensation, also require some measure of individual evaluation.

A few additional examples will illustrate the use of individual evaluation pay further, again with linkages to other alternative compensation models. One school that has received considerable national attention for its professional development and compensation system is the Vaughn Next Century Learning Center, a charter school in Los Angeles.[34] The school has developed a set of teaching standards around specific subject areas, lesson planning, and classroom management with rubrics to describe specific levels of performance on a four-point scale. Teachers rate their own performance using these rubrics, and they are observed by peer reviewers and instructional coordinators who also rate performance, with reviews occurring three times per year. The school places a heavy emphasis on feedback, monitors progress, furnishes mentors for less experienced teachers, and provides individualized staff development based on teacher performance review.

Vaughn uses a base pay system and additional compensation for advanced degrees, but the school also offers bonuses based on the performance review.[35] The Vaughn model utilizes a bonus system instead of a contingency system around individual teaching performance, and failure to achieve the minimum bonus level works similarly to an individual evaluation pay model in which a teacher fails to earn the expected increase on the salary scale. The bonus structure gives the Vaughn model a less punitive air, and teachers who earn low scores are also provided with intervention and assistance to improve their performance. Vaughn also allows teachers to receive bonuses for achieving goals around student attendance, discipline, parental involvement, and teamwork, as well as for schoolwide student achievement and for individual extra responsibilities.

The Douglas County compensation system incorporates individual evaluation pay as a feature of the base salary scale, with options for salary increase linked to evaluation.[36] Each year, teachers are rated as *proficient* or *unsatisfactory*; proficient teachers receive an annual salary increase, while unsatisfactory teachers do not. Teachers may also apply for a higher designation through the Outstanding Teacher Program, which involves submission and review of an Outstanding Teacher Portfolio. The portfolio includes artifacts from classroom practice and the teacher's reflections on the three evaluation categories: assessment and instruction, content and pedagogy, and collaboration and partnership, as well as reflections on client surveys and philosophy of education.

The Denver Public Schools have developed a compensation model that incorporates individual evaluation pay along with other components.[37] Based on the results of a four-year pilot of a pay-for-performance system relying largely on individual goal setting by teachers and related evaluation, the district developed and proposed a more comprehensive model that provides additional compensation for teachers based on student growth, professional evaluations, developing knowledge and skills, and responding to market demands. Different elements within these four areas can provide teachers with salary increases or with one-time bonuses. In the case of professional evaluation, teachers will receive salary increases linked to satisfactory evaluation ratings. One key aspect of the Denver proposal is an emphasis on ensuring funding and avoiding quotas; as illustrated in earlier examples, lack of funding or inability to support the number of teachers who qualify for certain compensation options may cause the failure or weak implementation of many alternative compensation models.

It is important to note that in each of these examples, individual evaluation pay is not the sole incentive or source of additional compensation within the teacher salary system. Moreover, teachers are highly involved in the evaluation process in each case, with options for setting individual goals, selecting data sources to demonstrate performance, and pursuing self-selected areas for growth. This combination of involvement and use of multiple sources is critical for the acceptance of the evaluation system and its linkage to compensation.

Focus on Teacher Quality

A compensation model that directly acknowledges exceptional performance by teachers with salary increases or bonuses assumes a basic connection between quality and compensation, a fundamental assumption that pay is an incentive for quality performance. Moreover, a compensation system that *does not* allow compensation increases for teachers who do not demonstrate satisfactory performance further underscores educational goals for teacher quality and consequent student learning. However, the myriad challenges associated with creating fair and valid evaluation systems linked to compensation require that individual evaluation models be implemented carefully and with extensive teacher support and communication, and suggest that an evaluation element might best be used in combination with other compensation options.

Nevertheless, a strong linkage between evaluation and compensation highlights a school district's emphasis on quality teaching, a message that has the potential to appeal to quality teachers and to limit the district's attractiveness to teachers who are less effective. With appropriate opportunities and support for professional development linked to individual and school goals, such a compensation model also supports the goal of developing quality teachers; and continued financial and resource support for the evaluation, professional development, and compensation system promotes the retention of quality teachers.

PERFORMANCE-BASED PAY[38]

Key Features and Assumptions

All of the models previously explored focused wholly or primarily on the behaviors and activities of the teacher, grounded in an assumption that measurable quality indicators in the teacher will relate to positive outcomes for students. Another type of compensation model addresses this assumption more directly by providing compensation for teachers based on the measured outcomes of their students. Although most of the models explored in this text do link compensation to some measure of *teacher* performance, we will use the term "performance-based pay" here to refer to alternative compensation models that provide bonuses to schools and/or teachers based on *student* achievement. Such compensation models delineate specific goals for growth and achievement and then reward the teachers and/or schools achieving their goals, as measured by such tools as standardized tests, division-developed tests, school- or teacher-developed tests, and student product development.

Performance-based pay models are grounded in the notion that the mission, goals, and major emphases across school programs should be focused on improving student achievement, and that teacher compensation should likewise be linked to this effort and outcome. Traditionally, teachers have been wary of performance-based pay models because of fairness issues around comparability of student groups, reliability and validity of assessments, and the varied roles performed by different teaching professionals. Moreover, because of the accumulation of education over time and in multiple contexts, they argue, it is difficult to determine the influence of one teacher over a group of students' performances, given the potential differences in students' previous educational experiences. Nevertheless, performance-based pay models are emerging around the country within the larger context of major accountability initiatives, and states and districts are now providing financial rewards for schools demonstrating high student achievement or performance improvement.

Performance-based pay models may take several different forms, based on decisions around key variables. First, the systems may provide bonuses for goals achieved at an *individual* level, by a given teacher's students, or at a *group* level, responding to the growth shown by teams, departments, schools, or school clusters. Second, performance-based pay models may involve bonuses paid out to staff members, or they may provide the bonuses directly to schools for school improvement initiatives and purchase of resources. Many of the emerging performance-based pay models utilize a value-added approach, assessing student *gains* or *change* over a specified period rather than criterion-based performance, in order to address concerns about the influence of individual teachers as opposed to collective influence over time. Recommendations for performance-based pay models center around defining criteria and measures for desired change, using group-based pay to foster collaboration over competition among individual teachers, and providing bonuses of some form and of sufficient amount to be motivating to the teachers involved.[39]

As with most of the other models discussed, one of the key elements of a successful performance-based pay model is the use of measures of performance that teachers perceive to be fair and valid. In this case, measures are assessments of student growth and achievement, and teachers must feel that the measures are valid and that expectations for classroom practice are aligned with the expectations for student learning. Moreover, as with the individual evaluation pay options, performance-based pay models are strengthened by the use of multiple data sources and by teacher involvement in goal setting and throughout the evaluation cycle.

Performance-based pay models usually incorporate a single-salary schedule as teachers' base pay and then provide bonuses for teachers, teacher groups, or schools demonstrating certain levels of performance. Most performance-based programs utilize a format in which bonuses must be re-earned each period in the program.

Advantages and Highlights

The major advantage of a performance-based pay model is its alignment to other school goals and its consequent focus on student learning and growth as the major emphasis of teacher practice. Some specific advantages of a performance-based pay model are detailed in Figure 4.12.

Specific additional advantages may also be noted for performance-based pay models that are based on *group* performance measures or on *individual* performance measures, as detailed in Figure 4.13.

Disadvantages and Concerns

The major disadvantages of the performance-based pay model center on fairness issues related to assessment, especially if a limited number of data sources are employed. In addition, the distinctions between group-based models and individually based models raise other concerns related to fairness. Some disadvantages of performance-based pay models in general appear in Figure 4.14, with specific attention to disadvantages of group- and individually based pay provided in Figure 4.15.

Examples of Performance–Based Pay Models

Increasing accountability pressures, increasing attention to teacher qualifications, and increasing pressure on school districts to demonstrate improvements in student achievement all contribute to an intensive focus on student performance outcomes. Compensation models incorporating

Figure 4.12   Advantages of Performance-Based Pay Models

- **Focus on outcomes and accountability:** Performance-based pay models reward teachers for the demonstrated outcomes of their classroom practice in terms of student achievement. Within a social climate placing heavy emphasis on demonstrated student achievement, such a model aligns teacher compensation with the major emphasis of school programs and the demands of the public.

- **Promotes monitoring of student progress:** As teachers work to encourage students toward achievement of the performance goals, they must carefully monitor student progress, engage in ongoing assessment, and use the data they collect for instructional planning. Thus teaching practice is carefully connected to documented student need.

- **Focus on improving student achievement:** At its most basic level, the purpose of the performance-based pay model is to promote student achievement. As a result, great effort is expended toward this central goal, and students can reap benefits in their overall growth and learning.

- **Support from experts in the field of teacher compensation:** The Consortium for Policy Research in Education (CPRE), a leading organization in the study of compensation systems around the country, advocates models that provide school-based bonuses for performance as a way of promoting student achievement and collaborative efforts toward common school goals. The CPRE has laid out some specific guidelines for the development and implementation of such systems, based on expert opinion and emerging findings from case studies.*

* Odden, 2000a; see also Kelley, Heneman, & Milanowski, 2000; Kelley, Odden, Milanowski, & Heneman, 2000.

Figure 4.13   Advantages of Group-Based and Individually Based Models of Performance-Based Pay

Group-Based Model

- **Promotes collaborative effort toward goals:** If performance-based pay is structured to reward group performance, then it can promote a climate in which teachers collaborate with and encourage one another toward continuous improvement. Moreover, if the compensation structure rewards school-level performance, it allows a central vision to drive schoolwide efforts and may be used to garner funds for school-based needs as well as staff bonuses, and it also helps to direct school resources toward the needed professional development and materials to support improvement goals.

- **Recognizes the additive effect of years of education:** In many group-based models, schools are rewarded based on the performance of students only in certain grade levels and in tests of certain subject areas. Yet these models may reward the entire staff of a school, recognizing that student learning across years is actually being measured by a given test and that staff members other than one year's classroom teacher can influence the child's overall learning process. Indeed, many group-based models foster a whole-school orientation toward student learning by providing bonuses not only to teachers but also to noninstructional support staff and all other employees of the school.

Individually Based Model

- **Allows recognition of outstanding teachers:** An individually based model that examines the performance of students in specific teachers' classrooms results in data that recognize those teachers who support outstanding levels of student achievement. Such a model can acknowledge teachers as effective and high performing based on outcome measures for the primary client of their practice, thereby providing direct acknowledgment of quality teaching and its main intended effect.

Figure 4.14   Disadvantages of the Performance-Based Pay Model

---

- ***Determining fair assessments:*** Fair and valid assessments are critical components of account-ability systems, all the more so when decisions about compensation are to be linked to the assessments. The specific measures to be used to assess student achievement must be valid and reliable, must be believed to be valid and reliable by teachers, and must be directly linked to standards of learning. Assessments that do not reflect these characteristics contribute to stress and frustration and will likely limit the motivational effect of a performance-based bonus model. The use of multiple sources of data is also critical to establishing fairness in a performance-based pay model.

- ***Test stress:*** The combination of the publicity of a performance-based pay model and the finan-cial incentive attached may influence high incidence of "teaching to the test" and teaching students more about test taking than about content. This may also contribute to high levels of stress for both students and teachers around test performance and greater emphasis on testing than on learning.

- ***Linking teacher effort to student performance:*** Although intuitively the idea that teaching influences student achievement makes sense, and although research is *beginning* to demon-strate strong linkages between teaching practice and student achievement,[*] still the specific con-nections are difficult to quantify and to link to compensation. One reason for this is the diversity in student populations and another is the additive effect of multiple years of schooling. Thus link-ing student achievement to the effects of one teacher for compensation purposes may not be valid or fair.

- ***"Haves" and "Have-nots":*** One of the concerns about performance-based pay models linked to the diversity in student populations is that individual classes, groups of classes, or schools may not have equitable opportunities to achieve performance standards because of the differ-ences in their student populations. This problem may be exacerbated if funding earmarked for performance awards continually goes to high-achieving schools, especially if there are significant differences in student populations in different schools within a district; such a situation would seem to reflect the adage that "the rich get richer, the poor get poorer." For this reason, school-based *improvement* goals are often used in performance-based pay models, rather than dis-trictwide performance standards.

- ***Quotas:*** Often, funding limits the amount of bonus money available and may, as a consequence, limit the number of schools or teachers who can receive recognition for achievement. This may have the result of increasing competition and resentment within and across schools based on the need to fight for scarce resources and recognition. Avoidance of quotas, to whatever degree pos-sible, is a critical consideration in establishing a performance-based pay model that encourages quality teaching for all.

- ***Cumbersome assessment system:*** Performance-based pay models presume the collection of extensive student performance data to be related to teacher quality and, therefore, linked to com-pensation. The implication of this is extensive assessment of students and follow-up grading and linkage to individuals or groups of teachers. To ensure consistency, these assessments are more likely to be districtwide or standardized assessments, which are more cumbersome and involve higher stakes than classroom assessment.

---

* Sanders & Horn, 1998.

performance-based pay have grown along with this public attention and pressure, as a means of promoting a positive perspective on accountability measures and supporting teachers who may feel as though they are working

Figure 4.15 Disadvantages Specific to Group-Based and Individually Based Models

---

Group-Based Systems

- **"Free rider" problem:** Group-based performance pay models are intended to diminish the influence of differences among student populations and to acknowledge the collective efforts of multiple professionals in supporting student learning. However, one potential problem with group-based models is the issue of the "free rider," a teacher or teachers who put in less effort than their colleagues but are rewarded because of the effect of all scores being combined toward group goals.

- **Fair distribution of bonus funds:** Group-based pay models can be designed to provide bonuses for grade level or departmental teams, for whole schools, for clusters of schools, or for other defined groups. One of the challenges of such a model, however, is determining if the bonus will be distributed equally or otherwise—to decide the size of the bonus to be received by different individuals within the group. Thus the model must determine ways for fair acknowledgment of teachers in nontested grades and subjects as well as classified and support personnel.

Individually Based Systems

- **Eligibility to participate:** Although the NCLB legislation has increased attention to accountability across grades and subjects, still not all teachers have responsibilities for subjects tested in high-stakes assessment systems, nor are students necessarily tested in all subjects at all grade levels. Consequently an issue emerges for performance-based pay models in terms of determining whether all teachers can be eligible for performance-based pay and, if so, how students in the nontested grades and classes are to be fairly assessed.

- **Publicity of results:** One of the major concerns about individual performance-based pay models is not focused on the compensation specifically, but rather on the publicity of the results. Similar to a concern noted in the individual evaluation pay section, if classroom-level results are used to determine bonuses, and if that information is made public, there is a concern about parental response and whether parents will attempt to avoid having their children placed in specific classes because of a given year's performance by specific teachers. Individually based performance pay models place a burden on individual teachers to perform that may be more stressful and detrimental than motivating, given the unique context of school settings.

---

under a microscope. Among some prominent school districts that have implemented bonuses to school staff for student achievement are Cincinnati, Columbus, Denver, Memphis, Miami-Dade, and New York City; among the districts that have paid out bonus funds to support school improvement needs are Boston, Minneapolis, Montgomery County, and Rochester.[40] Moreover, some states are making bonus funds available to school districts who achieve yearly performance expectations, with various guidelines for distribution of funds to individual schools and personnel. Many of the examples of compensation models discussed in previous sections also incorporate performance-based pay elements within their structures; several are described in the following paragraphs.

The Denver Public Schools piloted an individually based model for performance-based pay from 1999–2003 and incorporated successful aspects of it into the proposed comprehensive model noted in the previous section.[41] The Denver pay-for-performance model is somewhat unusual in that it rewards teachers on an individual basis for student achievement. Teachers are asked annually to work with their administrators to identify two student growth objectives that are linked to baseline data and not related to state assessment system results. The pilot program provided bonuses for teachers who met one or both objectives; the newly proposed system, on the other hand, allocates bonuses for teachers who meet one objective and a salary increase for any teacher who meets both.

The Douglas County Public Schools incorporate performance-based pay into their comprehensive compensation model as well. In Douglas County, as in Denver, performance-based bonuses are available based upon achievement of specified goals for student performance; however, in the case of Douglas County, these bonuses are available to groups rather than individual teachers. Another difference is that the Douglas County program is voluntary; each school may only submit one Group Incentive Plan per year for review and oversight from the Group Incentive Board, and that plan may include teachers, either schoolwide or a smaller group of teachers within the school. Evaluation occurs through a report developed by the group at the end of the year, reviewed by the Group Incentive Board for evidence that the goals were attained and that bonuses should be rewarded.[42] Similarly, the Vaughn Next Century Learning Center provides bonuses to all teachers and administrators when students meet the expectations of the state accountability system.[43]

In the Milken TAP schools, performance bonuses are carefully divided across a range of measures. As noted in the previous section, 50 percent of the bonus is tied to teacher knowledge and skills and 50 percent to student performance. However, within the latter a further designation is made: 30 percent (of the overall total) is group-based, tied to schoolwide student achievement, and the remaining 20 percent is available to reward individual teachers for the achievement of their students.[44]

The state of Florida serves as an example of performance-based pay bonuses provided from the state level with flexibility of implementation at the local level. Florida has authorized a "School Recognition Program," through which schools may receive bonuses based on achievement of the state-determined "A" level of performance or through improvement of at least one performance grade. Bonuses are allocated to schools based on student enrollment. Then, decisions are made by staff and the school advisory council at the school level for how to allocate these total funds, with options to use them for faculty and staff bonuses, educational materials, and/or hiring of temporary personnel to support ongoing student achievement.[45]

Focus on Teacher Quality

Performance-based pay models send a clear message that teacher quality is primarily demonstrated in student achievement. These models link compensation elements directly to central goals of the school district and to the demands of the public, the government, and the educational system at large. In these ways, performance-based pay models should be attractive to quality teachers and should have the effect of retaining quality teachers in a school district over time. At the same time, though, the complexity of the teaching process and the variability that students bring to their classrooms suggest the need to allow performance-based pay models to reward student growth not solely linked to state accountability systems. Current legislation already requires schools to demonstrate student performance at requisite levels, so bonuses related to the state accountability systems are limited in their strength as added incentive for quality teachers. On the other hand, as described in several of the examples noted, performance-based pay models can alternatively provide the possibility for teachers to set student growth goals enhancing and broadening what the state requires, and to work in collaboration with other teachers to achieve those goals. Linked with other options for professional development and growth, this model provides effective support and recognition of quality teaching.

CREATIVE COMPENSATION: OTHER WAYS OF RECOGNIZING TEACHER QUALITY[46]

A total compensation package encompasses more than just salary; teachers may receive additional benefits such as insurance, paid leave, retirement contributions, and job enhancement options as a part of their compensation from their school district. Some of these benefits were discussed in Chapter 3, with emphasis on how a benefits package influences the competitiveness of a school district's compensation model. In reflecting upon the various compensation models explored in this chapter, school districts must carefully consider not only how to structure the benefits system relative to a salary schedule but how the different alternative compensation models may influence that benefits system as well.

For example, one key decision point around each alternative model is whether additional compensation goes to teachers in the form of a *bonus* or a *salary increase*; generally, a salary increase has implications for increasing benefits that a bonus may not. Moreover, the rate at which salary increases occur has an influence on benefits planning, especially when considering methods for retaining teachers with a lot of experience: Retirement payouts are often linked to salaries earned in the last few years of teaching, so large increases and bonuses for teachers nearing retirement must also account for retirement implications over a longer period. Nevertheless, such late-career increases have the potential to be influential in recruiting and retaining more experienced teachers; teacher unions argue that a steeper salary curve late in the career represents "deferred compensation" for teachers' earlier low salaries. Current economic conditions and budget shortfalls are prompting many states to debate the structures of their retirement systems for public employees, including consideration of more individual flexibility in retirement options. Any revisions to an existing compensation system must reflect attention to retirement contributions from employer and employee, as well as the eventual budget implications for payouts to the retiring teaching force.[47]

At the same time, although districts must carefully weigh the retirement implications of large salary increases for teachers with extensive experience, they must also consider the potential of an attractive retirement package for recruiting and retaining experienced teachers. Retirement system formats for public employees are currently under debate in many states, with options for greater flexibility being weighed against budget shortfalls and overall economic conditions.

Market-Based Compensation

School districts may also incorporate other types of bonus and benefit options into compensation models to attract, develop, and retain quality teachers. Signing bonuses, which represent incentives for teachers to take positions with a school district, have been a popular compensation option among school districts and states facing teacher shortage issues.[48] One major consideration that has not been specifically addressed in the previous models is the concept of *market-based compensation*, or providing more attractive compensation options for teachers who can fill positions in critical shortage areas.[49] High-poverty and urban schools throughout the country often include on their faculties greater numbers of uncertified and out-of-field teachers than schools in areas of higher socioeconomic status (SES), and these schools often present working conditions that may make them less attractive to quality teachers. As discussed in Chapter 1, evidence suggests that individual teachers are more influential in student performance than most other factors of the school context.[50] Certain subject and specialty areas also suffer from critical shortages of teachers; mathematics, science, and special education are among the areas often cited as needing more teachers.[51] Consequently, providing a bonus to teachers who are qualified to fulfill teaching roles in schools and subject areas with critical shortages may be a way of attracting quality teachers to such schools and thus positively influencing student performance.[52] Examples of market-based compensation at work include the following:

- The Milken TAP model, described in several examples elsewhere in this chapter, includes market considerations as one key principle, providing opportunities for teachers who take on positions in critical shortage areas to receive additional compensation. Early results related to the program have found evidence of some quality teachers moving from higher SES to lower SES schools in order to participate in TAP.[53] Such movement may be related to other aspects of the TAP model, not merely the market-based compensation model, but results are positive regardless.

- The proposed comprehensive compensation model in the Denver Public Schools also incorporates incentives for teachers to work in "hard-to-staff assignments" and "hard-to-staff schools." These incentives are given in the form of bonuses distributed across the year in which a teacher works in one of these contexts.[54]

Working Conditions and Support Structures for Growth

Chapter 3 detailed aspects of working conditions that might influence competitiveness and thus the decisions of quality teachers to seek and maintain employment with a given school district. These elements are critical to consider in developing a comprehensive compensation model because they may be decision-making points for quality teachers in choosing among school districts with similar base salaries. Moreover, working conditions are clearly important to consider in pursuing the goals of developing and retaining quality teachers. The models discussed in this chapter have primarily focused on bonuses or salary increases provided to teachers *after* their achievement of given criteria; however, another form of compensation that also may enhance working conditions is the provision of funds for capacity building, or financial support for ongoing professional development.

Attention to the support structure provided for developing quality teachers is also important in restructuring compensation systems, both for the goal of developing and the goal of attracting quality teachers. A recent study of the signing bonus program established in Massachusetts in the late 1990s found that teachers were more attracted to the program for its accelerated alternative certification route than by the signing bonus itself, and that despite the bonus, teachers in the program were frustrated by limited opportunities for capacity building once in schools. Indeed, working conditions and new teachers' abilities to achieve the intrinsic rewards they expected from teaching influenced retention of these teachers far beyond the bonus they received.[55]

SUMMARY

This chapter has explored an array of options for teacher compensation, ranging from the traditional single-salary schedule to various models that acknowledge specific elements of teacher and student performance. Each model bears advantages and disadvantages that must be carefully weighed in considering elements to build into a comprehensive compensation model, and the examples provided have illustrated both the potential and the pitfalls of some of the options. In developing a compensation model that will link effectively to teacher quality, school districts should consider the various options addressed here and question what will be most feasible within their own context, and how to avoid common pitfalls, such as insufficient funding, unhealthy competition, and perceptions of compensation models as punitive rather than supportive. Moreover, school districts must continue to reflect upon compensation as one piece within their larger culture and to keep in mind that teachers seek not only financial rewards but also less tangible rewards, such as growth for themselves and their students. The next chapter will revisit key assumptions and principles in designing a compensation model and will then draw upon the models given here to suggest an optimal structure.

Building a Model Teacher Compensation System

What Will Work Best for Us?

he basic premise of *Teacher Pay and Teacher Quality* is that how a school district compensates its teachers is both a reflection of the value that the district places on teachers' work and an investment in the quality of the outcomes of teachers' efforts. In a simple *inputs-processes-products* model, quality teachers lead to quality teaching, which, in turn, leads to quality student learning. This central premise highlights three foundational assumptions upon which a model for teacher compensation can be built. Chapter 4 provided background information, analysis, and examples of the major current models of teacher compensation. The purpose of this chapter is to continue the discussion of compensation options by examining various teacher compensation models.

ASSUMPTIONS ABOUT COMPENSATION SYSTEMS

The important work of designing a comprehensive approach to paying teachers and promoting quality must begin with examining the basic assumptions about the purpose and the inherent nature of compensation in an educational organization. In other words, the professional and lay leaders of a school district must ask themselves:

- What do we aim to accomplish through our compensation system?
- Relatedly, what do we believe must be the basic characteristics of a compensation system that will accomplish this aim?

We offer three assumptions that answer these questions.

Assumption #1: Teacher quality leads to student learning, and student learning is our business.

The purpose of schools, broadly speaking, is to promote student learning and achievement. As we shared in Chapter 1, and as a growing body of evidence indicates, the quality of teachers is the single-most significant variable within the control of school districts that can influence student achievement.[1] The reasoning, then, becomes quite simple: A school district must invest in the quality of its teachers in order to improve the quality of student outcomes. The aim of teacher compensation in the eyes of the school district, therefore, is to improve student learning *by ensuring the quality of the students' teachers*. In this regard, teacher compensation is, quite simply, utilitarian in its purpose.

Assumption #2: Money matters.

We cannot rely on teachers' sense of altruism anymore as the predominant motivation that attracts and retains teachers in the profession. The classic argument that teachers are willing to be paid less than other professionals because of their personal sense of calling and the intrinsic rewards of helping other people cannot be relied upon. Indeed, if we applied this same, outdated rationale to other professions, couldn't we argue that doctors should be paid far less, given the extraordinarily powerful motivation of saving lives? Couldn't we argue that lawyers should be paid less because they enjoy the emotional satisfaction of protecting the rights of innocent people?

Susan Moore Johnson and the Project on the New Generation of Teachers (2004) investigated the changing nature of the teacher workforce in the United States, attempting to identify the motivators for those who choose to enter the profession, those who remain in the profession, and those who leave the profession.[2] Moore Johnson and her colleagues concluded that the new generation of teachers, although motivated at their core by a desire to make a difference in students' lives, also brings new expectations about how they will be compensated, rewarded, and supported in their chosen profession:

> They expect to be paid well . . . for the important work that they do. They expect variety in what they do with differentiated roles and opportunities to advance in the profession. They want the

chance to collaborate with colleagues and to work in organizations that support them.[3]

Assumption #3: Compensation is not an endgame; rather, it is integral to attracting, developing, and retaining effective teachers.

The traditional impression of compensation is that it is something that comes at the end of a process as a means of reward for activity and/or outputs. Although compensation does play this role, a systems approach to compensation suggests myriad roles that begin as early as an individual deciding to become a teacher and progressing through her preservice preparation, induction, service, and development in the profession. Compensation is not simply a rewards system; rather, it is an integral element of a system intentionally designed to attract, develop, and retain effective teachers.

Relatedly, the imperative for *effective* teachers is also an element of a systemic view of compensation. The main intended aim of education is student learning; therefore, all elements of the educational system at large should be related—whether proximally or distally—to this intended aim. Thus the compensation system should be related to and supportive of the aim of student learning. Every component of the compensation system should promote the connection between effective teaching and student learning. Simply put, the focus must be on the *quality* of the teachers.

DESIGN PRINCIPLES: CONSIDERATIONS IN TEACHER COMPENSATION

Given these three assumptions, what should a compensation system look like? There is no one best answer. We do not promote a one-size-fits-all approach to designing teacher compensation systems. Too many variables can affect the needs, opportunities, and limitations with which a school district is working. An urban district may be wrestling with a specific need to attract new teachers in critical shortage areas such as math, science, and foreign language. A rural district may be grappling with an aging teacher population and the prospect of mass retirements. A suburban district may have a curse of riches, whereby several local universities offer graduate coursework, but teachers are taking and completing classes indiscriminately and without regard to aligning their ongoing professional development with the strategic aims of the district. One district may be in a state that provides a stipend to teachers who earn National Board certification, while another district is in a state that does not.

There are nearly 15,000 school districts in the United States, each with extensive authority to devise its own compensation system. Each district, then, must exercise considerable judgment to meet local needs and to respond to local opportunities in designing its teacher compensation system. Nevertheless, in designing a teacher compensation system that intentionally aims to link teacher pay with teacher quality, there *are* certain design principles that should be considered.

Competitiveness

A teacher compensation system must be competitive, primarily with other school districts but also with other careers. However, a restructured teacher compensation system should not simply cost more. While increasing teacher pay would undoubtedly be welcomed, it would represent a growth in the current system, but not a fundamental change. The design of the compensation system should be aimed at creating a competitive compensation package, which means a compensation package that meets the needs and the reasonable wants of the targeted individuals that the system is designed to attract, support, and retain. In the case of schools, the target individuals are high-quality teachers.

Strategic Flexibility

A teacher compensation system should provide flexibility to the organization so the organization can strategically respond to changing needs and opportunities. Depending upon its particular challenges and strengths, a school district should question whether its compensation system readily allows district leadership to focus priorities on attracting teachers to critical shortage areas, or meet the need of imminent retirements, or align professional development with organizational goals. The traditional salary schedule, based on years of service and professional coursework alone, is extraordinarily limited in this sense.

Comprehensiveness

A teacher compensation system must incorporate all components of compensation that comprise the means of "paying" teachers for their work. In Chapter 3, elements of compensation such as noncash benefits, working conditions, and contract days were discussed to illustrate the principle of comprehensiveness. In addition, a compensation system must address other elements that are more directly related to the development of quality teachers, that is, to their contributions to and effects upon student learning.

Clarity

As noted at the opening of this chapter, a compensation system reflects the values and investments of the school district. In this sense, a compensation system communicates that which is important to the school district in pursuing its mission. What's more, this communication speaks directly to teachers but also to the public and the lay school board that support and set direction for the school district, respectively. If the compensation system is complex and unwieldy, an opportunity to communicate and pursue organizational goals may be confused or lost. Distrust may even result, as complex systems are sometimes construed as being shell games. Thus a compensation system should have a certain transparency and simplicity of design that can readily be communicated and understood.

Appropriateness

Although simplicity and communicativeness of design are desirable, the appropriateness of a compensation system cannot be sacrificed. Compensation systems *are* complex. One of the attractions of the traditional salary schedule is that it is relatively simple in design and easy to understand. However, as discussed in previous chapters, the simple design of the salary schedule does not make an appropriate compensation system. A compensation system must be appropriate in two fundamental ways:

- A compensation system must serve the purpose of attracting, developing, and retaining quality teachers. This design principle is compromised, if not violated, if the compensation system perpetuates, for example, the retention of *ineffective* teachers who do not positively contribute to student learning.
- A compensation system must be reliable in its implementation. In other words, the compensation system must be as fair and objective as possible so that quality indicators are the standard by which decisions about compensation are made, and not by chance, guess work, dishonest opinion, or erroneous factors.

These five design principles should guide the work of a school district developing a comprehensive teacher compensation system aimed at attracting, developing, and retaining quality teachers.

DESIGNING A COMPENSATION SYSTEM AIMED AT QUALITY

It would be misleading to say that the education profession's broad reliance on the uniform salary schedule has been solely to blame for dissatisfaction with teacher compensation in general or the current trends in teacher attrition, but it is clear that the monolithic salary schedule has not helped to combat these problems. Over time, this realization has led to other questions—practical and philosophical questions that any school district using a salary schedule could ask:

- How do we reward the early career teacher who outperforms most veterans?
- Should the teacher evaluated as "unsatisfactory" in an annual performance review still receive an annual step increase on the salary schedule?

- Should we invest additional resources in the competent teacher who pursues meaningful professional development and improves to a level of performance above the school district's expectations?
- Should we differentially compensate the teacher leader who contributes to the school beyond her own classroom, thereby positively influencing the performance of other teachers and indirectly contributing to the academic achievement of students not in her own classroom?
- Should we differentially compensate the teacher who sets specific, measurable, and meaningful goals of academic progress for her students; designs and implements strategies to achieve those goals; and then provides evidence of their achievement?
- How should the school district recognize and promote the teacher who achieves the highest professional standard of national certification?
- How do we account for the phenomenon that academic growth in a student is a collective enterprise, built upon the contributions of multiple teachers over successive years and, therefore, dependent upon collaboration?

In designing a comprehensive teacher compensation system, such questions become indicators of quality, for each is couched in terms that are directly related to student learning and achievement.

A COMPONENT-PARTS APPROACH TO TEACHER COMPENSATION

The premise of a "components-part" approach to designing a teacher compensation system is to provide competitiveness, strategic flexibility, comprehensiveness, clarity, and appropriateness of teacher pay in order to attract, develop, and retain quality teachers in support of the educational mission. There are at least five broad, salary-related components that, coupled with a nonsalary benefits package, can effectively create a *system* of compensation—a system that, upon even cursory review, is clearly intended to affect the quality of teaching and learning in schools. These five, broad types of compensation components include the following:

- Pay based on individual performance evaluation
- Pay based on targeted professional development
- Pay based on performing additional professional responsibilities
- Pay based on accomplishing recognition of professional excellence
- Pay based on group-attained impacts on student achievement

At the foundation of these compensation components is the presence of a competitive, stable base salary structure. The base salary component may be in the form of a traditional multilane salary schedule, a single-lane salary schedule, or a career ladder model with salary ranges embedded within the career levels. These variations on the salary schedule are considered in greater detail in the final section of this chapter. The point here is that the five broad categories of compensation components listed above provide multiple avenues for teachers to earn pay beyond a base salary for their job performance and, concomitantly, for a school district to promote and reward quality performance.

In introducing the concept of a component approach to designing a teacher compensation model, it warrants mentioning early in the discussion that components are intended to work in conjunction as a *comprehensive* approach to meeting a school district's goals of attracting, developing, and retaining quality teachers. Thus the intention is for *all* of the component categories to be adopted and, in time, to be implemented as part of a comprehensively restructured teacher compensation system.

By the same token, however, the component parts that comprise the recommended compensation model are, in fact, *stand-alone components* in their individual designs. Therefore, given conditions or circumstances within a school district, the School Board, administration, or designated advisory committees could decide against implementing one or more of the components, yet still have a compensation system substantially different from and improved upon a conventional single-salary schedule.

A MODEL FOR TEACHER COMPENSATION

What would a comprehensive compensation system built upon a competitive base salary schedule and complemented by the five compensation categories look like? In the following pages, we propose a model for teacher compensation that identifies specific components:

- Performance Evaluation
- Professional Development: Knowledge and Skills Acquisition
- Additional Responsibility Pay
- Extraordinary Performance
- Group-Based Pay

The interplay of these five components of a comprehensive compensation system is depicted in the conceptual model presented as Figure 5.1. The model assumes, first and foremost, a competitive base salary schedule. Then, there are several compensation options, incentives, and rewards available to teachers to promote and recognize performance. All teachers, for instance, may participate in *Knowledge Acquisition* (i.e., the completion of advanced coursework or degrees); *Skills Block Acquisition* (i.e., the completion and demonstrated acquisition of new professional

Figure 5.1   A Model for Teacher Compensation

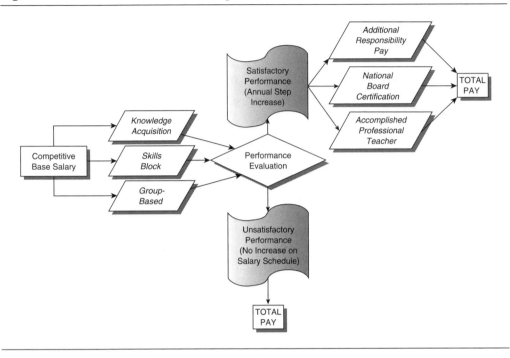

skills); or *Group-Based Pay* (i.e., projects demonstrating value-added student achievement).

A second series of compensation options are also available to teachers, but the availability of these is dictated by outcomes on the school district's *Performance Evaluation* system. Specifically, if a teacher receives a *satisfactory* evaluation, then he or she is eligible to receive an *Annual Step Increase*; pursue distinction as an *Accomplished Professional Teacher* through individual goal setting and documented student achievement; receive additional pay if certified by the *National Board for Professional Teaching Standards*; and participate in all options under *Additional Responsibility Pay*.

The elements of the compensation model are presented in another form in Figure 5.2. Less conceptual in its representation of the components of a comprehensive compensation system, Figure 5.2 depicts the relationship between a multilane salary schedule and the additional, quality-based components of the plan. In this model, the salary steps remain a foundational component. Knowledge acquisition components are represented in the conventional designation of salary lanes, typically defined by advanced coursework. (For purposes of this illustration, four lanes are shown, although some districts have more salary lanes, and some have fewer.) Performance Evaluation serves as the determinant of all other compensation options for teachers—those components available to all teachers and those available only to "satisfactory" teachers.

Figure 5.2   Multilane Salary Schedule With Bonus Components

Salary Steps	Possible Salary Lanes				Determines "Satisfactory" or "Unsatisfactory" Performance	Components Available to All Teachers			
1 2 3 4 5 . . .	Bachelor's	Bachelor's + 15	Master's	Master's Plus	Performance Evaluation	Skills Blocks	Additional Responsibility*	Group-Based Pay

Components Available Only to "Satisfactory" Teachers

Additional Responsibility*
Accomplished Professional Teacher
National Board Certification

* Some elements of Additional Responsibility Pay (e.g., activity sponsor stipend) may be available to all teachers. Other elements of Additional Responsibility Pay (e.g., service on designated division-wide committees) may be available only to "Satisfactory" teachers.

A CLOSER LOOK AT THE COMPONENTS OF COMPENSATION

The Role of Performance Evaluation

An essential feature of the compensation model is that the annual step increase in salary associated with many salary schedules and represented in Figures 5.1 and 5.2 is replaced by a reliance on an *annual performance review* to determine eligibility for the annual step increase. The fundamental purpose of a district's performance evaluation system is to determine whether a teacher's job performance is, broadly speaking, satisfactory or unsatisfactory. A teacher whose performance is satisfactory receives an annual step increase, and the other six compensation components are available to him or her to pursue. A teacher whose performance is evaluated as unsatisfactory receives no annual step increase to his or her base salary. This teacher is frozen on the salary schedule until he or she fulfills the goals of an improvement assistance plan. Furthermore, the compensation components of Accomplished Professional Teacher, NBPTS Certification, and certain options under Additional Responsibility Pay are not available to this teacher.

The effective use of performance evaluation in teacher compensation is based on two assumptions. First, a school district must design and institutionalize a valid and reliable performance evaluation review. Several models are available, and we strongly recommend evaluation systems that move beyond a classic observation-only approach to systems that are designed upon professional roles and responsibilities, academic goal setting, and multiple evaluation sources, including both observation and portfolio development.[4]

The second assumption in place when using performance evaluation as a compensation component is that longevity matters. While research is mixed (as noted in Chapter 4) on whether veteran teachers have a greater effect on student learning than novice teachers, there are other factors beyond the lack of empirical evidence about student achievement that should be valued. The longevity of teachers matters in terms of feelings of loyalty to a school district and also in savings in the costs of recruitment, hiring, induction, and professional development. Of course, these advantages are gained at the risk that compensating for years of experience can unintentionally promote professional complacency and the "dead wood" phenomenon of not being able to hire new teachers because some ineffective veterans won't move on. These are fair concerns about the role of longevity in compensation, but they are mostly exaggerated when longevity is the main factor upon which a compensation system is built, as with the traditional salary schedule used by most school districts. These potentially negative effects are greatly mitigated when (1) performance evaluation is used as the gateway to annual salary increases and (2) years of service are complemented by compensation components that focus on quality and achievement, such as knowledge and skills acquisition, additional performance pay, group-based performance incentives, and others.

The Role of Professional Development: Knowledge and Skills Acquisition

A second set of compensation components consists of knowledge acquisition and skills blocks completion, each operationalized as a distinctive element of professional development.

An essential feature of the model is the redefinition of the lanes in a conventional salary schedule with the designation of knowledge acquisition components.[5] Knowledge acquisition is the completion of advanced coursework and/or advanced degrees, typically the operational definition of lanes on conventional salary schedules. The multilane salary schedule model is characteristic of most school districts in the United States and in other industrialized nations. The proposed compensation model recommends that school districts retain a multilane salary schedule in part because of the prevalence and long history of this salary structure. Furthermore, there is research that suggests teachers with master's degrees tend to be more effective than those without master's degrees, but there is no clear indication in educational research regarding the value of advanced coursework beyond the master's level. However, there are also recommended amendments to how the knowledge acquisition component is implemented in order to relate compensation to quality teaching.

In the context of an integrated evaluation and compensation system, the knowledge acquisition component can serve as a means for a district to identify specific content and endorsement areas that qualify for additional pay, rather than the more common practice of simply encouraging teachers to complete graduate work of their choosing. For instance, a school district responding to a mandate to ensure that teachers are highly qualified to teach in certain content areas may elect to reward teachers who complete additional preparation or advanced degrees in those subjects. Another school district may target the need to develop teacher leaders in schools with the goal that they might contribute more effectively to shared decision making in a distributed leadership model of school administration; thus the district might pay teachers for earning endorsements or degrees in educational leadership.

Skills block is similar to the knowledge acquisition component in that it offers additional pay for completion of a designated training program and the subsequent demonstration of mastery and application of the targeted skill.[6] Unlike knowledge acquisition, however, skills blocks do not equate to graduate credit hours or advanced degrees. Nor do skills blocks require separate lanes on the salary schedule. Instead, they are intended to serve as a bonus compensation component available to all teachers on an annual basis. Skills blocks are intended to complement the professional development opportunities traditionally provided through advanced coursework. Skills blocks are identified and provided by the school district and closely linked to a school's or the division's goals. Therefore a teacher may be pursuing an advanced degree with a university while also completing skills block sessions with the school district. Indeed, teachers could participate in as many skills block training programs as appropriate and available.

In a study regarding the impact of induction on the retention and attrition rates of first-year teachers, researchers found that novice teachers who experienced little or no formal induction activities were twice as likely to leave the profession or transfer from their school or school district than novice teachers who had experienced formal induction activities, including collaboration and networking with other teachers and the provision of extra resources.[7] This finding highlights the role that professional development—seen here in the guise of growing into the professional roles and responsibilities of teaching with the formal support of the school and school district—plays in the retention of novice teachers. Presumably, these novice teachers have already required the investment of time, materials, and other resources in their recruitment, application, interviewing, selection, and hiring processes. Presumably, these teachers, in their selection and hiring, have met the district's criteria of quality and preparedness in order to be hired. The additional investment in these teachers of formal induction experiences can assist the novices in developing the essential skills necessary to make the transition from preservice to inservice teacher.

To implement the skills block component, a school district must consider several issues. First, a district must create the infrastructure to identify and offer skills blocks to teachers. A sufficient number of skills blocks should be offered annually to provide ample opportunity for teacher participation. But, as suggested previously, skills block offerings should be targeted to specific school or district goals, not simply offered for the sake of offering a training program. Second, demonstration of mastery and application of new skills should be the standard for "completion" of a skills block. This changes the nature of professional development from one of delivery and "seat time" to one of assimilation and application. It also requires more time and expertise to evaluate a teacher's mastery of the given skills. Third, the school district will need to devise a method for tracking skills block completion. College transcripts are a convenient means of tracking the knowledge acquisition component, but there is no universal transcript system for skills block acquisition. An internal tracking system would need to be developed.

The Role of the Additional Responsibilities

Additional Responsibility Pay entails compensating teachers for performing designated extra duties. While this concept is not new to education—coaches and activity sponsors, for example, have traditionally received stipends—it is a distinct compensation component in the context of the proposed model. The model reflects a more expanded definition of additional responsibility pay, comprised of three main categories that represent different roles or responsibilities beyond those expected of the typical classroom teacher:

- *Additional duty pay,* such as coaching and club sponsorship
- *School-based responsibility pay,* which is a sum available to each school to pay individual teachers for additional responsibilities deemed vital at a given school, such as after-school tutoring, school leadership team work, or providing professional development within the school
- *Districtwide responsibility pay,* which is a sum available at the division level to pay individual teachers for additional responsibilities deemed vital to the school district, such as membership on certain committees or task forces

A compensation system should recognize and value the contributions that some teachers make to schools and school districts beyond their expected duties. Stipends alone are not enough; they are typically fixed and often disproportionate to the expertise and time required to accomplish them and can even interfere with the centrality of the mission. Stipends are important but must be complemented with other components to meet district priorities and ensure quality in the meeting of additional responsibilities.

The Role of Extraordinary Performance

A teacher compensation system should differentiate among performers and should reward excellence. The advent of the National Board for Professional Teaching Standards (NBPTS) marked a broadly accepted means of recognizing excellence in teaching. In recent years, the practice of rewarding teachers for earning certification from the National Board for Professional Teaching Standards has become increasingly common among school districts and states. Such rewards are typically in the form of up-front monetary assistance to support a teacher's effort to earn NBPTS certification or a bonus paid to a teacher over the duration of the certificate (10 years). In many instances, both the professional development support money and the bonus stipend are available to teachers who seek and earn National Board certification. The proposed model for restructuring teacher compensation retains this component, recognizing the broad support in the field and among the public and acknowledging the growing trend toward institutionalizing the NBPTS process. Nonetheless, prior to implementing this step—or periodically after doing so—educational decision makers should carefully consider the efficacy of extra pay for National Board certification, or any other recognition type of pay for that matter. As of March 2005, more than 40,200 teachers had received their National Board certification,[8] and the numbers are likely to continue to increase. Yet, the value-added effects of National Board certification have come under increased scrutiny in recent years, with some researchers finding favorable results[9] and others suggesting less favorable results.[10]

Whereas NBPTS represents a national standard and process of certifying excellence in teaching, a potentially important complement to this component is a *local* or *district-based* process for promoting, recognizing, and rewarding excellence. A comprehensive compensation system is further strengthened by the development of an *Accomplished Professional Teacher (APT)* program.

A program targeting accomplished professional teachers reflects the fact that many districts are developing localized programs for recognizing and rewarding effective teachers, similar in concept to NBPTS certification. However, there are distinguishing differences. First, because it is a locally developed program unique to a given school district, the school district has the latitude to adjust the requirements and goals of the program to align with its strategic goals. A second distinguishing difference between a localized program and NBPTS certification is an emphasis on student achievement. While highly touted and broadly respected for its rigor, NBPTS certification is focused primarily on *process variables* of teaching—that is, how the teacher teaches. A localized program recognizing accomplished professional teachers could be focused more on *output variables*—that is, the results of a teacher's work as demonstrated by student achievement. This compensation component is a means of paying for performance.

Processes and guidelines need to be established in order to implement a program to reward accomplished professional teachers. These criteria may minimally include the following:

- No "needs improvement" or "unacceptable" ratings on most recent performance evaluation
- A defined number of "exceeds expectations" or "superior performance" ratings on the most recent performance evaluation
- Demonstration of sustained academic growth through documented academic goal setting and student achievement
- Documentation of meeting certain responsibilities specified by the district and linked to strategic goals (e.g., demonstration of specified skills blocks)

Specifically defining the criteria for the accomplished professional teacher program would be a key implementation step for a school district in adopting this compensation component as part of the restructured compensation system. An accomplished professional teacher program would also require new elements of administrative oversight, not only for setting guidelines for the program but also for approving applications for APT designation and responding to possible appeals from teachers who may not qualify.

The aim of recognizing accomplished professional teachers at the local level is twofold. First, a district can structure the focus and guidelines of the recognition and reward program in order to strategically align with and support the achievement of its organizational goals. Second, an APT program provides a school district with a *value-added* measure of teacher quality. At the core of recognizing accomplished teachers is the criterion of documented student achievement. Given that this compensation component is elective, the insidious and competitive effects of merit pay plans are minimized. Teachers elect to participate, identify learning goals aligned with the district's priorities, and set about achieving those goals. With documented success, students gain academically, the district gains academically, and teachers gain both professionally and monetarily.

The Role of Group-Based Performance Pay

Group-Based Pay is additional compensation paid as an annual bonus to a defined group of teachers who specify an academic achievement goal for an identified target group of students, develop and implement strategies to achieve the goal, and demonstrate the attainment of the goal by the students. This component is gaining increasing popularity and use in the field at large, partly because of its clear link to documented student achievement and its emphasis on building collaborative working relationships among teachers in school settings.

A teacher compensation system should not unintentionally damage other elements of an effective educational organization. For instance, the failure of many merit pay systems has been the result of the competitiveness that was generated among teachers. Teaching is a cumulative process, both horizontally and vertically within a school system. A compensation system that pits individuals against each other, ultimately, seems counter to the basic sequence of the educational process. With this in mind, logistical issues must be addressed when designing a group-based performance pay component.

1. The definition of group must be determined. A group could include an entire school, two or more departments in a school, two or more departments or grade levels among multiple schools, or a designated minimum number of teachers who share responsibility for a designated minimum number of students. While current research tends to support definitions of groups in larger rather than smaller terms and as extant administrative arrangements (e.g., formal departments) rather than ad hoc arrangements (e.g., a group of teachers who simply chose to work together), there is no definitive rule as to what should constitute a group.

2. The means of demonstrating student achievement must be determined. For purposes of recognizing and rewarding teachers for student achievement, achievement should be defined in terms of the "value-added" factor. In other words, the evaluation and compensation should not hold teachers individually accountable for a standard that is cumulative in its attainment.

3. Administrative processes must be developed whereby an eligible group would submit a proposal, including (1) baseline assessment data, (2) specific goals, (3) specific strategies, and (4) means of evaluation. An evaluation would be required following completion of the plan.

4. Limits on how many group-based pay projects an individual teacher is eligible to participate in would need to be established (e.g., one group-based pay project per year).

5. Administrative processes and guidelines such as definitions, approval processes, and appeals processes would need to be developed and institutionalized.

Methodologies for demonstrating value-added achievement have received much attention and refinement in recent years; however, these methodologies are, to a large degree, currently out of reach for smaller and nonwealthy school districts. A school system needs a robust data collection system to correlate student achievement reliably with individual teachers, not to mention to ensure that the measures of student achievement are, themselves, valid and reliable. Thus there are practical limits to group-based pay-for-performance, but the related problems are surmountable in most settings when the design issues cited above are addressed.

COMPENSATION AND QUALITY

A component parts model for teacher compensation is built upon the premise that a multilane salary schedule is a valid, fair, broadly accepted, and feasible means of paying teachers for what they know and do. It also recognizes that compensation is part of an integrated system of job responsibilities, evaluation, professional growth, and accountability. As such, the comprehensive model complements the traditional salary schedule with seven specific compensation components that are designed to attract, develop, and retain quality teachers, as depicted in Figure 5.3.

A comprehensive and systemic approach to teacher compensation is intended to focus a district and its teachers on quality teaching and student achievement. Specific advantages include the following:

1. The comprehensive model provides teachers multiple incentives and pathways to increase their total annual compensation, while also promoting and achieving the goals of the school district.

2. The salary schedule provides a fair, equitable, easy-to-understand, and easy-to-implement system of base salary.

3. The clarity and familiarity of a salary schedule may aid recruiting efforts because it is relatively easy to explain. The bonus components may provide additional, attractive incentives to prospective employees.

Figure 5.3   Comparison of Compensation Components and Organizational Goals

District Aims for Quality Teachers	Compensation Components							
	Base Salary	Performance Evaluation Program (PEP)	Knowledge Acquisition	Skills Block	Additional Responsibility Pay	Accomplished Professional Teacher	National Board for Professional Teaching Standards (NBPTS)	Group-Based Pay
Attracting Teachers	✓		✓	✓	✓	✓	✓	✓
Developing Teachers		✓	✓	✓		✓	✓	✓
Retaining Teachers	✓	✓	✓	✓	✓	✓	✓	✓

4. The salary schedule provides the opportunity for a district to periodically manipulate the number of lanes and the value of steps as strategic goals change. Market forces—such as critical shortage areas, high numbers of retirement-eligible teachers, and competition from other school districts—are all ones to which the school district must periodically respond.

5. The knowledge acquisition and skills block components promote and reward professional growth and development.

6. The model positions the district to promote goals, such as acquiring new skills or earning endorsement in critical shortage areas.

7. The model allows the district to reward effective teachers and to differentiate the compensation of teachers based on performance.

8. Teachers need not top out, as occurs on conventional salary schedules, because the option of bonuses is present for teachers at all steps on the salary schedule. There are continuing incentives for teachers to meet and exceed the expectations of the school district.

9. The Accomplished Professional Teacher (APT) and group-based pay components are tied to student achievement, thereby linking student achievement, teacher performance, teacher evaluation, and teacher compensation. Moreover, adopting these components now—even in a very basic form—positions the school district for using achievement data to recognize individual performance as well as group performance as a district's capacity (i.e., data tracking infrastructure and availability of assessments) improves over time.

10. The group-based pay component encourages collaboration. Research suggests that collaboration improves teacher effectiveness.

11. Combining a multilane salary schedule with a system of pay-for-performance allows for *internal equity* (i.e., fairness, in terms of equal pay for equal responsibilities) and *external competitiveness* (i.e., the addition of component bonuses being attractive to potential applicants).

12. Restructuring a teacher compensation system around a salary schedule similar to a district's current schedule and with the addition of component compensation pieces designed to attract, develop, and retain quality teachers is *an innovative, but not radical, approach* to restructuring the compensation system.

ALTERNATIVES TO CONSIDER

While the model we propose for teacher compensation attempts to account for current research and innovations in the field, there are alternatives available that may better serve the needs of an individual school district.

Three of those alternatives bear special mention here.

1. Opting to accelerate teachers on the salary schedule as a pay incentive instead of offering bonuses for successful participation in various compensation components.

2. Opting to restructure the current salary schedule to eliminate all degree/advanced coursework lanes in favor of a single-lane salary schedule.

3. Opting to replace the current salary schedule with a salary schedule embedded within a career ladder.

We explore these three alternatives in greater detail in the following paragraphs.

An Alternative to Consider: Accelerating
Teachers on the Salary Schedule

The foundation of our proposed model for teacher compensation system is a competitive base salary schedule. And, as previously described, the salary schedule is improved upon with a total of seven pay-for-performance components that are designed to promote and recognize teacher effectiveness. In the proposed model, these seven components are designed to serve as vehicles for bonus compensation to a teacher's base salary. A *bonus system* provides pay above the base salary as determined on the salary schedule. Thus a first-year teacher may be paid a base salary of $35,000, but she may increase her take-home pay for that year, for example, by successfully completing a skills block component for a $250 stipend and participating in a group-based pay project that paid $450. Hence, in addition to her annual salary of $35,000, this teacher would have earned a bonus of $700.

However, there is an alternative to the bonus pay structure: the use of an *accelerative system*. Whereas the bonus system pays additional money to teachers upon successful completion of one of the pay-for-performance components, an accelerative system rewards a teacher by moving her one or more steps on the salary schedule. So, the same first-year teacher earning $35,000 may be compensated for her successful participation in a skills block component and a group-based pay project with a two-step jump on the salary schedule, resulting in a $1,650 raise *in addition to* the regular annual step increase.

The concept of using accelerative components also has support in educational research. Some research suggests that teacher experience tends to be correlated with teacher effectiveness, especially during a teacher's first ten years. Then there tends to be a 10-year plateau until year 20. The trend after year 20 suggests a curvilinear pattern, during which time teacher effectiveness tends to decline.[11] Of course, trends do not necessarily

Figure 5.4   Examples of Accelerative Pay Options

Example 1

Bonus Pay	Acceleration on the Salary Schedule
Additional Responsibility	Knowledge Acquisition (advanced degree)
Group-Based Pay	Skills Block
National Board Certification	Accomplished Professional Teacher

Example 2

Bonus Pay	Acceleration on the Salary Schedule
Additional Responsibility	Accomplished Professional Teacher
Knowledge Acquisition (advanced degree)	National Board Certification
Skills Block	Group-Based Pay

Example 3

Bonus Pay	Acceleration on the Salary Schedule
Additional Responsibility	Knowledge Acquisition (advanced degree)
	Skills Block
	Accomplished Professional Teacher
	National Board Certification
	Group-Based Pay

characterize the performance of individual teachers. Teachers can be highly effective in their first years; teachers can be at their best in their last years in the classroom. As a trend, however, the research suggests that the traditional salary schedule that rewards teachers with annual step increases may be rewarding teachers for their longevity with the school district, but not necessarily for their increasing effectiveness. Thus the option of allowing teachers to accelerate on the salary schedule based on their performance holds some appeal.

It is important to note, however, that the bonus and accelerative systems are not necessarily exclusive of each other. Another option for rewarding teachers' achievement of pay-for-performance components is a *hybrid system*. A hybrid system uses bonus pay for some components and accelerative pay for others. For purposes of illustration, Figure 5.4 provides several examples for how the bonus and accelerative systems of pay-for-performance could be used in tandem.

There are several advantages to the option of using accelerative components in a comprehensive compensation system:

1. For teachers, it amounts to a permanent increase in base salary.

2. Steps on the salary schedule are not connected solely to years of experience; instead, steps on the salary schedule become equated with past and current performance.

3. Using accelerative components permits a district more latitude in responding to changes in the labor market by offering higher salaries in critical shortage areas, such as math, science, and special education. For example, a first-year science teacher could be placed on Step 3 of the salary schedule as an incentive for joining the district. (Notably, this same policy could be used with a traditional salary schedule, as well.)

Several disadvantages are also evident:

1. As teachers accelerate on the salary schedule, topping out may become more common.

2. Accelerating teachers on the salary schedule amounts to a permanent commitment of funds by the school district. A teacher is *perpetually rewarded* when accelerated on the salary schedule because his or her base salary is increased.

3. Accelerating on the salary schedule may be a less visible or obvious way of increasing compensation as compared with bonus pay; therefore, accelerative components may have less motivational effect for some teachers.

Another Alternative to Consider: Single-Lane Salary Schedule

A second option to consider in tailoring the model of a comprehensive compensation system to a school district's needs is to replace the multilane salary schedule with a single-lane salary schedule. This alternative effectively takes the lanes that differentiate pay based on advanced degrees or coursework and relegates them to a bonus compensation component, similar to the skills block. Figure 5.5 provides a model for how a single-lane salary schedule could be integrated with the seven compensation components.

Within this option would also be the alternative to combine the single-lane salary concept with the concept of accelerative components. Figure 5.6 provides a model for this integrative approach. As suggested in the figure, this is a *hybrid* model that combines the use of bonus components (for skills block, additional responsibility pay, and group-based pay) with accelerative components (for knowledge acquisition, APT, and NBPTS certification).

The model of the single-lane salary schedule is appealing for several reasons:

Figure 5.5   Single-Lane Salary Schedule With Bonus Components

Salary Steps		Determines "Satisfactory" or "Unsatisfactory" Performance	Components Available to All Teachers			
1	$33,000	Performance Evaluation	Knowledge Acquisition	Skills Blocks	Additional Responsibility*	Group-Based Pay
2	.					
3	.					
4	.					
.	.					
.	.					
.	.					
15	$71,000					

Components Available Only to "Satisfactory" Teachers

Additional Responsibility*
Accomplished Professional Teacher
National Board Certification

* Some elements of Additional Responsibility Pay (e.g., activity sponsor stipend) may be available to all teachers. Other elements of Additional Responsibility Pay (e.g., service on designated division-wide committees) may be available only to "Satisfactory" teachers.

Figure 5.6   Single-Lane Salary Schedule With Bonus *and* Accelerative Components

Salary Steps		Determines "Satisfactory" or "Unsatisfactory" Performance	Bonus Components		
1	$33,000	Performance Evaluation*	Skills Blocks	Additional Responsibility	Group-Based Pay
2	.				
3	.				
4	.				
.	.				
.	.				
.	.				
15	$71,000				

* Progress on the salary schedule can be accomplished by earning a satisfactory performance evaluation. Further acceleration on the salary schedule can be accomplished by successfully completing one or more of three Accelerative Components: (1) Knowledge Acquisition, (2) Accomplished Professional Teacher, and (3) National Board Certification.

1. Eliminating the lanes for advanced coursework and degrees equates knowledge acquisition with other components in the compensation system, such as skills block and group-based pay. Currently, in most districts, advanced coursework or an advanced degree is the *only* way for a teacher to increase his or her permanent salary base.

2. Eliminating lanes has support in educational research, which indicates that teacher effectiveness tends to increase when a teacher possesses a master's degree, yet a similar effect has not been demonstrated for coursework or degrees *beyond* the master's.[12]

3. By eliminating salary lanes, the school district has the choice of offering bonuses or acceleration on the salary steps as the method for rewarding teachers who successfully attain the knowledge acquisition component.

4. The single-lane salary schedule is simple in design and easy to both understand and communicate.

For all of the attractiveness of the single-lane salary schedule, there are also disadvantages:

1. While the single-lane salary schedule is simple in design, it is complex in implementation. There are a series of decisions that would accompany a school district's adoption of a single-lane schedule, such as, "How will new hires with master's degrees (whether novice or veteran) be placed on the salary schedule?"

2. The loss of lanes may be viewed as a disincentive to new hires (whether novice or experienced teachers) because competing districts have lanes for advanced coursework and degrees. Knowledge acquisition lanes are present in the salary schedules of most school districts and are a component of teacher compensation in 20 other industrialized nations.[13] Therefore departing from a multilane salary schedule represents a significant departure from convention.

3. While there is research that suggests that advanced degrees or coursework up to and including a master's degree are associated with improved teacher effectiveness, there is no solid research base to answer the question about the validity of coursework and degrees *beyond* the master's degree.

4. A single-lane salary schedule would require either an *elongated salary schedule* or *compressed salary schedule* in order to convert from a multilane salary schedule. Consider the hypothetical case of Lincoln Public Schools (LPS). A single-lane salary schedule would require approximately 30 steps because the district's current salary steps and lanes would need to be collapsed into a single salary column. If LPS's salary range is from $33,000 to $71,000, then the factor of difference between the lowest and highest salary is 2.15 or 215 percent. There are two fundamental ways to translate the current multilane salary schedule into a single-lane schedule. The first option is an *elongated salary schedule*. An *elongated salary schedule* contains more steps with smaller increases between steps. An elongated salary schedule allows for greater differentiation in pay among teachers. Such a salary

schedule would have approximately 30 steps and, given the current range of pay, each step would equate to an increase of approximately $1,250. The second option is a *compressed salary schedule*. A compressed salary schedule would contain fewer steps with larger increases between steps. A compressed schedule would be more intermittent, providing a salary increase every other year or perhaps every third year in association with the performance evaluation cycle. Such a salary schedule would have approximately 15 steps and, given the current range of pay, each step would equate to an increase of approximately $2,500.

A Third Alternative: The Career Ladder Model

Teaching is characteristically described as a "flat" profession because of the absence of a career path associated with being a classroom teacher. With the exception of taking on extra duties such as department chair in a high school or grade-level leader in an elementary school, there is little to distinguish a first-year teacher from a 20-year veteran in terms of either responsibility or professional status. A career ladder is an attempt to address the flat nature of the teaching profession by structuring specific levels of professional distinction and commensurate salary to which teachers aspire over the course of their careers.

Figure 5.7 provides a model of a career ladder, within the context of a comprehensive, components-based compensation system. In this model, four distinct stages of a teacher's career are defined: *Novice, Career, Accomplished,* and *Master Teacher.* Down the left-hand column are the basic components of the comprehensive compensation system, as previously described. A career ladder, essentially, is an alternate means of combining these compensation components into a schedule for determining teacher salaries. For example, the Novice Teacher level would be defined by a certain range of salary, perhaps $33,000–$39,600. With satisfactory evaluations, a teacher would earn annual step increases within this range for five years. This concept is illustrated in Figure 5.8, which provides an example of what career levels would be available to a teacher based upon the length of his service with the school district—that is, a teacher's step on the embedded salary schedule. Between Steps 3 and 5 in Figure 5.8, a Novice Teacher would then be eligible to apply for Career Teacher designation. To earn that designation, the teacher would have to meet the criteria identified for each *performance measure* appropriate to the advancement.

The concept of the career ladder, arguably, is growing in support and not only among school districts. The state of Virginia, for example, initiated the development of a proposal for a multitiered licensure system. The intent of this proposal was to provide a statewide mechanism for recognizing various levels of professional distinction and increasing responsibility for teacher leaders—those teachers who actively and constructively contribute to the leadership and achievement of their schools, districts, and professions *while remaining in the classroom.*

Figure 5.7   Career Ladder Model

Performance Measures	Novice Teacher	Career Teacher	Accomplished Teacher	Master Teacher
Years Experience (includes salary ranges similar to steps)	Pretenure	Must hold tenure	May require a minimum number of years experience	May require a minimum number of years experience
Performance Evaluation	Satisfactory evaluation required to earn tenure	Performance must meet expectations in all responsibilities and exceed expectations in certain designated responsibilities for a designated period of time	Performance must meet expectations in all responsibilities and exceed expectations in certain designated responsibilities for a designated period of time	Performance must meet expectations in all responsibilities and exceed expectations in certain designated responsibilities for a designated period of time
Knowledge Acquisition	Bachelor's degree	Bachelor's +15	Master's	Master's
Skills Block	Designated skills blocks required	Designated skills blocks required	Designated skills blocks required	Evidence of leadership in skills blocks
Additional Responsibility	May apply	May apply	Evidence of additional responsibility/ leadership (paid or unpaid)	Evidence of additional responsibility/ leadership (paid or unpaid)
Group-Based Pay		Participation in successful group-based pay project	Leadership of successful group-based pay project	Leadership of designated number of successful group-based pay projects
Accomplished Professional Teacher (APT)		May apply	Accomplished Professional Teacher (APT) designation required	Meets prerequisites for APT, but does not have to apply
National Board Certification		May apply	May apply	National Board Certification required

Career ladders are not new to education. In 1984, there were at least six statewide initiatives to implement career ladders in the nation, including Arizona, Missouri, North Carolina, Tennessee, Texas, and Utah. However, by the late 1990s, half of these states—North Carolina, Tennessee, and Texas—had abandoned career ladders.[14] It is worth noting that North Carolina has since gone on to become one of the states leading in the

Figure 5.8   Illustrations of Salary Steps Embedded Within a Career Ladder

Salary Steps	Novice Teacher	Career Teacher	Accomplished Teacher	Master Teacher
1				
2				
3				
4				
5				
6				
7				
8				
9				
10				
11				
12				
13				
14				
15				
16				
17				
18				
19				
20				

percentage of National Board Certified teachers, a program that is widely viewed as the gold standard of professional recognition. Meanwhile, Tennessee has received considerable national attention for its statewide "value-added" program, which provides school-based rewards for improved academic achievement and which is laying the groundwork for a compensation system that may recognize individual teachers. Indeed, the focus on school-based gains and rewards has grown during the past decades, as Tennessee has been joined by at least 21 other states—including Florida, Georgia, Indiana, Kentucky, North Carolina, South Carolina, and Texas—in implementing "whole-school incentive programs."[15]

Career ladders hold a great deal of intuitive appeal to teachers, policymakers, and the public. However, the track record is not favorable concerning the career ladder model. Nevertheless, the concept holds a great number of appealing features:

1. Career advancement is based on multiple criteria, not simply length of service, advanced coursework, or administrator judgment.

2. Teachers are rewarded for acquiring new knowledge and skills.

3. Performance measures such as Accomplished Professional Teacher and group-based pay are tied to demonstrated student achievement.

4. A career ladder holds a great deal of intuitive appeal to prospective teachers, especially when comparing the teaching profession to other career options.

5. A career ladder model can be designed to include comprehensive compensation components.

Although there are advantages to a career ladder model, there are also disadvantages evident in such a compensation system:

1. Career ladders are oftentimes viewed as an alternative to a salary schedule; however, career ladders actually have salary steps embedded within the career levels or lanes.

2. Once a teacher has acquired a lane, it constitutes a permanent pay raise rather than a bonus, diminishing the district's ability to analyze and reward professional performance regularly through bonuses.

3. There is a weak basis in actual practice in the field for career ladders, as exemplified by the frequent failures of innovations in the 1980s, 1990s, and even of more contemporary cases.

4. A career ladder may be a discouragement to novice teachers who enter the profession with a master's degree from a graduate-level initial teacher preparation program. These teachers may not be attracted to a career ladder unless there is a means of rewarding the master's degree as early as Step 1.

5. A career ladder would require an "opt-in" plan and a plan for transitioning teachers from the current salary schedule to an equivalent point on the career ladder. In addition, the school district would need to operate dual salary systems until a full conversion is made.

6. A career ladder may promote competition and divisiveness among teachers.

7. Career ladders are susceptible to *evaluation inflation*—when the vast majority of teachers earn the highest evaluation ratings. If this occurs within the context of a career ladder compensation model, then a school district's personnel costs can become unsustainable because of the number of teachers earning salaries in the highest ranges.

CONCLUDING THOUGHTS: DESIGNING A COMPENSATION SYSTEM

The idea of paying somebody to perform work is a simple-enough concept. However, the actual practice of using pay as a means of fostering, supporting, and rewarding *quality* performance is more complicated. In this chapter, we have presented a comprehensive model for teacher compensation that aims a school district's resources squarely at the issue of quality. This model is founded on three basic assumptions:

1. Teacher quality leads to student learning, and student learning is the main idea.

2. Money matters.

3. Compensation is not an endgame; rather, it is integral to attracting, developing, and retaining effective teachers.

With these three assumptions in mind, a compensation system should adhere to five basic design principles. These design principles may command varying degrees of emphasis in a given school district, but each must be considered and weighed when exploring the options available for compensating professional teachers. By design, a comprehensive compensation system that aims for teacher quality should provide for the following:

1. Competitiveness

2. Strategic flexibility

3. Comprehensiveness

4. Clarity

5. Appropriateness

With these foundational parameters clearly in mind, the decisions surrounding the specific combination and organization of the compensation components reviewed in this chapter can be selected deliberately and constructively. In the next chapter, we take a look at key points to move from the development and design of a comprehensive compensation system to the implementation of it.

6

From Planning to Implementation

How Do We Make This Change?

Implementation of a restructured teacher compensation system that focuses on teacher quality issues is a complex and time-intensive process. Thus it is helpful to outline the key steps that should occur to optimize the design, communication, implementation, and evaluation of the system. It also should be noted that any implementation plan should have an evolutionary quality to it. In other words, no implementation plan can predict all of the possible distracters, barriers, and opportunities that may arise during the course of implementation. Given this, the implementation plan must be sufficiently structured as to provide a clear road map to where the school district wants to be, while also being flexible enough to allow the district leadership to respond to unforeseen conditions of change.

Figure 6.1 depicts the steps in an implementation plan for restructuring a teacher compensation system. The implementation plan consists of five steps, each of which segues into the one that follows.

The implementation of a component parts teacher compensation system requires attention to a number of key issues within the district. Several of these issues are relevant across the different components; others are more specifically tied to selected options. First and foremost, any compensation

Figure 6.1   Implementation Plan

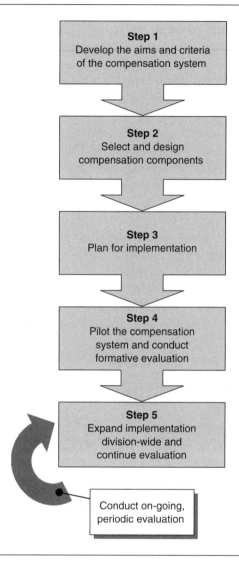

reform initiatives must acknowledge that, although some additional funding may be required and available, budget constraints are a significant challenge to new programs. Consequently, compensation initiatives must focus on improving compensation within the boundaries of sustainable funding. Given careful design, we hope we have been able to show—and will attempt to demonstrate in this chapter—that it is feasible for the additional cost to a school district of this model of a component compensation system to be a little as approximately 2 percent of the current salary line.

Second, the present discussion of the implementation of a restructured teacher compensation system assumes a school district's move away from a conventional multilane salary schedule. As previously noted, salary schedules are the most prevalent of teacher compensation systems in the United States, as well as other industrialized nations, and the focus on compensation reform during the past several decades has been aimed at addressing the shortcomings of a system designed only to reward longevity and advanced coursework, without regard to quality of performance or relevance of professional development.

Third, many of the compensation components advocated by the model presented in Chapter 5 require careful definitions of expectations, criteria, boundaries, and measurement strategies. These are weighty decisions not only requiring technical expertise but also necessitating considerable administrative support and the collaborative involvement of stakeholders, namely teachers.

Fourth, several of the components advocated in the compensation model require the investment of professional development time and funding; thus they carry the implication of a close collaboration between individuals and/or departments charged with professional development and human resources in a school district. Compensation reform is not just the responsibility of the finance department or chief financial officer.

Finally, as with any new initiative, the involvement of multiple stakeholders and attention to clear and regular communication are crucial to the implementation of change. We'll give this specific attention as we explore the steps involved with implementing a restructured teacher compensation system.

STEP 1: DEVELOP THE AIMS AND CRITERIA OF THE COMPENSATION SYSTEM

A basic premise of sound organizational planning and implementation is that all of the initiatives, projects, efforts, and systems of the organization are "pointing in the same direction." That is to say, the intentional, efficient, and, ultimately, effective organization aligns its resources and processes to achieve its intended mission. Schools and school districts are no different.

The purpose of any school district, regardless of the particular wording of its unique mission statement, is student learning. And the basic premise upon which educational systems are designed is that quality teaching leads to student learning. So, to what aim must all systems within an organization be pointed? Whether the "system" is the curriculum, the student discipline code, or the buildings-and-grounds operation, the ultimate aim of each must be student learning. The same holds true for teacher compensation. Ultimately, the teacher compensation system must be designed to promote student achievement through quality teachers.

This fundamental assumption about the aim of teacher compensation systems was presented in the previous chapter, providing the foundation for a model of a comprehensive components-based compensation system. A school district looking to develop a more intentional and effective approach to paying teachers must be clear about its own assumptions.

- Do your school district's leadership and professional staff accept the assumption that compensation is not an endgame or a simple remuneration for services rendered, but is, in fact, an integral element of a teacher's career continuum from being attracted to the district, developing and improving as a teacher, and remaining with the district?

- What other assumptions does your district make about the role of compensation in the lives, motivations, and performance outcomes of its teachers?

Step one of implementing a restructured compensation system is to be clear about these assumptions and their relationship to the broader aims of the educational system.

Also as described in the previous chapter, a district's aims and assumptions should inform the foundational principles upon which a restructured compensation system is to be designed. This process is analogous to meeting with an architect early in the process of designing a new house. The client may say, "We want lots of natural light in the house. We want to be able to watch the sunset at dinnertime. We need to be able to work from home." These statements are akin to design principles. At this point, there's no need to get into the details of how many windows the house should have, where the kitchen's going to be, or what the home office will look like, but the basic criteria from which such design components will be derived are evident.

In Chapters 2 and 5, we presented five design principles for a comprehensive compensation system aimed at teacher quality:

1. Competitiveness

2. Strategic flexibility

3. Comprehensiveness

4. Clarity

5. Appropriateness

Whether a school district accepts these, refines them, or adds to them, the point is that the district leadership must be intentional about the criteria that will characterize the design of a compensation system aimed at ensuring student learning through promoting teacher quality.

STEP 2: SELECT COMPENSATION COMPONENTS

Assumptions and design principles drive the creation of a teacher compensation system. As we advocate and describe in detail in Chapter 5, a comprehensive teacher compensation system built from a menu of interrelated compensation components best serves the needs of school districts facing challenges of changing teacher demographics. Thus the second step in implementing a restructured approach to teacher compensation is to decide upon the specific components that will comprise the compensation system for the district. We review the components here, but also provide an additional variable for consideration: funding. Simply put, the components that ultimately comprise a district's compensation system must be fiscally feasible. Although the financial ramifications of each component will be different in any given district, we offer here some practical illustrations of funding implications to further inform decision making.

Competitive Base Salary

The creation of a competitive base salary is at the foundation of structuring an effective and comprehensive teacher compensation model. The competitiveness of the salary schedule is dependent upon external and internal influences: the salary schedule of competing school districts and the demographics of the school district's existing teacher workforce. When a school district's base salary schedule is designed to be competitive given these factors, it can be a tool for attracting and retaining quality teachers. A competitive salary schedule also serves as the foundation upon which to build other compensation components that can serve not only to attract and retain quality teachers but also to develop them.

Benchmarking is the process of comparing the salary schedules of competing school districts at selected points and identifying the points at which salaries are similar or dissimilar within a given range. In practice, a school district may benchmark its salary schedule to another school district by comparing a representative sample of the entire range of the salary schedule or by comprehensively comparing every point on its own salary schedule with corresponding points on the salary schedules of its competitors. Figure 6.2 presents a sample comparison of Lincoln Public Schools (LPS) and two of its neighboring—that is, *competing*—school districts. The shading in the figure indicates the school district with the highest *total pay* for a teacher after each given period of service, calculated here in five-year increments.

This benchmarking exercise for LPS illustrates a classic problem in determining the competitiveness of a base salary. The issue is not with LPS's competitiveness. Indeed, for early career teachers, LPS provides the highest cumulative salary at all degree levels. However, it becomes evident from this analysis that LPS's competitiveness *diminishes* for veteran teachers. The salary schedule by itself, then, may do more to attract teachers, but less to retain them.

Figure 6.2   Benchmarking of Salary Lanes at Selected Steps

Data Table of the Total Sum After 5 Years of Service

District	BA/BS	BA + 15	MA	MA + 30	PhD
LPS	$181,489	$189,735	$211,189	$230,986	$240,887
District 1	$180,589	$189,698	$199,260	$209,303	$219,851
District 2	$180,993	$187,294	$202,730	$210,187	$218,617

Data Table of the Total Sum After 10 Years of Service

District	BA/BS	BA + 15	MA	MA + 30	PhD
LPS	$404,223	$421,319	$471,875	$511,472	$531,269
District 1	$406,758	$427,176	$448,612	$471,122	$494,761
District 2	$400,039	$412,640	$443,511	$458,448	$475,288

Data Table of the Total Sum After 15 Years of Service

District	BA/BS	BA + 15	MA	MA + 30	PhD
LPS	$643,457	$688,606	$780,073	$839,469	$869,163
District 1	$655,518	$727,091	$763,519	$801,781	$841,950
District 2	$661,967	$680,868	$727,174	$749,591	$774,841

Data Table of the Total Sum After 20 Years of Service

District	BA/BS	BA + 15	MA	MA + 30	PhD
LPS	$883,692	$961,843	$1,101,149	$1,180,355	$1,219,932
District 1	$908,004	$1,049,339	$1,101,872	$1,157,065	$1,214,991
District 2	$969,248	$994,450	$1,056,190	$1,086,087	$1,119,746

Data Table of the Total Sum After 25 Years of Service

District	BA/BS	BA + 15	MA	MA + 30	PhD
LPS	$1,127,927	$1,239,080	$1,426,225	$1,525,240	$1,574,701
District 1	$1,168,074	$1,381,271	$1,450,393	$1,523,025	$1,599,242
District 2	$1,296,183	$1,327,690	$1,412,760	$1,450,137	$1,492,206

Data Table of the Total Sum After 30 Years of Service

District	BA/BS	BA + 15	MA	MA + 30	PhD
LPS	$1,372,162	$1,516,318	$1,751,301	$1,870,125	$1,929,471
District 1	$1,435,949	$1,723,176	$1,809,373	$1,899,970	$1,995,022
District 2	$1,623,118	$1,660,930	$1,781,445	$1,826,302	$1,876,781

Note: For each lane and step comparison, the highest salary among the districts is highlighted in gray.

The knee-jerk reaction to benchmarking is to conclude that more money must be committed to salary in order to be competitive with neighboring districts. If LPS pursued this course, here are some possible financial ramifications:

1. LPS tends to pay teachers *less* at the Bachelor's and Bachelor's + 15 levels than either of the other districts; therefore, there potentially would be a net *cost* to replicate either competitor's salary schedule at these levels.

2. LPS tends to pay teachers *more* at the Master's and Master's + 30 levels than the other districts; therefore, there potentially would be a net *cost savings* to replicate either competitor's salary schedule at these levels.

3. For teachers at the doctoral level, LPS tends to pay less than District 1 but more than District 2; therefore, there potentially would be a net *cost* to replicate District 1's salary schedule at this level or a net *cost savings* to replicate District 2's doctoral lane.

4. If LPS were to convert wholesale—that is, per teacher across the entire salary schedule—from its current salary schedule to District 1's salary schedule, there would be a net *cost* of approximately $133,000. However, if LPS were to convert wholesale to District 2's salary schedule, then LPS could realize a *savings* of approximately $642,000.

Benchmarking opens a window on the issue of competitiveness; however, as illustrated, the decisions that ensue are not necessarily self-evident. LPS must ask some more questions:

- With which district(s) do we wish to compete?
- What range of differentiation between our salary schedule and our competitors' is acceptable to us? Dollar figures will rarely be exactly the same on salary schedules with literally scores of cells in them, so the district may decide that a percentage difference of plus or minus 2 percent is acceptable, but a difference of more than 2 percent (whether above or below the competitor) is unacceptable.
- At what year-increments on the salary schedule do we want to be most competitive?

This last question points to another important variable in ensuring the competitiveness of a school district's salary schedule: the profile of the district's current teacher workforce. Demographics that indicate large pockets of teachers within a certain age range can have implications for converting to a new salary schedule and also for recruitment, employment, and retention decisions. Looking again at LPS, Figure 6.3 depicts the district's teacher workforce by age, thereby providing insight into the distribution of novice, midcareer, and veteran teachers.

In LPS, slightly more than 40 percent of all its teachers are or will be eligible for full or partial retirement benefits within the next five years.

Figure 6.3   Distribution of Teachers by Age in LPS

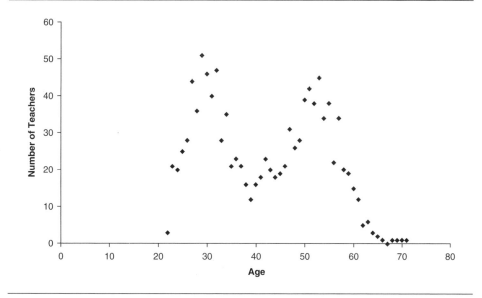

This is a significant demographic factor, representing a profile of a teaching force that is on the cusp of a significant turnover beginning now and continuing for approximately the next decade. The school district is faced with several ways to address this need:

- Option 1—Attract new teachers to replace those retiring. A salary that is competitive at points of entry into the profession, notably steps 1–3, is one solution.
- Option 2—Weigh more heavily those steps on which most retirement-eligible teachers are being paid as a way of encouraging teachers to continue working and to lessen the impact of the potential teacher shortage.
- Option 3—Midload the salary schedule to attract and retain midcareer teachers, which is the population segment currently least represented in the LPS teacher workforce.

When viewed through the lens of teacher demographics and strategic imperatives, a "competitive" base salary can mean something quite different than simply bumping up the salary schedule to top those of the neighboring school districts.

Performance Evaluation

The performance evaluation component of a comprehensive compensation system links a district's teacher evaluation system to teacher pay. In concept, this point is simple enough: A teacher's performance is reviewed on a regular basis by her supervisor, typically a principal or assistant principal, and this review is used to determine the teacher's progression on the salary schedule. If her performance meets or exceeds expectations, she earns an annual merit increase—that is, she progresses on the salary schedule. If her performance needs significant improvement or is unsatisfactory, she does not gain an annual increase.

Although simple enough in concept, linking the evaluation system to the compensation system requires careful attention to two fundamental factors.

1. The evaluation system must be *valid*—that is, it must evaluate the knowledge, skills, and dispositions associated with quality teaching.[1]

2. The evaluation system must be *reliable*. A commonplace, and often warranted, criticism of teacher evaluation systems is that they are too subjective and, therefore, too unreliable to serve as a basis for high-stakes decisions, such as compensation. However, this points to a need to redress a district's *teacher evaluation system*, rather than decoupling performance evaluation and compensation.

Teacher evaluation systems continue to evolve and improve, as does the feasibility and propriety of using teacher evaluation for objectively and appropriately linking teacher performance to student learning.[2] However, we strongly caution that integrating performance evaluation into a compensation system as a "trigger" for annual step increases is dependent upon the presence of a trustworthy means of evaluating teacher performance.

What are the funding implications for implementing performance evaluation as part of a teacher compensation system? There are two possible answers. First, if a school district already has a valid and reliable system for regularly evaluating the performance of teachers in place, then there are essentially no additional costs for integrating teacher evaluation into a comprehensive compensation plan. The evaluation system simply becomes the gate to determining a teacher's progression or stasis on the salary schedule. The second possible answer regarding the cost of this compensation component is for a school district that does *not* have a trusted and fair performance evaluation system in place. For such a district, the additional costs are associated with the development and implementation of a new evaluation system.

Professional Development: Knowledge and Skills Acquisition

For many school districts in the United States, the integration of knowledge and skills acquisition components into their teacher compensation systems would involve both minor and potentially significant changes. Knowledge and skills acquisition, as described in Chapter 5, typically takes the form of conventional graduate-level coursework or specifically designed professional development programs. These elements currently exist in many school districts. For example, school districts typically budget for professional development for teachers. Also, most salary schedules in school districts include salary lanes, which differentiate pay among teachers based upon accumulated graduate-level credit (e.g., bachelor's degree plus 15 credits) and upon the attainment of advanced degrees (e.g., master's degree, certificate of advanced study, or doctoral degree). In addition, many school districts also blend these two elements in that they will fund all or a portion of a teacher's continuing education through tuition assistance programs. For school districts that already employ these practices, shifting to a *knowledge acquisition* component requires attention to two basic issues. First, a district would need to decide whether to retain its conventional salary schedule that includes lanes or whether to eliminate lanes in favor of either bonuses or acceleration on a single-lane salary schedule, as discussed in the previous chapter. The second basic issue for a school district to address in implementing a knowledge acquisition component is the set of decision rules that it would put in place to determine what specific coursework and/or experiences the school district will identify to support and reward teachers for completing. The resolution of this important issue is the factor that links knowledge acquisition as a compensation component to knowledge acquisition as a teacher—and district—quality component.

What is the fiscal impact of the knowledge acquisition component? Again, much depends on the current funding of a district's salary lanes and its professional development budget. If these are intact and funded, then the fiscal impact is minimal, if any. Of course, the case is quite different for the rare district that has little or no professional development fund, nor salary lanes. Clearly, such a school district would need to assess the potential impact dependent upon the strategic goals that it is intending to achieve through knowledge acquisition, the number of teachers potentially involved, the availability of courses or programs, the costs of such courses and programs, and the funding stream.

Similar to the knowledge acquisition component, the *skills block* component of a comprehensive compensation system aims to link teacher development, teacher quality, and teacher compensation. Although the two components are close in nature, a distinguishing feature about a skills block is that it is focused upon an identified skill set for a teacher to develop and that compensation for attainment of the skill set is contingent upon demonstrated mastery and use of the skill in a teacher's job function. To implement skills blocks, a district must attend to the following key issues:

1. Identify the skill sets necessary for teachers to meet the goals of the school district

2. Create the means of offering useful and appropriate professional development experiences supporting the skill sets

3. Devise a means of evaluating teacher mastery of skills block content to demonstrate impact on student learning

4. Design a system for tracking skills blocks for purposes of compensation, including whether to compensate teachers in the form of bonuses or acceleration on the salary schedule

5. Ensure the availability of a sufficient number of skills blocks to sustain this as a viable compensation component

The implementation of skills blocks represents, for many school districts, a significantly new element of professional development and compensation, both of which have financial implications. In administering the program, there are costs associated with identifying, offering, and tracking skills blocks, the specific costs of which are dependent upon the district's size, current professional development programs, and current administrative organization. In terms of actual compensation for teachers, the most significant decision is the level of pay for successful completion and demonstration of a skills block.

Returning to our example of LPS, the district decides that skills blocks will be an effective complement to the knowledge acquisition component, primarily because skills blocks are seen as targeted, timely, performance-driven professional development that will more immediately impact the district's goals than conventional coursework. The district also anticipates that not all of its 1,300 teachers will annually participate in skills blocks because (1) the district itself is limited in its capacity to develop and mount its own "homegrown" professional development and (2) the focused nature of skills blocks means that the district is not taking a one-size-fits-all approach to professional development. For instance, one year the district may focus on reading instruction skills for primary grade teachers, while the next year the district may target teaching-for-meaning skills of high school math teachers. This amounts to a determination that only about one-quarter of the LPS teacher workforce will be involved with skills block compensation in a given year, and the district decides to design compensation as a one-time bonus, as opposed to a sustained increase in base pay. In the case of LPS, then, a $150,000 budget for skills block pay for 23 percent of their teachers each year translates into a $500 pay bonus for 300 teachers.

Additional Responsibility Pay

Pay for additional responsibility is another component of a comprehensive compensation system that is extant in many school districts; however, it is often incomplete and unaligned with a district's strategic goals.

First and foremost, a district must reassess the practices through which certain teachers earn stipends for fulfilling additional roles. More often than not, such stipends are limited to athletic coaches and, in more limited ways, to club sponsors and pseudoadministrative roles, such as high school department chairs. The practice of paying stipends varies widely, district to district; therefore, a district that intends to use its compensation system as a means of attracting quality professionals and retaining them will integrate the payment of additional duty stipends into its comprehensive compensation plan.

A basic premise of any compensation system, as noted in Chapter 5, should be that whom a district pays, what a district pays them for, and how much a district pays them is a reflection of the value that the district places on certain roles and intended outcomes. What message, then, is sent by the school district that compensates one teacher with a stipend of several thousand dollars for serving as a varsity coach, but expects another teacher to serve on a districtwide curriculum alignment committee for no compensation? This rhetorical question is not intended to question whether a varsity coach deserves a certain and substantive level of compensation for specialized knowledge and significant after-hours commitment—in fact, the coach is arguably not being compensated enough. But that is a different issue to be addressed. The point at hand is that a school district should begin its implementation of additional responsibility pay by comprehensively reviewing *all* of the roles for which teachers do, should, and could receive additional compensation. As described in the previous chapter, these duties can typically be classified as additional duty, school-based, and district-based pay.

What are the fiscal impacts of paying teachers for additional responsibility? Again, much depends on what compensation a district already provides and whether current compensation needs to be (1) increased and (2) expanded to include roles for which teachers are not currently paid. In addition, as with other compensation components, a district must decide on the relative merits of bonus and accelerative pay structures for additional responsibility pay.

The sample case of LPS illustrates the impact for one district. LPS determined it would continue to provide stipends for conventional additional responsibilities (e.g., coaching and club sponsorship) and that it would also provide a new pool of funds for individual schools and for central office departments to compensate teachers for important, ongoing, and, frankly, time-intensive professional work (e.g., curriculum development and textbook adoption). Based on a review of activity over recent years, the district determined that approximately 50 percent of its teacher force fulfilled formal roles of additional responsibility in their schools, although far, far fewer than that had been compensated in the past. In addition, the district determined that about 3 percent of its teachers fulfilled such roles at the district level. Based on a teacher population of 1,300 and making no immediate changes in its stipend rates for current stipend positions, LPS's budget for additional responsibility pay becomes as follows:

Type of Pay	$/Teacher	Total Funding
Additional duty pay	variable	$313,000
School-based pay	650 teachers @ $200/teacher	$130,000
Districtwide pay	40 teachers @ $1,000/teacher	$40,000
TOTAL		$483,000

Again, the impact on any given school district is going to be unique, depending upon its strategic intentions and fiscal resources. The previous example illustrates one district's decision making, based on an attempt not to change its existing practices of compensating teachers for traditional extra duties during its first year of a comprehensive compensation and a simultaneous decision to compensate teachers for the important contributions being made to achieving the district's core mission through committee work and service.

Extraordinary Performance

The intent of compensating teachers for *Extraordinary Performance* is to promote and reward excellence in teaching. As previously explained in Chapter 5, the National Board for Professional Teaching Standards (NBPTS) certification program provides a widely accepted, stand-alone system for identifying quality teachers, but a school district can also develop its own system for recognizing accomplished professional teachers in lieu of or complementary to National Board certification.

What should a school district consider when deciding whether to create a local system for recognizing extraordinary performance? First, a district may want to design and implement a system to recognize accomplished professional teachers if there are specific strategic goals that such a system would help to promote. Such goals can then become essential criteria for the recognition and additional compensation. Second, a locally developed compensation program for rewarding excellent performance may be attractive to a school district that does not have a systemized means for documenting teacher impact on student achievement, but wants to promote voluntary and innovative means for teachers to do so. Third, a district may decide that National Board certification is not well aligned with promoting needs that are particular to the school district. In this case, the district may decide to forego inclusion of NBPTS as a compensation component. However, the demoralizing effects of *not* recognizing nationally certified teachers may be more damaging than the resources needed to support such a program.

Administrative costs for implementing and overseeing a compensation component for accomplished professional teachers can be significant. As suggested in the description of this compensation component in Chapter 5, the initial investment to develop and design such a program would be both time and resource intensive, given the need to ensure a valid and reliable program for evaluating extraordinary performance. After the initial design of the program, the administrative costs would primarily consist of additional responsibility pay for a standing Accomplished Professional Teacher (APT) Advisory Committee—and these teachers would, of course, receive additional responsibility pay—to serve in interpreting guidelines, evaluating applications, and responding to appeals. In addition, a district would need to create a system for tracking participation in the program for payroll purposes. LPS, for example, estimates that roughly 10 percent of its 1,300 teachers will successfully participate in its APT program, for which the compensation bonus is $2,250 per teacher. In addition, the district budgets several thousand dollars for administrative costs. The district's total budget is $325,000.

The decision points around the National Board certification component are similar to those for a locally devised recognition program, although less complex because the National Board for Professional Teaching Standards already exists and operates independent of school districts. Thus the critical issues to consider include whether the NBPTS component should be an integral component of a district's teacher compensation system, what local criteria a teacher must meet to qualify (e.g., satisfactory evaluations), and how and from what source to compensate teachers for successfully meeting this component. In deciding *how* to compensate teachers related to this component of the compensation system, a district must decide whether to pay teachers an *up-front incentive* to pursue National Board certification, a *continuing stipend* for having received national certification, or *both*.

Returning again to LPS, the district decides *not* to provide an incentive for NBPTS for two reasons: (1) National Board is an individual, voluntary activity and (2) teachers in LPS also have the option of the local Accomplished Professional Teacher program, which is less cost intensive. The district does decide, however, to provide a continuing stipend for those teachers who have achieved National Board certification. With this in mind, the district reviews its current number of NBPTS teachers, which is relatively low because there are limited state incentives for the certification, and they estimate the number of new participants. Assuming that about 1 percent of LPS's teachers (about 15) will achieve National Board certification and assigning $3,000 per teacher, the new required funding equals $45,000 for the district.

Group-Based Pay

As described in previous chapters, group-based pay-for-performance has garnered attention and increasing prominence in recent years. Group-based pay provides a means for recognizing and rewarding teachers' *collective* efforts that result in demonstrated student achievement, while reducing or eliminating the unintended negative consequence of merit pay systems that tend to promote counterproductive competition among teachers, antithetical to the aim of creating communities of learners within schools. However, group-based pay introduces a different complication into the teacher pay equation: paying teachers equally and collectively for work and outcomes in which they may not equally contribute.

In designing and implementing group-based pay, a school district has three basic decisions to make, the answers to which will set the foundation of this compensation component.

- Will all teachers be compelled to participate in this compensation component, or will it be voluntary?
- How will we define "groups"—by school; by department, team, or grade-level; or by choice of teachers?
- How will we operationally define "student achievement"—by certain predetermined, extant assessments, such as standardized test results, or will teachers have latitude to develop their own curriculum-based assessments to measure student learning gains?

Once these decisions are made, a district must address the administrative organization and support that are required to put the component in place and sustain it. For example, processes and criteria must be established for applying and successfully completing pay-for-performance projects, a system must be developed for tracking successful participation in group-based pay projects for purposes of evaluation and pay, and a representative districtwide committee should be established to oversee the program, establishing procedures, ensuring compliance, and resolving disputes.

A district must also ensure against the single greatest threat to performance-based pay, whether linked to group or individual performance. The component must be consistently and sustainably funded. Administrative costs for implementing and overseeing the group-based pay component would need to be included in determining funding implications. After the initial design of the program, the administrative costs would primarily consist of additional responsibility pay for a standing advisory committee to serve in interpreting guidelines, evaluating applications, and responding to appeals. Bonus money for group-based pay would be the greatest budget item. Looking to the example of LPS, the district leadership answers the three foundational questions by deciding: (1) participation in group-based pay will be voluntary; (2) "groups" will be defined by grade level at the elementary level, core teams at the middle schools, and departments at the high schools; and (3) student achievement measures can be identified and developed by groups. With these organizing principles in place and administrative procedures in development, the district turns to the question of funding for this compensation component.

The district sets the value of successful participation in group-based pay-for-performance projects at $500 per teacher. Based on polling of teachers, the district estimates that up to 50 percent of the 1,300 teachers in LPS will participate in the compensation option:

650 teachers (50% of 1,300 teachers) × $500/year = $325,000

Selecting Compensation Components

In implementing a restructured teacher compensation system, a district must begin with two steps: (1) develop the aims and criteria of the compensation system and (2) select the compensation components from which the system will be designed. We have presented six components to be considered in the design of a comprehensive compensation system:

1. Competitive base pay

2. Performance evaluation pay

3. Knowledge- and skills-acquisition pay

4. Additional responsibility pay

5. Extraordinary performance pay

6. Group-based pay

The operative term when selecting among these compensation components is *comprehensive.* While each of these components holds merit in and of itself as a means of paying teachers for their roles, contributions, and achievements with students, a district severely limits its ability to meet multiple aims of a compensation system without coupling several—if not *all*—of these components into the design of a comprehensive compensation system.

Thus when undertaking Step 2 of the implementation process—selecting among the compensation components—a district must wisely revisit the aims and criteria that it established in Step 1 of the process as a means of ensuring that the restructured compensation system will be designed to accomplish what is intended.

STEP 3: PLAN FOR IMPLEMENTATION

The actual selection of given compensation components and the design of the comprehensive compensation system that results from Steps 1 and 2 will greatly determine the specific implementation issues with which a district must contend. For instance, if a district designs a model for teacher compensation that is similar to its current model, then the implementation of the new components will be less complex and issues of change less challenging. For a district that pursues a wholesale restructuring of its teacher compensation system, the implementation issues are, clearly, far more intricate, thereby requiring a far more complex series of implementation steps.

Whether a district is pursuing relatively unobtrusive change or a complete reconstitution of its teacher compensation system, a series of implementation issues are apparent. In the following list, we discuss five broad categories of implementation issues.

1. *Alignment with the strategic plan.* Most school districts engage in long-range strategic planning in order to marshal resources and set organizational direction to meet the mission statement and achieve the vision of the school district. Teacher compensation, as a significant system within the organization, should be aligned in its purpose and, to the extent appropriate, should be supportive of the goals of the district's strategic plan. For example, if a district has set a strategic goal to address the need of reaching students from diverse ethnic backgrounds and has identified teacher training in cultural competency as a means to achieve that end, then a comprehensive compensation system with knowledge and skills acquisition components integral to it aligns well with and supports this focus of the strategic plan.

2. *Prerequisite conditions and systems in place.* When a teacher plans for instruction, it is important for her to take into account her students' prior learning. What should students already know in order to engage in the planned lesson? Considering the prerequisites of each of the selected components of a compensation system is equally important to a school district implementing a comprehensive system for paying teachers. A school district must ask, "What are the required associated or tangential systems in place to support each of the selected compensation components?" Consider the performance evaluation component, for example. While the component may be attractive to a district for its promise of linking the evaluation of teacher performance to teacher pay, the component is essentially unavailable to that district if it does not already have in place a valid and reliable means of evaluating teacher performance. If principals are unable to complete the required number of formal observations and evaluation conferences during a given evaluation cycle, if teachers have persistent concerns about the subjectivity of the evaluation system, or if other concerns about the fairness and objectivity of the evaluation system are evident, then that district is not in a position to implement that particular compensation component. The presence of a trustworthy teacher evaluation system is a prerequisite for a performance evaluation compensation component, just as a system for professional development is a prerequisite for knowledge and skills acquisition components, and a student achievement data management system is potentially a prerequisite for a group-based pay component.

3. *Logistical details of each component spelled out.* As discussed in much greater detail under the heading "Step 2: Select Compensation Components" previously in this chapter, there are a host of administrative details to which a district's leadership must attend in order to put each of the components

into place. Without reviewing those again here, we simply reiterate that "the devil is in the details." And, if the details are left unattended, they will certainly be the undoing of even the best-intentioned compensation system.

4. *Timeline considered.* When a good idea is at hand, it seems to be human nature to want implementation to be immediate. In restructuring a system as complex as teacher compensation, immediate implementation simply is not possible. The more different the new model is from the current compensation system, the more complicated and time consuming the implementation will be. Indeed, this principle holds true among the various components as well. A school district can ask, "On what timeline will various components be 'rolled out'?" For example, a school district decides to significantly restructure its teacher compensation system, which currently consists of a conventional multilane salary schedule. Thus there are several components that can be addressed sooner and others that will require a good deal more time. The district can, for instance, redefine its salary lanes and its tuition-assistance program to better approximate a knowledge acquisition component, expand the positions of additional responsibility eligible for stipends, and begin compensating National Board certified teachers with little or no lead time or disruption to the current compensation system. On the other hand, the implementation of skills blocks, an accomplished professional teacher program, and group-based pay will need to be staggered in their development and integration into the system.

5. *Transitioning processes in place.* Related to the issue of timing is the issue of transitioning. Transitioning is consideration of the issues of how teachers—real people drawing real salaries as their livelihoods—will move from the current compensation system to the restructured compensation system without being penalized. Just consider some of the concerns related to transitioning to a more competitive base salary schedule. In the case of LPS, as presented previously in this chapter and illustrated in Figure 6.2, the school is highly competitive in some lanes and steps on its existing salary schedule but is far less competitive at others. If the district adopts a more uniformly competitive salary schedule, then what concessions are made for those teachers who are presently making more on the current salary schedule at a given step than they would at the same step on a revised salary schedule?

The implementation issues noted previously are loosely ordered in terms of the sequence in which they are likely to be addressed, but they are not discrete. In other words, one is likely to segue into another, and details associated with a previous topic may go unresolved while a district is already pursuing the next issue. In some instances, certain topics may demand more or less time, energy, attention, and resources to resolve, depending upon a school district's particular circumstances and needs.

It is also important to note that there are two critically important issues that have not yet been addressed, but which will be influential—positively or negatively—in any school district. These topics are *communication* and *funding*. Because of the ubiquitous and significant roles that these play in implementing a restructured teacher compensation system, the issues of communication and funding are addressed separately and in greater detail in the following sections.

Communication

In Chapter 5, we identified *clarity and communication* as one of five design principles of an effective compensation system. This design principle requires that a system for paying teachers be simple and easy to communicate. The district leadership that attends to clarity recognizes the importance of making the compensation system understandable to all of its various constituents—teachers, administrators, and the public, alike. But, as we cautioned earlier, a district cannot artificially simplify its compensation system and thereby jeopardize the integrity of the system just for the sake of simplicity. Compensation systems are complex. For this reason, a district must also create a communication plan to facilitate the implementation of its restructured compensation system.

Sometimes a communication plan is misunderstood to be a slick public relations campaign, a marketing initiative, or, even more pejoratively, propaganda. These characterizations misrepresent the purpose of communication in pursing reform in a complex, public institution such as a school district. The purpose of a district's communication efforts should be threefold:

1. To inform people about the new compensation system so it is accurately understood

2. To solicit feedback about the new compensation system in order to identify and correct weaknesses in its purpose or design

3. To foster support for the compensation system in order to initiate, unveil, and, eventually, institutionalize the change

Of course, a communication plan is dependent in large part on the actual compensation model that a school district decides to pursue. Thus, in this section, only the fundamentally salient issues of a communication plan are addressed. Once a district makes key decisions regarding the design and implementation of the restructured compensation system, then the specific details of a communication plan need to be further developed. Here, we address the particular role of *constituents*.

A central tenet of good communication is to know your audience. Educational practice is replete with examples of failed compensation systems that were poorly communicated and little understood by the people they most affected. In the case of teacher compensation, the obvious and main audience consists of teachers, who, quite literally, have a vested interest in the district's compensation system. For this reason, a district must provide opportunities for teachers to have a voice in the various processes of developing, designing, implementing, and evaluating its compensation system. Without participation in the process, teachers are less likely to trust changes and will view such changes as being thrust upon them, rather than as favorable changes. Change of any sort is typically viewed with consternation and suspicion, which breed resistance to being open to new ideas or to willingness to lend support. Informing teachers, soliciting input, responding to concerns, and seeking support are vital communication strategies in pursuing a restructured approach to teacher compensation. As noted in a report by the Southern Regional Education Board, "A new teacher compensation system will not succeed without a critical mass of teachers who 'buy in.'"[3]

Districts must also give particular consideration to communication with teacher unions. Teacher unions may be local or state labor organizations that wield contract bargaining authority, or they may be affiliations of national teacher organizations such as the National Education Association (NEA) or the American Federation of Teachers (AFT), which represent professional teachers' interests. Broadly and historically speaking, teacher unions have strongly supported efforts to increase base teacher pay, but they have opposed plans that pit teacher-against-teacher for limited pots of money or that rely on invalid or subjective measures of performance.[4] Nevertheless, several notable, recent examples of union support for differentiated compensation models suggest at least a discontent with the traditional uniform salary schedule and a willingness to pursue new compensation models that more directly support and reflect the core mission of teaching and learning in schools.

The Cincinnati Public Schools garnered considerable national attention for its initiative at the turn of the millennium to restructure its compensation system into a career ladder. It is worth noting that the district effort was supported by the Ohio Department of Education (ODOE), which had been exploring the possibility of creating a statewide career ladder system for purposes of teacher license, with the broad-reaching intent of eventually having all Ohio school districts compensate teachers according to a career ladder model. At the time, Cincinnati Public Schools served as a proving ground for the state's initiative. However, the economic downturn following the 1990s had profound effects on the state's efforts and, according to a presentation by representatives of the ODOE at a meeting in March 2002, the statewide career ladder initiative was slowed due to budget considerations. Then, in May of that year, the Cincinnati Federation of Teachers (CFT) held a vote among its members to decide whether to support implementation of the career ladder compensation model beyond the pilot year. Cincinnati teachers rejected the proposed career ladder model by a vote of 1,892 to 73. Reasons cited for rejecting the plan included a fear that the restructured system would be susceptible to budget fluctuations, would result ultimately in lower pay for teachers, had an inadequate piloting phase, and had inadequate ties to professional development.[5]

Denver Public Schools has also pursued a new model of teacher compensation in recent years and has done so in close partnership with the Denver Classroom Teachers Association (DCTA). The restructured compensation system in Denver is focused on a pay-for-performance plan, rather than a career ladder model, as in Cincinnati. As of the spring of 2005, the plan was supported by the Denver Public Schools leadership and approved by the DCTA membership. In the fall of 2005, Denver voters approved a $25 million levy to pay for the new system. As promising as the scenario seems, there is some irony in the fact that in the spring of 2005, the Denver Classroom Teachers Association battled with Denver Public Schools and threatened a walkout. What was the source of contention? The district and the teachers' association had locked horns over step increases on the district's uniform salary schedule. Therefore, even in the midst of innovative compensation reform, the centrality of the salary schedule in establishing an equitable base salary for all teachers remains a core focus of teacher unions.

Denver's current experiences also point to a third important constituency in the compensation equation: the public. In a nationally representative public poll conducted in November 2004, more than 70 percent of the general public believed that the way teachers are traditionally paid needed to be changed.[6] There seems to be a commonly held belief that teachers—especially the most effective ones—are not paid what they should. Hence, there is a willingness among much of the public in the United States to pay teachers accordingly. But the same poll also found that barely 60 percent of the general public favored increasing teacher salaries across the board. Rather, respondents favored increased pay for teachers working in high-poverty schools, teachers in hard-to-staff subject areas, and teachers who demonstrated gains in student achievement. What are the implications for school districts? In designing and communicating a restructured compensation system, a district must be cognizant of the local community's views on teacher compensation, which may or may not reflect the findings of the 2004 poll. Then, a district must give particular attention to communicating the proposed compensation plan in clear, layman's terms.

A simple example of a potential communication pitfall, for instance, is found in our use of the concept of a "knowledge acquisition" component. Without reviewing the extensive explanations offered in this and previous chapters, it's clear enough that the term is specialized and probably largely meaningless to the general public. The role, then, of communication is to *translate* the term into clearer language: "Our compensation system will address our need for teachers in hard-to-staff subject areas such as math and science by paying teachers who already have or who work to earn licensure in one of these critical shortage subjects." Communication with the public must be honest and accessible, while not being mired in detail or patronizing. After all, public support is vital, whether in concrete ways such as Denver's situation where the public actually voted to assess taxes to support a new compensation plan, or in situations where public support is important in a more generalized sense of acceptance and approval of the direction set by the district.

Another key constituent group in the implementation of a teacher compensation system is building-level administrators, that is, principals and assistant principals. In the comprehensive model of teacher compensation that we have presented, several components focus directly on the *quality* of teachers. Teacher quality is promoted, developed, and rewarded in this compensation system, be it through demonstrated and targeted professional development; the consistent meeting or exceeding of the district's performance standards; performance of additional duties or responsibilities that contribute to the educational program; achievement of recognized professional excellence; or demonstrated and significant contributions to a collaborative impact on student achievement. Each of these components requires the involvement and support, and sometimes the direction setting and evaluation, of a school-level leader. In our experience, the success of conceptually strong designs for teacher compensation and teacher evaluation has hinged upon a district's subsequent success in developing the requisite knowledge, skills, and commitment of principals and assistant principals who serve the practical, daily role of leading the instructional program.

Communication is a central means of ensuring successful implementation of a restructured teacher compensation system, and a district's leadership must consider the perspectives, needs, and roles of various constituent groups within the district in order to develop a communication plan. Figure 6.4 presents an analysis of several key groups—namely teachers, school administrators, and community members—and the generalized views that each may hold regarding the potential opportunities and threats from each group's perspectives. This understanding helps to shape a plan for communicating information about the proposed compensation model to different constituencies.

Inherent to communicating effectively with multiple constituent groups, each of which brings varying perspectives, is the need to approach communication through multiple avenues. While the circumstances, recourses, and particular history of a school district will all bear on determining the most effective means of communication, Figure 6.5 lists several possible methods for promoting a district's chosen compensation plan. Rather than select a few strategies, the best method is to build support for the plan across the various constituency groups by employing multiple avenues for communication.

Figure 6.4   Opportunities-Threat Force Field Analysis

Constituents	Opportunities	Threats
Teachers	+ Potential for increased pay + Incentives to demonstrably improve professional knowledge and skills + Incentives to achieve professional excellence + Incentives to collaborate and demonstrably improve student achievement + Attractiveness of joining the district + Incentives to remain with the district over time	− Concerns about subjectivity of performance evaluations − Concerns about inequities among rewards − Potential for comparatively slower growth in income over time − Concerns about sustainability of unconventional compensation components over time
School Administrators	+ Better qualified and skilled teachers + Availability of incentives for teachers to take on additional roles at school level, which may ease administrative loads of school leaders + Potential for improved student achievement as a result of systemic approach to teacher compensation promoting teacher quality	− Increased administrative responsibilities in implementing many of the components − Increased supervisory responsibilities required of several components − Increased interpersonal burden due to high-stakes role of annual teacher evaluations—pressure to inflate evaluations
The Public: Parents, Taxpayers, Businesses	+ Improved teacher quality + Improved student achievement + Stable population of teachers in hard-to-staff subject areas + Increased competitiveness of school district, attractive to new businesses and residents + Better educated students compete for better paying jobs supporting the tax base for all + As schools improve, property values go up + Reduced need and expense of retraining/remediating graduates	− Increased district budget − Tax increases

Budgeting for Sustainability

Ultimately, implementation of a teacher compensation system is dependent upon adequate and sustainable funding. Of course, a multiplicity of variables is at play in any district's effort to identify budgetary implications for restructuring its teacher compensation system. Funding is impacted, for example, by the size of the district, the taxing authority of the school board, the demographics of the teaching population, the economic demographics of the community, the district's current budget commitments, the structure of the district's current teacher compensation system, and much, much more. Although we obviously cannot account for all the variables here and the myriad budgetary implications for the nearly 14,000 school districts in the nation, we return to LPS by way of an example.

Figure 6.5   Promoting the Plan

Method	Deployment Issues
Focus Groups	• Teachers • School administrators • Community and business leaders • Students • Neighborhood groups
Grass Roots Campaign	• Mobilize parent groups • Mobilize teacher groups
Fact Sheets	• Mail/e-mail to school district employees • Mail/e-mail to key communicators • Place in public places (e.g., schools, libraries, grocery stores) • Post on district Web site
Key Communicators	• Local business people, community and church leaders, realtors, etc.
Media: Print, TV, Radio, Electronic	• Press releases • Letters-to-the-editor • Human interest stories • Guests on talk radio • School district newsletter • School district Web site and listserv
Presentations	• School Board meetings • Public hearings • School faculty meetings • PTA meetings • Civic association meetings
Neighborhood Coffees	• Local neighborhoods

In reviewing innovative compensation models and working with school districts that have pursued implementation, we have seen that a comprehensive component-based system for teacher compensation can require as little as a 2 percent increase in a district's current budget for teacher pay. It is important to note, however, that this 2 percent increase does *not* account for such initial and ongoing costs as benchmarking a base salary schedule or designing and administering new compensation components (e.g., the administrative costs associated with developing and overseeing a system for identifying accomplished professional teachers).

In Chapter 5, we reviewed each of the components in a comprehensive teacher compensation system and, using LPS as the example, illustrated realistic estimates of the associated costs. How do these costs add up? Figure 6.6 summarizes the funding implications of implementing the proposed model based upon these estimates.

Building from the LPS salary budget, the anticipated cost of each of the proposed components is calculated as a percentage. The cost of implementation is estimated to be $1,548,000 or 1.78 percent of the current budget. Notably, the costs of designing and administering the various components are not reflected in this budget, only the recurrent costs of

Figure 6.6   Financial Summary of Compensation Components

Lincoln Public Schools Restructured Compensation Plan Financial Summary		
LPS's Salary Costs Under Conventional Compensation System		
Salary Costs	$86,790,318	
LPS's Salary Costs Under Restructured Compensation System*		
	Estimated Component Costs	% of Conventional Salary Cost
Knowledge Acquisition	$200,000	0.23%
Skills Block	$150,000[†]	0.17%
Additional Responsibility Pay	$503,000	0.57%
Accomplished Professional Teacher	$325,000[†]	0.37%
National Board Certification	$45,000	0.05%
Group-Based Pay for Performance	$325,000	0.37%
TOTAL COSTS **(not including base salaries)**	**$1,548,000**	**1.78%**

* Calculations are based on participation and cost rates as indicated in scenarios from Chapter 5.
[†] Does not include costs for delivery of staff development program.

compensation to teachers. On the other hand, the 1.78 percent increase in the budget does not include the current costs associated with some of these components, such as more than $300,000 currently budgeted for additional responsibility pay and $200,000 for knowledge acquisition. Considering these currently budgeted items, the additional percentage increase for LPS would be 1.21 percent of the current total salary budget.

In addition to reviewing the cost of implementing the proposed model for the school district, it is important to consider the potential impact on individual teachers regarding compensation. Figure 6.7 provides a comparative example of three hypothetical teachers.

In Figure 6.7, *Teacher A* has a bachelor's degree, is on Step 4 of the salary schedule, and has received an unsatisfactory evaluation. Teacher A's salary is frozen for the contract year at $37,946. In addition, Teacher A is not eligible to participate in any of the optional compensation components; therefore, he receives no increase in pay.

By comparison in Figure 6.7, *Teacher B,* like Teacher A, also has a bachelor's degree and is on Step 4 of the salary schedule. Teacher B, however, receives a satisfactory evaluation and, therefore, an annual step increase as well. Teacher B also has successfully participated in four optional compensation components, including a skills block, a school-based additional responsibility, a group-based pay project, and achievement of Accomplished Professional Teacher designation for the first time. In addition to her step increase, Teacher B has earned $2,900 or 6.8 percent of her salary for her exceptional performance.

Figure 6.7   Illustrations of Impact of Proposed Compensation Plan on Teacher Salaries

Proposed Compensation Components for Participating Teachers[1]	Teacher A: Bachelor's Frozen at Step 4 due to IAP*	Teacher B: Bachelor's Moving From Step 4 to Step 5	Teacher C: Master's at Step 14
Base Salary	$37,946	$39,596	$64,015
Step Increase	0	$1,650	N/A†
Knowledge Acquisition Pay[2]	0	0	0
Skills Block Pay[3]	0	$500	$500
Additional Responsibility Pay • Additional duty pay[4] • School-based pay • Division-wide pay	 0 0 0	 0 $400 0	 $1,000 $400 $1,000
Accomplished Professional Teacher	0	$1,500	$1,500
National Board Certification	0	0	$2,500
Group-Based Pay for Performance	0	$500	$500
TOTAL SALARY	**$37,946**	**$44,146**	**$71,415**
Total Dollar Increase From Compensation Components	0	$2,900	$7,400
Components as Percentage Increase of Base Salary[5]	0	6.8%	11.6%

Note: This analysis does not take into account the impact of revisions in the base salary schedule. Rather, the figure provides examples of how the compensation components would affect total annual teacher pay.

* IAP = Improvement Assistance Plan for unsatisfactory performance.

† Assumes no salary increase at Step 14 on current LPS salary schedule due to topping out.

1. Salary impact for the three teacher examples is based on the LPS salary schedule.

2. Assumes no lane change on current salary schedule.

3. Assumes acquisition of one skills block.

4. Assumes assignment for one extra duty pay under current salary structure.

5. Percentages rounded to nearest tenth.

Teacher C in Figure 6.7 is an experienced teacher on Step 14 with a master's degree. According to the current salary schedule, she has topped out and is not eligible for a step increase. However, Teacher C is an excellent teacher and a committed professional who participates in nearly every optional compensation component. Despite the absence of a step increase, Teacher C receives $7,400 in additional compensation, amounting to the equivalent of an 11.6 percent bonus for the year.

Such scenarios demonstrate the real impact of the compensation system on teacher pay and are constructive in developing and implementing both a budget and a communication plan.

STEP 4: PILOT THE RESTRUCTURED COMPENSATION SYSTEM

The fourth major step in implementing a restructured compensation system is to pilot the program. The primary purpose of piloting the system is to identify and remedy any unforeseen barriers or unintended consequences. The pilot is a trial run, intended to identify strengths and weaknesses of the design and implementation and to make improvements before full-scale implementation of the new system. Several guideline actions are necessary for a pilot study.

- Design the pilot project to include fail-safe structures to protect participants, evaluation methods designed to make decisions based on actual results, and administrative implementation structures (e.g., an APT committee, a skills block training sequence) in order to test the actual components in action.
- Secure resources (i.e., funds and administrative support) for implementation of the pilot project.
- Identify participants, including teachers, administrators, and building locations. It is preferable that participation be voluntary.
- Conduct training for participants.
- Implement the pilot for a designated period of time.
- Conduct formative evaluation, avoiding premature decisions and allowing the program to operate for an agreed-upon period of time in order to avoid knee-jerk resistance to change that is oftentimes associated with new programs.
- Revise individual components of the comprehensive model as necessary and continue implementation.
- Conduct summative evaluation of the pilot project at the designated end of the pilot.
- Use evaluation results to design a plan for districtwide expansion.

STEP 5: DISTRICTWIDE IMPLEMENTATION AND EVALUATION

Based on the outcomes of the pilot project, plans for expansion of the restructured compensation system to districtwide implementation can be made. Indeed, the outline for conducting the pilot study largely provides the structure for districtwide implementation, as reflected in the following implementation guidelines.

- Identify a means of transitioning teachers from the old compensation system to the new one. The particular compensation model selected will drive this step. If the selected model is based on a multilane salary schedule, then all teachers can be transitioned into the new system seamlessly. If the selected model is greatly different from the current system, then provisions will need to be made for (1) transitioning teachers in to the new system and/or (2) allowing current teachers to opt to participate in the new system.
- Finalize evaluation methods. If possible, evaluation methods would mirror those used in the pilot study, thereby providing baseline data for purposes of comparison.
- Put administrative structures in place (e.g., APT committee, criteria for group-based pay, system for tracking skills block completion).
- Secure resources (i.e., the funds and administrative support) for implementation of a new compensation system. This step needs to be coordinated with the budget cycle, which may be tied to the fiscal year rather than the academic calendar.
- Determine a distinct period of time during which the system will be implemented without substantive change in order to provide time for it to become established.
- Conduct initial training for all participants and make provisions for ongoing training, as needed.
- Conduct formative evaluation, avoiding premature decisions and allowing the program to operate for the agreed-upon period of time. Establishing a "no judgment" time period in advance of implementation can be useful in avoiding reactionary decisions about a new program based on discomfort with change or unfamiliarity.
- Revise individual components or the comprehensive model as necessary and continue implementation.
- Conduct summative or comprehensive evaluation of the project at a designated point in time.
- Use evaluation results to refine and improve the new compensation system.
- Plan for ongoing, periodic evaluation of the system.

The purpose of program evaluation is twofold. First, program evaluation provides data and a standard of judgment by which to assess the effectiveness of a program and to identify areas of strengths and weaknesses that may be built or improved upon, respectively. This is typically referred to as *formative evaluation*. Formative evaluation is conducted during the course of implementation and is intended to provide the kinds of corrective feedback or data that can allow for corrections in design or implementation of the program. As such, formative evaluation will play a central role in the pilot phase of the project. However, ongoing, periodic evaluation is also a component of the division-wide implementation of a

new compensation system. Therefore, formative evaluation has an important role to play in the division's ongoing implementation of a new teacher
compensation system.

Second, program evaluation provides data and a standard of judgment
by which to assess the worth, value, or merit of a program. This is typically
referred to as *summative evaluation.* Summative evaluation is conducted at
a point in time determined to be a concluding point or significant
milestone in a program's implementation. For example, a school district
could determine in advance of implementation that the new compensation
plan will be allowed to operate for a specific number of years (e.g., three
years) before making any substantive changes to it. The purpose of providing this window for implementation is to permit sufficient time for the
new system to become institutionalized within the school division and
familiar to its users (i.e., teachers and administrators). Then, after this
period of time has elapsed, summative data are collected and analyzed to
evaluate the effectiveness of the new compensation system in meeting the
district's intended goals.

Whether formative or summative in nature, evaluation methods
should be tied to the goals of the intended program. In the case of a
restructured compensation system, the broad goals are to attract, develop,
and retain quality teachers. Thus the evaluation criteria should speak to
the accomplishment of these goals. Figure 6.8 presents information that
indicates each of these goals, as well as suggested evaluation questions,
possible data sources, and the intended use for each.

CONCLUDING THOUGHTS:
TEACHER QUALITY AND TEACHER PAY

Implementation, communication, funding, and evaluation of a new
teacher compensation system are ultimately dependent upon the selection
of a model for restructuring. In this chapter we have provided an outline
for addressing pertinent issues related to implementation, communication, funding, and evaluation, while allowing sufficient flexibility to
accommodate the particularities of a given compensation model or changing conditions. And, throughout the book, we have attempted to make a
strong, logical connection between teacher quality and teacher pay. For too
long, these two essential elements of a public school system have been
only loosely connected.

What seems to be constant in any consideration for connecting teacher
quality and pay is that any teacher compensation system needs to balance
internal equity (i.e., fairness, in terms of equal pay for equal responsibilities)
and *external competitiveness* (i.e., the provision of compensation components that makes the district attractive to prospective and current
teachers). We understand and appreciate the intent and history of the

Figure 6.8 Evaluation Criteria for Implementing a Restructured Teacher Compensation System

Goals	Guiding Questions	Possible Data Sources	Purpose	
			Formative	Summative
Attract	Does the district attract an adequate quantity of quality teachers to fill existing and projected needs?	Applications and hiring data	•	•
	What attracts teachers to apply to the district?	Survey data	•	
	Why do teachers select the district?	Survey data	•	
	Why do teachers *not* select the district?	Survey data	•	
Develop	Are our teachers having their professional development needs met?	Survey data • Teachers • Administrators	•	
	Is there evidence that teacher effectiveness is improving or being sustained?	Performance evaluation data sources	•	•
	Is student achievement improving?	Standardized test scores	•	•
		Group-based pay results	•	•
Retain	Does the district retain quality teachers?	Comparative analysis of performance evaluation results and student achievement	•	•
	How many teachers leave the district annually?	Exit data	•	
	Why do teachers leave the district?	Exit survey	•	
	Why do teachers stay with the district?	Survey	•	

conventional multilane salary schedule in terms of internal equity, but we also see its limits in terms of external competitiveness. For these reasons, we suggest that school districts pursue the development, design, and implementation of a comprehensive teacher compensation system that aims to attract, develop, and retain quality teachers by aligning all of its compensation components toward this end. A comprehensive, components-based model for compensation provides teachers multiple incentives and pathways to increase their total annual compensation, while also promoting and achieving the goals of the school district.

We conclude with a few thoughts to guide a district's newly implemented teacher compensation system:

- Make changes that are productive and different, but not radical. Few people are comfortable with radical changes related to their salary.
- Gain a critical mass of support among key constituent groups, such as policymakers (school board), district administrators, teachers, and community members, but do not expect absolute consensus before moving forward.
- Communicate early and often, and remember that communication should flow in at least two directions.
- Ensure sustained political will. Ultimately, compensation is a decision of taxpayers and policymakers.
- Make sure that your compensation system is fair, easily communicated and understood, and feasible.

And remember, compensation is not simply about paying people for their work. When designed and used intentionally as a system, teacher compensation is about attracting, developing, and retaining quality teachers in support of the core mission and goals of the school district.

Endnotes

CHAPTER 1

1. Wright, S. P., Horn, S. P., & Sanders, W. L. (1997). Teacher and classroom context effects on student achievement: Implications for teacher evaluation. *Journal of Personnel Evaluation in Education, 11,* 63.

2. Nye, B., Konstantopoulos, S., & Hedges, L. V. (2004). How large are teacher effects? *Educational Evaluation and Policy Analysis, 26,* 247.

3. Nye, Konstantopoulos, & Hedges, 2004, p. 253.

4. No Child Left Behind Act of 2001, Pub. L. No. 107–110, 115 Stat. 1425 (2002).

5. Stronge, J. H. (2002). *Qualities of effective teachers.* Washington, DC: Association for Supervision and Curriculum Development.

6. Thompson, D. C., & Wood, R. C. (1998). *Money and schools: A handbook for practitioners.* Boston: Allyn & Bacon.

7. Ingersoll, R. M. (2001). Teacher turnover and teacher shortages: An organizational analysis. *American Educational Research Journal, 38,* 499–534; Ingersoll, R. M., & Smith, T. M. (2003). The wrong solution to the teacher shortage. *Educational Leadership, 60*(8), 30–33; Liu, X., & Meyer, J. P. (2005). Teachers' perceptions of their jobs: A multilevel analysis of the Teacher Follow-Up Survey for 1994–1995. *Teachers College Record, 107,* 985–1003; Odden, A., & Kelley, C. (2002). *Paying teachers for what they know and do: New and smarter compensation strategies to improve schools* (2nd ed.). Thousand Oaks, CA: Corwin.

8. Ingersoll, 2001; Ingersoll & Smith, 2003.

9. Johnson, S. M. (1986). Incentives for teachers: What motivates, what matters. *Educational Administration Quarterly, 22,* 54–79; Johnson, S. M. (1990). *Teachers at work: Achieving success in our schools.* New York: Basic Books; Liu, E., Johnson, S. M., & Peske, H. G. (2004). New teachers and the Massachusetts signing bonus: The limits of inducements. *Educational Evaluation and Policy Analysis, 26,* 217–236.

10. Deci, E. L., Koestner, R., & Ryan, R. M. (2001). Extrinsic rewards and intrinsic motivation in education: Reconsidered once again. *Review of Educational Research, 71,* 1–27; Kohn, A. (1993, October 17). For best results, forget the bonus. *New York Times.* Retrieved June 2, 2005, from http://www.alfiekohn.org/managing/fbrftb.htm; Ryan, R. M., & Deci, E. L. (2000). Intrinsic and extrinsic motivations: Classic definitions and new directions. *Contemporary Educational Psychology, 25,* 54–67 (p. 56).

11. Odden, A., Kellor, E., Heneman, H., & Milanowski, A. (1999). *School-based performance award programs: Design and administration issues synthesized from eight programs.* Madison: Wisconsin Center for Education Research.

12. Ryan & Deci, 2000, p. 56.

13. Deci, Koestner, & Ryan, 2001; Ryan & Deci, 2000.

14. Rebore, R. W. (2001). *Human resources administration in education* (6th ed.). Boston: Allyn & Bacon; Odden & Kelley, 2002; Vroom, V. H. (1964). *Work and motivation.* New York: John Wiley.

15. Ryan & Deci, 2000.

16. Ryan & Deci, 2000, p. 59.

17. Tschannen-Moran, M., Hoy, A. W., & Hoy, W. K. (1998). Teacher efficacy: Its meaning and measure. *Review of Educational Research, 68*(2), 202–248.

18. Ryan & Deci, 2000.

19. For example, Kohn, 1993.

20. Odden, A. (2000a). *Emerging findings in teacher compensation.* Retrieved June 1, 2005, from http://www.wcer.wisc.edu/cpre/tcomp/research/general/findings.asp

21. Firestone, W. A. (1994). Redesigning teacher salary systems for educational reform. *American Educational Research Journal, 31,* 549–574.

22. Jenkins, G. D., Jr., Gupta, N., Mitra, A., & Shaw, J. D. (1998). Are financial incentives related to performance? A meta-analytic review of empirical research. *Journal of Applied Psychology, 83,* 777–787; Rebore, 2001.

23. Odden & Kelley, 2002.

24. Ibid.

25. Wright, Horn, & Sanders, 1997.

26. Peterson, B. (2000). *Merit: To pay or not to pay.* Retrieved April 4, 2005, from http://www.rethinkingschools.org/Archives/14_03/mert143.shtm

27. Weld, J. (1998, June 3). Beyond the salary carrot. *Education Week, 17*(38), 33.

28. Deci, Koestner, & Ryan, 2001.

29. Firestone, 1994; Odden & Kelley, 2002.

30. Thompson, D. C., & Wood, R. C. (1998). *Money and schools: A handbook for practitioners.* Larchmont, NY: Eye on Education.

31. Firestone, 1994; Odden & Kelley, 2002.

32. Firestone, 1994.

33. Odden & Kelley, 2002; Sharpes, D. (1987). Incentive pay and the promotion of teaching proficiencies. *The Clearing House, 60,* 406–408.

34. Johnson, 1986.

35. Hanushek, 1994, p. 86, quoted in Odden & Kelley, 2002.

36. Thompson & Wood, 1998; Ballou, D., & Podgursky, M. (1993). Teachers' attitudes toward merit pay: Examining conventional wisdom. *Industrial and Labor Relations Review, 47,* 50–61; Nelson, W. (2001). Timequake alert: Why payment by results is the worst "new" reform to share the educational world, again and again. *Phi Delta Kappan, 82,* 384–389.

37. Firestone, 1994.

38. Johnson, 1986.

39. Quoted in Odden & Kelley, 2002, p. 34.

40. Ebmeier, H., & Hart, A. W. (1992). The effects of a career-ladder program on school organizational process. *Educational Evaluation and Policy Analysis, 14,* 261–281; Firestone, 1994; Jesness, J. (2001, April 4). Teacher merit pay. *Education

Week, 20(29), 37, 39; Keiffer-Barone, S., & Ware, K. (2001). Growing great teachers in Cincinnati. *Educational Leadership, 58*(8), 56–59; Makkonen, R. (2004). Taking care of novice teachers. *Harvard Education Letter, 20*(3), 1–4; Odden & Kelley, 2002.

41. Jesness, 2001.

42. NBPTS. (2001). *The impact of National Board Certification on teachers: A survey of National Board Certified teachers and assessors.* Retrieved April 4, 2005, from http://www.nbpts.org/pdf/ResRpt.pdf; Wright, Sanders, & Horn, 1997.

43. Kelley, C., Odden, A., Milanowski, A., & Heneman, H. (2000). *The motivational effects of school-based performance awards* (CPRE Policy Briefs, RB-29). Philadelphia: University of Pennsylvania, Consortium for Policy Research in Education.

44. Gursky, D. (1992, April). Not without merit pay. *Teacher Magazine,* 23–25.

45. Spencer, J. (2005, April 4). HISD has incentives to change merit pay. *Houston Chronicle* online. Retrieved April 11, 2005, from http://www.chron.com/cs/CDA/ssistory.mpl/metropolitan/3116498

46. Odden, A. (2001). The new school finance. *Phi Delta Kappan, 83*(1), 85–91.

47. Kelley, Odden, et al., 2000.

48. Ibid.

49. Gursky, 1992, p. 24.

50. Nelson, 2001.

51. Conley, S. C., Gould, J., Muncey, D. E., & White, N. (2001). Negotiating a pay-for performance program encouraged by state mandate. *Journal of Personnel Evaluation in Education, 15,* 137–148.

52. Cascio, W. F. (2003). *Managing human resources: Productivity, quality of work life, profits* (6th ed.). Boston: McGraw-Hill/Irwin.

53. Solmon, L. C., & Podgursky, M. (2000). *The pros and cons of performance-based compensation.* Santa Monica, CA: Milken Family Foundation. (ERIC Document Reproduction Service No. ED445393)

54. Ramirez, A. (2001). How merit pay undermines education. *Educational Leadership, 58*(5), 16–20.

55. Risher, H. (1999). Merit pay can be a hard sell. *Public Management, 81*(7), 8–13.

56. Ibid.

57. Solmon & Podgursky, 2000.

58. Ibid.

59. Odden & Kelley, 2002.

60. Alexander, K., & Salmon, R. G. (1995). *Public school finance.* Boston: Allyn & Bacon; Swanson, A. D., & King, R. A. (1997). *School finance: Its economics and politics* (2nd ed.). New York: Longman.

61. Nelson, F. H., & Drown, R. (2003). *Survey and analysis of teacher salary trends 2002.* Washington, DC: American Federation of Teachers.

62. Odden & Kelley, 2002.

63. Ingersoll, R. M. (1999). *Teacher shortages, teacher turnover, and the organization of schools: A CTP working paper.* Seattle, WA: Center for the Study of Teaching and Policy.

64. Odden, A., Kelley, C., Heneman, H., & Milanowski, A. (2001). *Enhancing teacher quality through knowledge- and skills-based pay* (CPRE Policy Brief RB-34). Philadelphia: University of Pennsylvania, Consortium for Policy Research in Education; Keiffer-Barone, S., & Ware, K. (2001). Growing great teachers in Cincinnati. *Educational Leadership, 58*(8), 56–59.

65. Sanders, W. L., & Horn, S. (1998). Research findings from the Tennessee Value-Added Assessment System (TVAAS) database: Implications for educational evaluation and research. *Journal of Personnel Evaluation in Education, 12,* 247–256.

66. Stronge, 2002.

67. Thompson & Wood, 1998.

68. Hoerr, T. R. (1998). A case for merit pay. *Phi Delta Kappan, 80,* 326.

69. Odden, 2001.

70. Stronge, 2002.

71. Murnane, R. J., Singer, J. D., Willet, J. B., Kemple, J. J., & Olsen, R. J. (1991). *Who will teach? Policies that matter.* Cambridge, MA: Harvard University Press.

72. Odden & Kelley, 2002.

73. Odden & Kelley, 2002.

74. Kelley, C. (1997). Teacher compensation and organization. *Educational Evaluation and Policy Analysis, 19,* 15–28; Odden, 2001.

75. Firestone, W. A. (1994). Redesigning teacher salary systems for educational reform. *American Educational Research Journal, 31,* 549–574; Mohrman, A. M., Jr., Mohrman, S. A., & Odden, A. R. (1996). Aligning teacher compensation with systemic school reform: Skill-based pay and group-based performance rewards. *Educational Evaluation and Policy Analysis, 18,* 51–71.

CHAPTER 2

1. Kouzes, J. M., & Posner, B. Z. (1995). *The leadership challenge: How to keep getting extraordinary things done in organizations.* San Francisco: Jossey-Bass; Nanus, B. (1992). *Visionary leadership.* San Francisco: Jossey-Bass.

2. DuFour, R., & Eaker, R. (1998). *Professional learning communities at work: Best practices for enhancing student achievement* (p. 84). Bloomington, IN: National Educational Service.

3. DuFour & Eaker, 1998, p. 58.

4. DuFour, R. (1997). Make the words of mission statements come to life. *Journal of Staff Development, 18*(3), 54–55; DuFour & Eaker, 1998.

5. DuFour, 1997.

6. Hassel, B. C. (2002, May). *Better pay for better teaching: Making teacher compensation pay off in the age of accountability.* Washington, DC: Progressive Policy Institute; Koppich, J. E., & Kerchner, C. T. (1999). Organizing the other half of teaching. In L. Darling-Hammond & G. Sykes (Eds.), *Teaching as the learning profession: Handbook of policy and practice* (pp. 315–340). San Francisco: Jossey-Bass.

7. Kelley, C. (1997). Teacher compensation and organization. *Educational Evaluation and Policy Analysis, 19,* 15–28; Odden, A. (2001). The new school finance. *Phi Delta Kappan, 83,* 85–91.

8. Firestone, W. A. (1994). Redesigning teacher salary systems for educational reform. *American Educational Research Journal, 31,* 549–574; Mohrman, A. M., Jr., Mohrman, S. A., & Odden, A. R. (1996). Aligning teacher compensation with systemic school reform: Skill-based pay and group-based performance rewards. *Educational Evaluation and Policy Analysis, 18,* 51–71.

9. Knoster, T. (1991, June). *Factors in managing complex change.* Presentation at the conference of The Association for People with Severe Disabilities (TASH), Washington, DC. Adapted from Ambrose, D. (1987). *Managing complex change.* Pittsburgh, PA: The Enterprise Group.

10. Liu, E., Johnson, S. M., & Peske, H. G. (2004). New teachers and the Massachusetts signing bonus: The limits of inducements. *Educational Evaluation and Policy Analysis, 26,* 217–236; McDonnell, L. M., & Elmore, R. F. (1987). Getting the job done: Alternative policy instruments. *Educational Evaluation and Policy Analysis, 9,* 133–152.

11. Ibid.

12. Stronge, J. H. (1997). Improving schools through teacher evaluation. In J. H. Stronge (Ed.), *Evaluating teaching: A guide to current thinking and best practice.* Thousand Oaks, CA: Corwin.

CHAPTER 3

1. Holcomb, E. (2001). *Asking the right questions: Techniques for collaboration and school change* (2nd ed.). Thousand Oaks, CA: Corwin Press.

2. Bryson, J. M. (1995). *Strategic planning for public and nonprofit organizations.* San Francisco: Jossey-Bass.

3. Gerald, D. E., & Hussar, W. J. (2000). Projections of education statistics to 2010. (NCES Publication No. NCES 2000–071). Washington, DC: U.S. Department of Education, Office of Educational Research and Improvement.

4. Hussar, W. J. (1999). Predicting the need for newly hired teachers in the United States to 2008–09. (NCES Publication No. NCES 1999–026). Washington, DC: U.S. Government Printing Office.

5. Edwards, V. B. (Ed.). (2000). Quality counts 2000 [Special Issue]. *Education Week, 29*(1).

6. Stewart, K. J., & Reed, S. B. (1999). Consumer price index research series using current methods, 1978–1998. In *Family Economics and Nutrition Review 13*(1), 101–104. (Taken from *Monthly Labor Review, 122*[6], pp. 29–38).

7. Martocchio, J. J. (2003). *Employee benefits: A primer for human resource professionals.* Boston: McGraw-Hill/Irwin.

8. Hoy, W. K., & Miskel, C. G. (2001). *Educational administration: Theory, research, and practice* (6th ed.). Boston, MA: McGraw-Hill.

9. Loeb, S., & Page, M. E. (2000). Examining the link between teacher wages and student outcomes: The importance of alternative labor market opportunities and non-pecuniary variation. *The Review of Economics and Statistics, 82*(3), 393–408.

10. Lankford, H., Wyckoff, J., & Papa, F. (2000). *The labor market for public school teachers: A descriptive analysis of New York State's teacher workforce.* Albany, NY: New York State Educational Finance Research Consortium.

11. Haycock, K. (2003). Toward a fair distribution of teacher talent. *Educational Leadership, 60*(4), 11–15.

12. Finn, J. D., & Achilles, C. M. (1999). Tennessee's class size study: Findings, implications, misconceptions. *Educational Evaluation and Policy Analysis, 21*(2), 97–109; Molnar, A., Smith, P., Zahorik, J., Palmer, A., Halbach, A., & Ehrle, K. (1999). Evaluating the SAGE program: A pilot program in targeted pupil-teacher reduction in Wisconsin. *Educational Evaluation and Policy Analysis, 21*(2), 165–177.

13. Southeast Center for Teaching Quality. (n.d.). *Listening to the experts: A report on the 2004 South Carolina teacher working conditions survey.* Retrieved April 11, 2005, from http://www.teachingquality.org/pdfs/TWC_SCFinalReport.pdf

CHAPTER 4

1. Note: Although performance-based pay could be read to refer to compensation based on *teacher or* student performance measures, in this text the term will be used to refer specifically to those compensation models that provide pay based on measures of *student achievement.* Individual responsibility pay refers more specifically to evaluated *teacher* behaviors as opposed to student outcomes.

2. The discussion of the single-salary schedule in this chapter does not include a specific example; readers may refer to the discussion in Chapter 3 of the LPS model and its connection to attracting, developing, and retaining quality teachers.

3. Key references for this section: Conley, S., & Odden, A. (1995). Linking teacher compensation to teacher career development. *Educational Evaluation and Policy Analysis, 17,* 219–237; Firestone, W. A. (1994). Redesigning teacher salary systems for educational reform. *American Educational Research Journal, 31,* 549–574; Hanushek, E. A. (1989). The impact of differential expenditures on school performance. *Educational Researcher, 18*(4), 45–62; Hoerr, T. R. (1998). A case for merit pay. *Phi Delta Kappan, 80,* 326; Mohrman, A. M., Jr., Mohrman, S. A., & Odden, A. R. (1996). Aligning teacher compensation with systemic school reform: Skill-based pay and group-based performance rewards. *Educational Evaluation and Policy Analysis, 18,* 51–71; Odden, A., & Kelley, C. (2002). *Paying teachers for what they know and do: New and smarter compensation strategies to improve schools* (2nd ed.). Thousand Oaks, CA: Corwin Press; Ramirez, A. (2001). How merit pay undermines education. *Educational Leadership, 58*(5), 16–20; Swanson, A. D., & King, R. A. (1997). *School finance: Its economics and politics* (2nd ed.). New York: Longman.

4. Odden & Kelley, 2002; Sharpes, D. (1987). Incentive pay and the promotion of teaching proficiencies. *The Clearing House, 60,* 406–408.

5 Odden & Kelley, 2002.

6. See Allen, R. M., & Casbergue, R. M. (2000). *Impact of teachers' recall on their effectiveness in mentoring novice teachers: The unexpected prowess of the transitional stage in the continuum from novice to expert.* Paper presented at the Annual Meeting of the American Educational Research Association, New Orleans, LA; Blair, J. (2000, October 25). ETS study links effective teaching methods to test-score gains. *Education Week, 20*(8), 24; Covino, E. A., & Iwanicki, E. (1996). Experienced teachers: Their constructs of effective teaching. *Journal of Personnel Evaluation in Education, 11,* 325–363; Darling-Hammond, L. (2000). Teacher quality and student achievement: A review of state policy evidence. *Educational Policy Analysis Archives, 8*(1). Retrieved March 21, 2000, from http://epaa.asu.edu/epaa/v8n1/; Durall, P. C. (1995) Years of experience and professional development : A correlation with higher reading scores. Dissertation from Murray State University. ERIC Document: ED386681; Fetler, M. (1999). High school staff characteristics and mathematics test results. *Educational Evaluation and Policy Analysis, 7*(9). Retrieved March 21, 2000, from http://epaa.asu.edu/epaa/v7n9.html; Glass, C. S. (2001). Factors influencing teaching strategies used with children who display attention deficit hyperactivity disorder characteristics. *Education, 122*(1), 70–80; Goldhaber, D. D., & Brewer, D. J. (2000). Does teacher certification matter? High school certification status and student achievement. *Educational Evaluation and Policy Analysis, 22,* 129–145.

7. Nelson, 1995, cited in Swanson & King, 1997, p. 445.

8. Key references for this section: Firestone, W. A. (1991). Merit pay and job enlargement as reforms: Incentives, implementation, and teacher response. *Educational Evaluation and Policy Analysis, 13,* 269–288; Firestone, 1994; Firestone, W. A.,

& Pennell, J. R. (1993). Teacher commitment, working conditions, and differential incentive policies. *Review of Educational Research, 63,* 489–525.

9. Firestone, 1994.

10. Office of Human Resources, Douglas County School District. (2001). Licensed staff pay for performance information. Retrieved June 1, 2005, from http://www1.dcsdk12.org/; Wolf, K., Lichtenstein, G., Bartlett, E., & Hartman, D. (1996). Professional development and teaching portfolios: The Douglas County outstanding teacher program. *Journal of Personnel Evaluation in Education, 10,* 279–286.

11. Douglas County School District. (2001). *Teacher compensation plan.* Castle Rock, CO: Author. Retrieved May 24, 2002, from http://www.dcsd.k12.co.us

12. Key references for this section: Conley & Odden, 1995; Ebmeier, H., & Hart, A. W. (1992). The effects of a career-ladder program on school organizational process. *Educational Evaluation and Policy Analysis, 14,* 261–281; Firestone, 1991; Firestone & Pennell, 1993; Jesness, J. (2001, April 4). Teacher merit pay. *Education Week, 20*(29), 37, 39; Keiffer-Barone, S., & Ware, K. (2001). Growing great teachers in Cincinnati. *Educational Leadership, 58*(8), 56–59; Makkonen, R. (2004). Taking care of novice teachers. *Harvard Education Letter, 20*(3), 1–4; Odden & Kelley, 2002; Risher, H. (2000). Paying for employee competence. *The School Administrator,* 21–24; Solmon, L. C., & Podgursky, M. (2000). *The pros and cons of performance-based compensation.* Santa Monica, CA: Milken Family Foundation. (ERIC Document Reproduction Service No. ED445393)

13. Poston, W. K., & Frase, L. E. (1991). Alternative compensation programs for teachers: Rolling boulders up the mountain of reform. *Phi Delta Kappan, 73,* 317–320.

14. Keiffer-Barone & Ware, 2001; Keller, 2002.

15. Cincinnati Public Schools. (2002). *Teacher evaluation system.* Retrieved June 1, 2005, from http://www.cps-k12.org/general/tchngprof/TES/TEStitle.html

16. Blair, J. (2001, September 19). Teacher performance-pay plan modified in Cincinnati. *Education Week, 21*(3), 3.

17. Laine, S. W. M. (2002). Pay for performance: New thinking in Iowa. *NCREL's Learning Point, 4*(1), 16–18.

18. Ibid.

19. Odden, A., & Wallace, M. (2004). Experimenting with teacher compensation. *School Administrator, 61*(9), 24–28.

20. Office of Human Resources, Douglas County School District, 2001.

21. Schiff, T. (2004, Spring). The path to multiple career paths. *What's on TAP, 2*(1), 5–6. Retrieved June 1, 2005, from http://www.mff.org/tap/

22. Dee, T. S., & Keys, B. J. (2004). Does merit pay reward good teachers? Evidence from a randomized experiment. *Journal of Policy Analysis and Management, 23,* 471–488.

23. Key references for this section: Bushweller, K. (1999). Bonus bucks for teachers. *The American School Board Journal, 186*(8), 21; Conley, S. C., Gould, J., Muncey, D. E., & White, N. (2001). Negotiating a pay-for performance program encouraged by state mandate. *Journal of Personnel Evaluation in Education, 15,* 137–148; Conley & Odden, 1995; Firestone, 1994; Milanowski, A., Odden, A., & Youngs, P. (1998). Teacher knowledge and skill assessments and teacher compensation: An overview of measurement and linkage issues. *Journal of Personnel Evaluation in Education, 12,* 83–101; Mohrman, Mohrman, & Odden, 1996; Nelson, W. (2001). Timequake alert: Why payment by results is the worst "new" reform to share the educational world, again and again. *Phi Delta Kappan, 82,* 384–389; Odden, A. (2000c). New and better forms of teacher compensation are possible.

Phi Delta Kappan, 81, 361–366; Odden, A. (2001). The new school finance. *Phi Delta Kappan, 83,* 85–91; Odden & Kelley, 2002; Odden, A., Kelley, C., Heneman, H., & Milanowski, A. (2001). *Enhancing teacher quality through knowledge- and skills-based pay* (CPRE Policy Brief RB-34). Philadelphia: University of Pennsylvania, Consortium for Policy Research in Education; Odden, A., Kellor, E., Heneman, H., & Milanowski, A. (1999). *School-based performance award programs: Design and administration issues synthesized from eight programs.* Madison: Wisconsin Center for Education Research; Risher, 2000; Solmon & Podgursky, 2000; Wolf, Lichtenstein, Bartlett, & Hartman, 1996.

24. Durall, 1995; Rowan, B., Chiang, F. S., & Miller, R. J. (1997). Using research on employees' performance to study the effects of teachers on student achievement. *Sociology of Education, 70,* 256–284; Wenglinsky, H. (2002). How schools matter: The link between teacher classroom practices and student academic performance. *Educational Policy Analysis Archives, 10*(12). Retrieved February 28, 2002, from http://epaa.asu.edu/epaa/v10n12/

25. Odden, 2000a.

26. Odden, A. (2000b). Initial findings from school district survey. Consortium for Policy Research in Education. Retrieved May 31, 2005, from http://www.wcer.wisc.edu/cpre/tcomp/research/ksbp/findings/district.asp

27. Office of Human Resources, Douglas County School District, 2001; Wyman, W., & Allen, M. (2001, June). *Pay-for-performance: Key questions and lessons from five current models.* ECS Issue Paper. Retrieved May 31, 2005, from http://www.ecs.org/clearinghouse/28/30/2830.htm

28. Milanowski, A. (2003, January 29). The varieties of knowledge and skill-based pay design: A comparison of seven new pay systems for K–12 teachers, *Education Policy Analysis Archives, 11*(4). Retrieved May 15, 2005, from http://epaa.asu.edu/epaa/v11n4/; Odden et al., 2001; Wyman & Allen, 2001.

29. Solmon, L. (2004, Spring). What we have learned about performance pay. *What's on TAP, 2*(1), 17. Retrieved June 1, 2005, from http://www.mff.org/tap/

30. Odden, 2000a.

31. Key references for this section: Ballou, D., & Podgursky, M. (1993). Teachers' attitudes toward merit pay: Examining conventional wisdom. *Industrial and Labor Relations Review, 47,* 50–61; Cascio, W. F. (2003). *Managing human resources: Productivity, quality of work life, profits* (6th ed.). Boston: McGraw-Hill/Irwin; Conley & Odden, 1995; Firestone, 1991, 1994; Firestone & Pennell, 1993; Hanushek, 1994; Hoerr, 1998; Holt, 2001; Nelson, 2001; Odden & Kelley, 2002; Thompson, D. C., & Wood, R. C. (1998). *Money and schools: A handbook for practitioners.* Larchmont, NY: Eye on Education.

32. Kimball, S. M. (2002). Analysis of feedback, enabling conditions and fairness perceptions of teachers in three school districts with new standards-based evaluation systems. *Journal of Personnel Evaluation in Education, 16,* 241–268; Stronge, J. H. (Ed.). (1997). *Evaluating teaching: A guide to current thinking and best practice.* Thousand Oaks, CA: Corwin Press.

33. Odden & Kelley, 2002.

34. Archer, J. (2000, June 14). Changing the rules of the game. *Education Week, 19*(40), 24–29; Vaughn Next Century Learning Center. (n.d.). *Teacher quality and professional growth.* Retrieved May 30, 2002, from http://www.vaughncharter.com

35. Vaughn Next Century Learning Center, n.d.

36. Office of Human Resources, Douglas County School District, 2001.

37. Joint Task Force on Teacher Compensation. (2004). *Tentative agreement between School District No. 1 and Denver Classroom Teachers Association on Professional Compensation System for teachers.* Retrieved June 1, 2005, from http://denverprocomp.org/generalinformation; Odden & Wallace, 2004.

38. Key references for this section: Archer, J. (2001, December 12). Denver pay plan offers lessons, review says. *Education Week, 21*(15), 5; Bushweller, 1999; Community Training and Assistance Center. (2001). *Pathway to results: Pay for performance in Denver.* Boston, MA: Author. Retrieved from http://www.denver.k12.co.us/pdf/PayForPerformance.pdf; Conley, Gould, Muncey, & White, 2001; Firestone, 1994; Goertz, M. E., & Duffy, M. C. (2001). *Assessment and accountability in the 50 states: 1999–2000* (CPRE Research Report Series RR-046). Philadelphia: University of Pennsylvania, Consortium for Policy Research in Education; Holt, 2001; Kelley, C., Heneman, H., & Milanowski, A. (2000). *School-based performance award programs, teacher motivation, and school performance: Findings from a study of three programs* (CPRE Research Report Series RR-44). Philadelphia: University of Pennsylvania, Consortium for Policy Research in Education; Kelley, C., Odden, A., Milanowski, A., & Heneman, H. (2000). *The motivational effects of school-based performance awards* (CPRE Policy Briefs, RB-29). Philadelphia: University of Pennsylvania, Consortium for Policy Research in Education; LaFee, S. (2000). Linking teacher pay to student scores. *The School Administrator,* 14–20; McCollum, S. (2001). How merit pay improves education. *Educational Leadership, 58*(5), 21–24; Nelson, 2001; Odden, 2000c; Odden, 2001; Odden & Kelley, 2002; Odden, Kellor, Heneman, & Milanowski, 1999; Solmon & Podgursky, 2000; Wolf, Lichtenstein, Bartlett, & Hartman, 1996.

39. Odden, 2000a.

40. Urbanski, A., & Erskine, R. (2000). School reform, TURN, and teacher compensation. *Phi Delta Kappan, 81,* 367–370.

41. Community Training and Assistance Center, 2001; Joint Task Force on Teacher Compensation, 2004.

42. Office of Human Resources, Douglas County School District, 2001; Wyman & Allen, 2001.

43. Archer, 2000; Odden & Wallace, 2004; Vaughn Next Century Learning Center, n.d.

44. Solmon, 2004.

45. Florida Department of Education. (2005). *Florida School Recognition Program.* Retrieved September 12, 2005, from http://www.firn.edu/doe/evaluation/schrmain.htm

46. Key references for this section: Leigh, A., & Mead, S. (2005, April). Lifting teacher performance. Progressive Policy Institute Policy report. Retrieved May 15, 2005, from http://www.ppionline.org/; Liu, E., Johnson, S. M., & Peske, H. G. (2004). New teachers and the Massachusetts signing bonus: The limits of inducements. *Educational Evaluation and Policy Analysis, 26,* 217–236; Martocchio, J. J. (2003). *Employee benefits: A primer for human resource professionals.* Boston: McGraw-Hill/Irwin; Schacter, J., & Schiff, T. (2004, Spring). The impact of the Teacher Advancement Program. *What's on TAP, 2*(1), 10–11. Retrieved June 1, 2005, from http://www.mff.org/tap/

47. Hoff, D. J. (2005, May 18). States facing fiscal strain of pensions. *Education Week.* Retrieved September 13, 2005, from http://www.edweek.org

48. Liu, Johnson, & Peske, 2004.

49. Leigh & Mead, 2005; Odden & Wallace, 2004.

50. Nye, B., Konstantopoulos, S., & Hedges, L. V. (2004). How large are teacher effects? *Educational Evaluation and Policy Analysis, 26,* 237–257.

51. Ingersoll, R. M. (2001). Teacher turnover and teacher shortages: An organizational analysis. *American Educational Research Journal, 38,* 499–534.

52. Leigh & Mead, 2005.

53. Schacter & Schiff, 2004.

54. Joint Task Force on Teacher Compensation, 2004.

55. Liu, Johnson, & Peske, 2004.

CHAPTER 5

1. Marzano, R. J., Pickering, D. J., & Pollock, J. E. (2001). *Classroom instruction that works.* Alexandria, VA: Association for Supervision and Curriculum Development. Sanders, W. L., & Horn, S. P. (1998). Research findings from the Tennessee Value-Added Assessment System (TVASS) database: Implications for educational evaluation and research. *Journal of Personnel Evaluation in Education, 12,* 247–256; Stronge, J. H. (2002). *Qualities of effective teachers.* Alexandria, VA: Association for Supervision and Curriculum Development.

2. Moore Johnson, S., & The Project on the Next Generation of Teachers. (2004). *Finders and keepers: Helping teachers survive and thrive in our schools.* San Francisco: Jossey-Bass.

3. Ibid, p. xii.

4. See Tucker, P. D., Stronge, J. H., & Gareis, C. (2002). *Handbook on teacher portfolios for evaluation and professional development.* Larchmont, NY: Eye On Education; and Tucker, P. D., & Stronge, J. H. (2005). *Linking teacher evaluation and student learning.* Alexandria, VA: Association for Supervision and Curriculum Development.

5. Odden, A., & Kelley, C. (2002). *Paying teachers for what they know and do* (2nd ed.). Thousand Oaks, CA: Corwin Press.

6. Ibid.

7. Smith, T. M., & Ingersoll, R. M. (2004). What are the effects of induction and mentoring on beginning teacher turnover? *American Educational Research Journal, 41*(3), 681–714.

8. NBPTS Web site. (n.d.). Retrieved March 5, 2005, from http://www.nbpts .org/nbct/nbctdir_bystate.cfm

9. See, for example: Bond, L., Smith, T., Baker, W., & Hattie, J. (2000). *The certification system of the National Board for Professional Teaching Standards: A construct and consequential validity study.* Greensboro, NC: Center for Educational Research and Evaluation, University of North Carolina at Greensboro; Cavalluzzo, L. C. (2004). *Is National Board Certification an effective signal of teacher quality?* Alexandria, VA: The CAN Corporation. Retrieved February 2, 2005, from http://www.cna .org/documents/CavaluzzoStudy.pdf; Vandevoort, L. G., Amrein-Beardsley, A., & Berliner, D. C. (2004, September 8). National Board Certified teachers and their students' achievement. *Education Policy Analysis Archives, 12*(46). Retrieved March 5, 2005, from http://epaa.asu.edu/epaa/v12n46/

10. See, for example, Stone, J. E. (2001). *The value-added achievement gains of NBPTS-certified teachers in Tennessee: A brief report.* Retrieved September 27, 2002, from http://www.education-consumers.com/briefs/stoneNBPTS.shtm

11. Fetler, M. (1999). High school staff characteristics and mathematics test results. *Educational Policy Analysis Archives, 7*(9). Retrieved June 8, 2005, from http://epaa.asu.edu/epaa/v7n9.html; Darling-Hammond, L. (2000). Teacher quality and student achievement: A review of state policy evidence. *Educational Policy Analysis Archives, 8*(1). Retrieved March 21, 2000, from http://epaa.asu .edu/epaa/v8n1/; Covino, E. A., & Iwanicki, E. (1996). Experienced teachers: Their constructs on effective teaching. *Journal of Personnel Evaluation in Education, 11*, 325–363; Allen, R. M., & Casbergue, R. M. (2000, April). *Impact of teachers' recall on their effectiveness in mentoring novice teachers: The unexpected prowess of the transitional stage in the continuum from novice to expert.* Paper presented at the Annual Meeting of the American Educational Research Association, New Orleans, LA.

12. Goldhaber, D. D., & Brewer, D. J. (2000). Does teacher certification matter? High school certification status and student achievement. *Educational Evaluation and Policy Analysis, 22*(2), 129–145; Fetler, 1999; Darling-Hammond, 2000.

13. Nelson, F. H. (1994, December). International comparison of teacher salaries and conditions of employment. *Developments in School Finance,* 111–127.

14. Cornett, L. M., & Gaines, G. F. (2002). Quality teachers: Can incentive policies make a difference? Atlanta, GA: Southern Regional Education Board.

15. Cornett & Gaines, 2002, pp. 12–14.

CHAPTER 6

1. Tucker, P. D., & Stronge, J. H. (2005). *Linking teacher evaluation and student learning.* Alexandria, VA: Association for Supervision and Curriculum Development; Stronge, J. H. (2002). *Qualities of effective teachers.* Alexandria, VA: Association for Supervision and Curriculum Development.

2. Tucker & Stronge (2005).

3. Cornett, L. (2002, August). Performance pay for teachers: What works and what doesn't? Excerpt from *Quality Teachers: Can Incentive Policies Make a Difference?* (p. 3). Atlanta, GA: Southern Regional Education Board.

4. Spencer, J. (2005, April 4). HISD has incentives to change merit pay. *Houston Chronicle.* Retrieved April 5, 2005, from http://www.chron.com/disp/ story.mpl/metropolitan/3116498.html

5. Keller, B. (2002, May 29). Cincinnati teachers rebuff performance pay. *Education Week, 21*(38), 5.

6. Keller, B. (2005, April). Poll finds support for changes in teacher pay. *Education Week, 24*(31), 5.

References

Alexander, K., & Salmon, R. G. (1995). *Public school finance.* Boston: Allyn & Bacon.

Allen, R. M., & Casbergue, R. M. (2000, April). *Impact of teachers' recall on their effectiveness in mentoring novice teachers: The unexpected prowess of the transitional stage in the continuum from novice to expert.* Paper presented at the Annual Meeting of the American Educational Research Association, New Orleans, LA.

Ambrose, D. (1987). *Managing complex change.* Pittsburgh, PA: The Enterprise Group.

Archer, J. (2000, June 14). Changing the rules of the game. *Education Week, 19*(40), 24–29.

Archer, J. (2001, January 10). Teacher re-creation. *Education Week, 20*(16), 46–50.

Archer, J. (2001, December 12). Denver pay plan offers lessons, review says. *Education Week, 21*(15), 5.

Ballou, D., & Podgursky, M. (1993). Teachers' attitudes toward merit pay: Examining conventional wisdom. *Industrial and Labor Relations Review, 47,* 50–61.

Blair, J. (2000, October 25). ETS study links effective teaching methods to test-score gains. *Education Week, 20*(8), 24.

Blair, J. (2001, September 19). Teacher performance-pay plan modified in Cincinnati. *Education Week, 21*(3), 3.

Bond, L., Smith, T., Baker, W., & Hattie, J. (2000). *The certification system of the National Board for Professional Teaching Standards: A construct and consequential validity study.* Greensboro, NC: Center for Educational Research and Evaluation.

Bryson, J. M. (1995). *Strategic planning for public and nonprofit organizations.* San Francisco: Jossey-Bass.

Bushweller, K. (1999). Bonus bucks for teachers. *The American School Board Journal, 186*(8), 21.

Cascio, W. F. (2003). *Managing human resources: Productivity, quality of work life, profits* (6th ed.). Boston: McGraw-Hill/Irwin.

Cavalluzzo, L. C. (2004). *Is National Board Certification an effective signal of teacher quality?* Alexandria, VA: The CAN Corporation. Retrieved February 2, 2005, from http://www.cna.org/documents/CavaluzzoStudy.pdf

Cincinnati Public Schools. (2002). *Teacher evaluation system.* Retrieved June 1, 2005, from http://www.cps-k12.org/general/tchngprof/TES/TEStitle.html

Community Training and Assistance Center. (2001). *Pathway to results: Pay for performance in Denver.* Boston: Author. Retrieved October 20, 2005, from http://www.denver.k12.co.us/pdf/PayForPerformance.pdf

Conley, S. C., Gould, J., Muncey, D. E., & White, N. (2001). Negotiating a pay-for performance program encouraged by state mandate. *Journal of Personnel Evaluation in Education, 15,* 137–148.

Conley, S., & Odden, A. (1995). Linking teacher compensation to teacher career development. *Educational Evaluation and Policy Analysis, 17,* 219–237.

Cornett, L. (2002, August). Performance pay for teachers: What works and what doesn't? Excerpt from *Quality teachers: Can incentive policies make a difference?* Atlanta, GA: Southern Regional Education Board.

Cornett, L. M., & Gaines, G. F. (2002). *Quality teachers: Can incentive policies make a difference?* (02E02). Atlanta, GA: Southern Regional Education Board.

Covino, E. A., & Iwanicki, E. (1996). Experienced teachers: Their constructs on effective teaching. *Journal of Personnel Evaluation in Education, 11,* 325–363.

Darling-Hammond, L. (2000). Teacher quality and student achievement: A review of state policy evidence. *Educational Policy Analysis Archives, 8*(1). Retrieved March 21, 2000, from http://epaa.asu.edu/epaa/v8n1/

Dee, T. S., & Keys, B. J. (2004). Does merit pay reward good teachers? Evidence from a randomized experiment. *Journal of Policy Analysis and Management, 23,* 471–488.

Douglas County School District. (2001). *Teacher compensation plan.* Castle Rock, CO: Author. Retrieved May 24, 2002, from http://www.dcsd.k12.co.us

DuFour, R. (1997). Make the words of mission statements come to life. *Journal of Staff Development, 18*(3), 54–55.

DuFour, R., & Eaker, R. (1998). *Professional learning communities at work: Best practices for enhancing student achievement.* Bloomington, IN: National Educational Service.

Durall, P. C. (1995). *Years of experience and professional development: A correlation with higher reading scores.* Dissertation from Murray State University, Murray, KY. (ERIC Document Reproduction Service No. ED386681)

Ebmeier, H., & Hart, A. W. (1992). The effects of a career-ladder program on school organizational process. *Educational Evaluation and Policy Analysis, 14,* 261–281.

Edwards, V. B. (Ed.). (2000). Quality counts 2000: Who should teach? [Special Issue]. *Education Week, 19*(18).

Fetler, M. (1999). High school staff characteristics and mathematics test results. *Educational Policy Analysis Archives, 7*(9). Retrieved June 8, 2005, from http://epaa.asu.edu/epaa/v7n9.html

Finn, J. D., & Achilles, C. M. (1999). Tennessee's class size study: Findings, implications, misconceptions. *Educational Evaluation and Policy Analysis, 21*(2), 97–109.

Firestone, W. A. (1991). Merit pay and job enlargement as reforms: Incentives, implementation, and teacher response. *Educational Evaluation and Policy Analysis, 13,* 269–288.

Firestone, W. A. (1994). Redesigning teacher salary systems for educational reform. *American Educational Research Journal, 31,* 549–574.

Firestone, W. A., & Pennell, J. R. (1993). Teacher commitment, working conditions, and differential incentive policies. *Review of Educational Research, 63,* 489–525.

Florida Department of Education. (2005). *Florida School Recognition Program.* Retrieved September 12, 2005, from http://www.firn.edu/doe/evaluation/schrmain.htm

Gerald, D. E., & Hussar, W. J. (2000). *Projections of education statistics to 2010* (NCES Publication No. NCES 2000-071). Washington, DC: U.S. Department of Education, Office of Educational Research and Improvement.

Glass, C. S. (2001). Factors influencing teaching strategies used with children who display attention deficit hyperactivity disorder characteristics. *Education, 122*(1), 70–80.

Goertz, M. E., & Duffy, M. C. (2001). *Assessment and accountability in the 50 states: 1999–2000* (CPRE Research Report Series RR-046). Philadelphia: University of Pennsylvania, Consortium for Policy Research in Education.

Goldhaber, D. D., & Brewer, D. J. (2000). Does teacher certification matter? High school certification status and student achievement. *Educational Evaluation and Policy Analysis, 22*(2), 129–145.

Gursky, D. (1992, April). Not without merit pay. *Teacher Magazine,* 23–25.

Hanushek, E. A. (1989). The impact of differential expenditures on school performance. *Educational Researcher, 18*(4), 45–62.

Hassel, B. C. (2002, May). *Better pay for better teaching: Making teacher compensation pay off in the age of accountability.* Washington, DC: Progressive Policy Institute.

Haycock, K. (2003). Toward a fair distribution of teacher talent. *Educational Leadership, 60*(4), 11–15.

Hoerr, T. R. (1998). A case for merit pay. *Phi Delta Kappan, 80,* 326.

Hoff, D. J. (2005, May 18). States facing fiscal strain of pensions. *Education Week.* Retrieved September 13, 2005, from http://www.edweek.org

Holcomb, E. (2001). *Asking the right questions: Techniques for collaboration and school change* (2nd ed.). Thousand Oaks, CA: Corwin.

Holt, M. (2001). Performance pay for teachers: The standards movement's last stand. *Phi Delta Kappan, 83,* 312–317.

Hoy, W. K., & Miskel, C. G. (2001). *Educational administration: Theory, research, and practice* (6th ed.). Boston: McGraw-Hill.

Hussar, W. J. (1999). Predicting the need for newly hired teachers in the United States to 2008–09 (NCES Publication No. NCES 1999-026). Washington, DC: U.S. Government Printing Office.

Ingersoll, R. M. (2001). Teacher turnover and teacher shortages: An organizational analysis. *American Educational Research Journal, 38,* 499–534.

Ingersoll, R. M., & Smith, T. M. (2003). The wrong solution to the teacher shortage. *Educational Leadership, 60*(8), 30–33.

Jenkins, G. D., Jr., Gupta, N., Mitra, A., & Shaw, J. D. (1998). Are financial incentives related to performance? A meta-analytic review of empirical research. *Journal of Applied Psychology, 83,* 777–787.

Jesness, J. (2001, April 4). Teacher merit pay. *Education Week, 20*(29), 37, 39.

Johnson, S. M. (1986). Incentives for teachers: What motivates, what matters. *Educational Administration Quarterly, 22,* 54–79.

Johnson, S. M. (1990). *Teachers at work: Achieving success in our schools.* New York: Basic Books.

Joint Task Force on Teacher Compensation. (2004). *Tentative agreement between School District No. 1 and Denver Classroom Teachers Association on Professional Compensation System for teachers.* Retrieved June 1, 2005, from http://denver-procomp.org/generalinformation

Keiffer-Barone, S., & Ware, K. (2001). Growing great teachers in Cincinnati. *Educational Leadership, 58*(8), 56–59.

Keller, B. (2002, May 29). Cincinnati teachers rebuff performance pay. *Education Week, 21*(38), 5.

Keller, B. (2005, April 13). Poll finds support for changes in teacher pay. *Education Week, 24*(31), 5.

Kelley, C. (1997). Teacher compensation and organization. *Educational Evaluation and Policy Analysis, 19,* 15–28.

Kelley, C., Heneman, H., & Milanowski, A. (2000). *School-based performance award programs, teacher motivation, and school performance: Findings from a study of three programs* (CPRE Research Report Series RR-44). Philadelphia: University of Pennsylvania, Consortium for Policy Research in Education.

Kelley, C., Odden, A., Milanowski, A., & Heneman, H. (2000). *The motivational effects of school-based performance awards* (CPRE Policy Briefs, RB-29). Philadelphia: University of Pennsylvania, Consortium for Policy Research in Education.

Kimball, S. M. (2002). Analysis of feedback, enabling conditions, and fairness perceptions of teachers in three school districts with new standards-based evaluation systems. *Journal of Personnel Evaluation in Education, 16,* 241–268.

Knoster, T. (1991, June). *Factors in managing complex change.* Presentation at the conference of The Association for People with Severe Disabilities (TASH), Washington, DC.

Kohn, A. (1993, October 17). For best results, forget the bonus. *New York Times.* Retrieved June 2, 2005, from http://www.alfiekohn.org/managing/fbrftb.htm

Koppich, J. E., & Kerchner, C. T. (1999). Organizing the other half of teaching. In L. Darling-Hammond & G. Sykes (Eds.), *Teaching as the learning profession: Handbook of policy and practice* (pp. 315–340). San Francisco: Jossey-Bass.

Kotter, J. (1996). *Leading change.* Boston: Harvard Business School Press.

Kouzes, J. M., & Posner, B. Z. (1995). *The leadership challenge: How to keep getting extraordinary things done in organizations.* San Francisco: Jossey-Bass.

LaFee, S. (2000). Linking teacher pay to student scores. *The School Administrator,* 14–20.

Laine, S. W. M. (2002). Pay for performance: New thinking in Iowa. *NCREL's Learning Point, 4*(1), 16–18.

Lankford, H., Wyckoff, J., & Papa, F. (2000). *The labor market for public school teachers: A descriptive analysis of New York State's teacher workforce.* Albany: New York State Educational Finance Research Consortium.

Leigh, A., & Mead, S. (2005, April). Lifting teacher performance. *Progressive Policy Institute Policy Report.* Retrieved May 15, 2005, from http://www.ppionline.org/

Liu, E., Johnson, S. M., & Peske, H. G. (2004). New teachers and the Massachusetts signing bonus: The limits of inducements. *Educational Evaluation and Policy Analysis, 26,* 217–236.

Liu, X., & Meyer, J. P. (2005). Teachers' perceptions of their jobs: A multilevel analysis of the Teacher Follow-Up Survey for 1994–1995. *Teachers College Record, 107,* 985–1003.

Loeb, S., & Page, M. E. (2000). Examining the link between teacher wages and student outcomes: The importance of alternative labor market opportunities and non-pecuniary variation. *The Review of Economics and Statistics, 82*(3), 393–408.

Makkonen, R. (2004). Taking care of novice teachers. *Harvard Education Letter, 20*(3), 1–4.

Martocchio, J. J. (2003). *Employee benefits: A primer for human resource professionals.* Boston: McGraw-Hill/Irwin.

Marzano, R. J., Pickering, D. J., & Pollock, J. E. (2001). *Classroom instruction that works.* Alexandria, VA: Association for Supervision and Curriculum Development.

McCollum, S. (2001). How merit pay improves education. *Educational Leadership, 58*(5), 21–24.

McDonnell, L. M., & Elmore, R. F. (1987). Getting the job done: Alternative policy instruments. *Educational Evaluation and Policy Analysis, 9,* 133–152.

Milanowski, A. (2003, January 29). The varieties of knowledge and skill-based pay design: A comparison of seven new pay systems for K–12 teachers. *Education Policy Analysis Archives, 11*(4). Retrieved May 15, 2005, from http://epaa.asu.edu/epaa/v11n4/

Milanowski, A., Odden, A., & Youngs, P. (1998). Teacher knowledge and skill assessments and teacher compensation: An overview of measurement and linkage issues. *Journal of Personnel Evaluation in Education, 12,* 83–101.

Mohrman, A. M., Jr., Mohrman, S. A., & Odden, A. R. (1996). Aligning teacher compensation with systemic school reform: Skill-based pay and group-based performance rewards. *Educational Evaluation and Policy Analysis, 18,* 51–71.

Molnar, A., Smith, P., Zahorik, J., Palmer, A., Halbach, A., & Ehrle, K. (1999). Evaluating the SAGE program: A pilot program in targeted pupil-teacher reduction in Wisconsin. *Educational Evaluation and Policy Analysis, 21*(2), 165–177.

Moore Johnson, S., & The Project on the Next Generation of Teachers. (2004). *Finders and keepers: Helping teachers survive and thrive in our schools.* San Francisco: Jossey-Bass.

Murnane, R. J., Singer, J. D., Willet, J. B., Kemple, J. J., & Olsen, R. J. (1991). *Who will teach? Policies that matter.* Cambridge, MA: Harvard University Press.

Nanus, B. (1992). *Visionary leadership.* San Francisco: Jossey-Bass.

NBPTS. (2001). *The impact of National Board Certification on teachers: A survey of National Board Certified teachers and assessors.* Retrieved April 4, 2005, from http://www.nbpts.org/pdf/ResRpt.pdf

NBPTS. (2002). *National board for professional teaching standards: Local and state action.* Retrieved April 4, 2005, from http://www.nbpts.org/state_local/ri.Action.html

Nelson, F. H. (1994, December). International comparison of teacher salaries and conditions of employment. *Developments in School Finance,* 111–127.

Nelson, F. H., & Drown, R. (2003). *Survey and analysis of teacher salary trends 2002.* Washington, DC: American Federation of Teachers.

Nelson, W. (2001). Timequake alert: Why payment by results is the worst "new" reform to share the educational world, again and again. *Phi Delta Kappan, 82,* 384–389.

No Child Left Behind Act of 2001, Pub. L. No. 107–110, 115 Stat. 1425 (2002).

Nye, B., Konstantopoulos, S., & Hedges, L. V. (2004). How large are teacher effects? *Educational Evaluation and Policy Analysis, 26,* 237–257.

Odden, A. (2000a). *Emerging findings in teacher compensation.* Retrieved June 1, 2005, from http://www.wcer.wisc.edu/cpre/tcomp/research/general/findings.asp

Odden, A. (2000b). *Initial findings from school district survey.* Retrieved May 31, 2005, from http://www.wcer.wisc.edu/cpre/tcomp/research/ksbp/findings/district.asp

Odden, A. (2000c). New and better forms of teacher compensation are possible. *Phi Delta Kappan, 81,* 361–366.

Odden, A. (2001). The new school finance. *Phi Delta Kappan, 83,* 85–91.

Odden, A., & Kelley, C. (2002). *Paying teachers for what they know and do: New and smarter compensation strategies to improve schools* (2nd ed.). Thousand Oaks, CA: Corwin.

Odden, A., Kelley, C., Heneman, H., & Milanowski, A. (2001). *Enhancing teacher quality through knowledge- and skills-based pay* (CPRE Policy Brief RB-34). Philadelphia: University of Pennsylvania, Consortium for Policy Research in Education.

Odden, A., Kellor, E., Heneman, H., & Milanowski, A. (1999). *School-based performance award programs: Design and administration issues synthesized from eight programs.* Madison: Wisconsin Center for Education Research.

Odden, A., & Wallace, M. (2004). Experimenting with teacher compensation. *School Administrator, 61*(9), 24–28.

Office of Human Resources, Douglas County School District. (2001). *Licensed staff pay for performance information.* Retrieved June 1, 2005, from http://www1 .dcsdk12.org/

Peterson, B. (2000). *Merit: To pay or not to pay.* Retrieved April 4, 2005, from http://www.rethinkingschools.org/Archives/14_03/mert143.shtm

Poston, W. K., & Frase, L. E. (1991). Alternative compensation programs for teachers: Rolling boulders up the mountain of reform. *Phi Delta Kappan, 73,* 317–320.

Ramirez, A. (2001). How merit pay undermines education. *Educational Leadership, 58*(5), 16–20.

Rebore, R. W. (2001). *Human resources administration in education* (6th ed.). Boston: Allyn & Bacon.

Risher, H. (1999). Merit pay can be a hard sell. *Public Management, 81*(7), 8–13.

Rowan, B., Chiang, F. S., & Miller, R. J. (1997). Using research on employees' performance to study the effects of teachers on student achievement. *Sociology of Education, 70,* 256–284.

Sanders, W. L., & Horn, S. (1998). Research findings from the Tennessee Value-Added Assessment System (TVAAS) database: Implications for educational evaluation and research. *Journal of Personnel Evaluation in Education, 12,* 247–256.

Schacter, J., & Schiff, T. (2004, Spring). The impact of the Teacher Advancement Program. *What's on TAP, 2*(1), 10–11. Retrieved June 1, 2005, from http://www .mff.org/tap/

Schiff, T. (2004, Spring). The path to multiple career paths. *What's on TAP, 2*(1), 5–6. Retrieved June 1, 2005, from http://www.mff.org/tap/

Sharpes, D. (1987). Incentive pay and the promotion of teaching proficiencies. *The Clearing House, 60,* 406–408.

Smith, T. M., & Ingersoll, R. M. (2004). What are the effects of induction and mentoring on beginning teacher turnover? *American Educational Research Journal, 41*(3), 681–714.

Solmon, L. (2004, Spring). What we have learned about performance pay. *What's on TAP, 2*(1), 17. Retrieved June 1, 2005, from http://www.mff.org/tap/

Solmon, L. C., & Podgursky, M. (2000). *The pros and cons of performance-based compensation.* Santa Monica, CA: Milken Family Foundation. (ERIC Document Reproduction Service No. ED445393)

Southeast Center for Teaching Quality. (n.d.). *Listening to the experts: A report on the 2004 South Carolina teacher working conditions survey.* Retrieved April 11, 2005, from http://www.teachingquality.org/pdfs/TWC_SCFinalReport.pdf

Spencer, J. (2005, April 4). HISD has incentives to change merit pay. *Houston Chronicle.* Retrieved April 5, 2005, from http://www.chron.com/disp/story.mpl/metropolitan/3116498.html

Stewart, K. J., & Reed, S. B. (1999). Consumer price index research series using current methods, 1978–1998. In *Family Economics and Nutrition Review 13*(1), 101–104. Taken from *Monthly Labor Review, 122*(6), 29–38.

Stone, J. E. (2001). *The value-added achievement gains of NBPTS-certified teachers in Tennessee: A brief report.* Retrieved September 27, 2002, from http://www.education-consumers.com/briefs/may2002.asp

Stronge, J. H. (2002). *Qualities of effective teachers.* Alexandria, VA: Association for Supervision and Curriculum Development.

Stronge, J. H. (Ed.). (2006). *Evaluating teaching: A guide to current thinking and best practice* (2nd ed.). Thousand Oaks, CA: Corwin.

Swanson, A. D., & King, R. A. (1997). *School finance: Its economics and politics* (2nd ed.). New York: Longman.

Thompson, D. C., & Wood, R. C. (1998). *Money and schools: A handbook for practitioners.* Larchmont, NY: Eye on Education.

Tschannen-Moran, M., Hoy, A. W., & Hoy, W. K. (1998). Teacher efficacy: Its meaning and measure. *Review of Educational Research, 68*(2), 202–248.

Tucker, P. D., & Stronge, J. H. (2005). *Linking teacher evaluation and student learning.* Alexandria, VA: Association for Supervision and Curriculum Development.

Tucker, P. D., Stronge, J. H., & Gareis, C. (2002). *Handbook on teacher portfolios for evaluation and professional development.* Larchmont, NY: Eye on Education.

Urbanski, A., & Erskine, R. (2000). School reform, TURN, and teacher compensation. *Phi Delta Kappan, 81,* 367–370.

Vandevoort, L. G., Amrein-Beardsley, A., & Berliner, D. C. (2004, September 8). National board certified teachers and their students' achievement. *Education Policy Analysis Archives, 12*(46). Retrieved March 5, 2005, from http://epaa.asu.edu/epaa/v12n46/

Vaughn Next Century Learning Center. (n.d.). *Teacher quality and professional growth.* Retrieved May 30, 2002, from http://www.vaughncharter.com

Vroom, V. H. (1964). *Work and motivation.* New York: John Wiley.

Weld, J. (1998, June 3). Beyond the salary carrot. *Education Week, 17*(38), 33.

Wenglinsky, H. (2002). How schools matter: The link between teacher classroom practices and student academic performance. *Educational Policy Analysis Archives, 10*(12). Retrieved February 28, 2002, from http://epaa.asu.edu/epaa/v10n12/

Wolf, K., Lichtenstein, G., Bartlett, E., & Hartman, D. (1996). Professional development and teaching portfolios: The Douglas County outstanding teacher program. *Journal of Personnel Evaluation in Education, 10,* 279–286.

Wright, S. P., Horn, S. P., & Sanders, W. L. (1997). Teacher and classroom context effects on student achievement: Implications for teacher evaluation. *Journal of Personnel Evaluation in Education, 11,* 57–67.

Wyman, W., & Allen, M. (2001, June). *Pay-for-performance: Key questions and lessons from five current models* (ECS Issue Paper). Retrieved May 31, 2005, from http://www.ecs.org/clearinghouse/28/30/2830.htm

Index

Page references followed by *fig* indicate an illustrated figure.

**CORWIN
PRESS**

The Corwin Press logo—a raven striding across an open book—represents the union of courage and learning. Corwin Press is committed to improving education for all learners by publishing books and other professional development resources for those serving the field of PreK–12 education. By providing practical, hands-on materials, Corwin Press continues to carry out the promise of its motto: **"Helping Educators Do Their Work Better."**